D0480307

Yesterday was Summer

previous books by the authors

Marian Pallister:
Villages of Southern Argyll (Birlinn)
Lost Argyll (Birlinn)

Yesterday was Summer

The Marion Campbell Story

Marian Pallister &
David Adams McGilp

ARGYLL PUBLISHING

First published by
Argyll Publishing
Glendaruel
Argyll PA22 3AE
Scotland
www.argyllpublishing.com

British Library Cataloguing-in-Publication Data.
A catalogue record for this book in available from the British Library.

ISBN 978 1 906134 03 7

Printing: St Edmundsbury Press

To JCMA
Thank you for listening

Marian Pallister

To Mandy & Niamh

David Adams McGilp

Marion Campbell was an isolated child, brought up in the Victorian manner by her middle-aged parents. Her cloak of fair hair hampered any attempt at adventure

Contents

Marion Campbell – the woman

Introduction 23
Chapter One: Kilberry – silver spoon or poisoned chalice 25
Chapter Two: A child out of her time 41
Chapter Three: Exile 61
Chapter Four: The learning curve 71
Chapter Five: Disappointments and aspirations 77
Chapter Six: A frustrating war 89
Chapter Seven: The homecoming 117
Chapter Eight: Life and love for a Renaissance woman 127
Chapter Nine: Miss Somebody 141
Chapter Ten: The influential years 155
Chapter Eleven: Politics and people 165
Chapter Twelve: The irony and the ecstasy 177
Epilogue 197

Marion Campbell – the work

Introduction 205
The Old Lady and the Books 209
Facets and Familiar Spirits 214
The Wide Blue Road 217
Unlocking the Treasure-House 220
Lances and Longships 223
Young Hugh 225
The Squire of Val 227
The Dark Twin 229
Argyll: The Enduring Heartland 236
For Love, and A Little Money 241
Magnus the Orkney Cat 251
When the Years Were Young 252
Revival and Remuneration 254
Alexander III: King of Scots 256
Feet First From Kilberry 260
Tidemarks 262
Acknowledgements 264
Bibliography 265
Index 269

John 'Jock' Campbell of Kilberry and his bride Marion Isabel Durand at their wedding in 1913. Jock's behaviour had already caused Marion concern during their engagement

In the six years after their wedding, the couple had experienced a disastrous First World War and had lost a baby daughter and a son. When Marion, here a toddler on her beloved father's knee, was born, she was especially precious to the Campbells of Kilberry

When her father died in 1927, Marion and her mother were excluded from Kilberry. A doll's house was eventually liberated for the devastated child, and Princess Carnation became a constant comforting companion

The Campbells of Kilberry led a gypsy life, avoiding high rates by vacating the castle. Here at St Briac in northern France in 1925, Marion was far from the home she loved

Ivy Arbuthnot, a Campbell cousin pictured here in her youth, came to the rescue in buying Kilberry and then leaving it to Marion

Was the Kilberry which Miss Campbell kept in her heart throughout the war years the fairy tale castle painted by E. Gardner – or the 1940s crumbling reality?

At St Margaret's PNEU school in Edinburgh in the 1930s, Marion was known as 'MCK' because of her insistence on the 'of Kilberry' title

Visits home from school were precious, even though she and her mother were Miss Arbuthnot's paying guests. In 1936, Marion posed in school uniform with her mother at the bottom of the castle steps while 'Auntie Ivy' and her dog Chappie stand at the door. The child is not named

No official pictures survive of Marion Campbell's presentation at Court, but this delightful portrait taken in 1938 is described as her 'coming out' photograph

By September of 1939, she was in the uniform of the ATS, her long hair slashed into the nape of her neck

Third Officer WREN M. Campbell who served on HMS *Heron* in 1942 was also running 5,000 acres long distance

Miss Ivy Arbuthnot's death saw Marion inherit Kilberry for a second time. Barely out of her teens she looked mature beyond her years as she carried flowers into the castle

During the war, she became close to her cousin Walter John Campbell, who also served in the Royal Navy. She would describe him in later years as 'the love of my life', and this portrait remained at her bedside until her death

Miss Campbell and her lifelong friend Mary Sandeman received many accolades for their meticulous recording of the ancient monuments of Mid Argyll. They also led many local 'digs' – here in 1968 they explored Dun Mhulig at Craignish

Her archaeological expertise led to many field trips. Here Miss Campbell is seen enthralling the crowd at 'Temple Wood' – the cairns exposed during the 1970s

A founder of the Auchindrain Folk Museum project, Marion Campbell battled to preserve not only vernacular buildings but evidence of ancient land use – and above all, the culture of Mid Argyll. In 1991, unable to travel the 80mile round trip any more, she gave an inspirational speech to those who would follow in her footsteps

On a boat trip to Eilean Mor, 1970s

Mary Sandeman

With a biography of Alexander III still to polish for the publishers, Miss Campbell found herself caught up in movie making when Charner Wallis bought the film rights to her children's books and the novel *Dark Twin*

Determined to see Kilberry's traditions continued, she introduced Miss Sarah Campbell of Kilberry (her heir John's daughter) to the mysteries of speech making when Charlie Sutherland retired as Kilberry postman in 1994

Her involvement with the SNP's ownership of Eilean Mor was a happy one. Here (above) she enjoys a trip to the island with William Wolfe (third from the right), Mary Sandeman (head just seen in the long grass at the right in front of Marion), and other supporters. In the photograph below, William Wolfe is on the left of Marion Campbell

Her support of the Scottish National Party – Miss Campbell is seen chairing a party conference at Dunoon – gave impetus to the campaigns which saw a record number of 'Nats' going to Westminster

Ordered chaos: Miss Campbell in her 'office' in the cottage down the drive from the castle. It was 1999. Her *magnum opus Alexander III* was published, early books were being given film treatments – but her list of work pending was a long one

Marion Campbell – the woman

by Marian Pallister

Introduction

Marion Campbell of Kilberry was a woman of wit, wisdom and a way with words. A member of a cadet family of the House of Argyll, she was proud of her Campbell lineage and of the county of her roots. She was a writer, an archaeologist and historian. She involved herself in politics and served on the County Council. She knew about birds and wild flowers, could turn a poem nicely, and had in her day farmed the land on which she lived, taking her Highland cattle to market and looking for a fair price. She lived in a castle and could be a little crusty. And is all of that not what one would expect of the daughter of a laird, privileged and pampered, finished at the best schools, leisured enough to indulge her many interests?

Perhaps so.

But although Marion Campbell was indeed the daughter of a laird, she was neither privileged nor pampered, her education was a struggle and her adult life was spent chasing elusive pennies to keep a roof over her head and food on her table.

That she became a respected archaeologist, that the rights to her children's books were eventually bought with a view to turning them into films and that she won the approval of academics for her history of Alexander III is due not to her genealogical status but to her sheer dogged determination.

Marion Campbell of Kilberry was the product of a sad union and of a hereditary system which favoured the male line. I make no apology for exploring so much of her parents' marriage and her early years, because it is my belief that the intensity, the tragedy, and the marginalisation experienced then made Miss Campbell the complex and talented woman of later years.

Miss Campbell created myths about her past which she may well have come to believe herself in time. Yet this was a family which kept all its correspondence, from *billet doux* to taxman's bills. School reports, doctors' diagnoses, lawyers' letters, telegrams, Naval communiqués, lovers' letters, friends' letters, manuscripts – they are all there from the day that Marion Durand said 'yes' to Jock Campbell and Kilberry Castle became home to yet another generation. Miss Campbell gave many hundreds of these documents to Murdo MacDonald, the Argyll archivist. Many more have been kept by her heir, the current John Campbell of Kilberry and his wife Charmian. These primary sources have informed my part of this biography and I am immensely grateful to John, Charmian and Murdo for the privilege of access.

Marian Pallister
January 2007

CHAPTER ONE

Kilberry – silver spoon or poisoned chalice?

The letter was written from Rivernook, Wraysbury, England, on July 13, 1913. It did not come from a teenager fluttering with the effects of a first romance but from a mature and accomplished young woman who had been presented at court more than a decade previously. Even so, there was an undercurrent of excitement in the words sent from Marion Isabel Durand to her friend in the summer of that last year of peace across Europe before the Great War. She wrote:

> Dearest Tessa,
>
> I have been struggling to get a few minutes to write you my news – will you ever be able to believe it, I wonder? I am engaged to Captain John Campbell of Kilberry, Molly's brother – and I am amazingly happy and well content. He is tall, dark, going grey – late of the 93rd Highlanders (now 'Argyll and Sutherland'). We hope to be married on August 27th – so as to go together to the Oban gathering on September 8th. It's a painful rush isn't it.
>
> You will have to come and stay with me at Kilberry – it's such a nice place. Please will you tell your Mother with my best love? I know I'm sure of her kind sympathy. Very much love dear Tessa and forgive such a short note.
>
> Ever your loving
> Marion Durand

In the same month seventy-five years later, another Marion wrote another letter which revealed that however 'nice' Kilberry – for four centuries the castle home of Campbells, situated on the west coast of

Argyll overlooking the Sound of Jura – may be, it did not necessarily offer the happiness envisaged by Marion Durand. The second Marion was daughter to the first. When she wrote her July letter, her whole life had been inextricably bound up in Kilberry. Now she was to say finally that the castle would no longer be her home and she wanted to pass it on to her second cousin, leaving her free to live out her days in a modest cottage within its grounds. There was no longer an estate to be inherited – no farms or shooting rights from which to derive an income. It was not, however, the obvious fact that a now crumbling castle was the prize on offer which prompted the lengthy letter detailing the proffered inheritance.

Miss Campbell of Kilberry was not about to inflict on John Campbell the emotional blackmail to which she felt she had been subjected from the moment she entered this world at 8.50 am on December 16, 1919. In her letter, she said:

> I am not about to tell you (or anyone else) what to do; my whole life seems to have been overshadowed by people's ideas of what I ought to do . . .

She linked the word 'overshadowed' to the interference of relatives, however well meaning, who from her birth claimed to know what was best for her. Much else overshadowed Marion Campbell's life – not least the marriage of which Marion Durand wrote to her friend Tessa in 1913.

Her parents' marriage was not one made in heaven and was destined to be troubled from the outset. The partnership was between a man with an acknowledged alcohol problem and a woman who shared his intellect but was not equipped to cope with such a flawed personality. He was the heir to Kilberry, an estate which was already in the hands of this branch of Campbells by 1600. In the eighteenth and early nineteenth centuries, income came from investments in Jamaica and the family home was at the arguably more pleasant Knockbuy on Loch Fyne. Then Marion's great-grandfather had Kilberry castle modernised by Edinburgh architect Thomas Brown and moved in for the birth of his son in 1844. This John Campbell succeeded in 1861. He was a military man serving in India when he inherited Kilberry and did not come back to Scotland until 1870. Then he too set about enhancing the castle with the help of a cash injection from his wife, Margaret Lloyd, whose family's fortune was made from Italian marble. It became a gothic Victorian pile enhanced by architects Peddie and Kinnear. The gardens were formal and attractive, there was a large glass conservatory, the five farms brought in good rents and shooting lets were a further source of income.

By the end of the nineteenth century, however, farm rents had peaked and were plummeting. When Marion's father John Campbell – Jock – took up the baton, the glory days were already over. He had been an intelligent and sensitive boy educated at Harrow and Eton, but was expected to follow his father's footsteps into the army. He joined the Argylls and was posted to India as a teenager and was sucked into a culture where heavy drinking was considered the manly norm. There were relationships but none which led to anything serious until he met Marion Durand, a friend of his sister Molly.

Marion was the eldest of General Sir Edward Durand's large family. She had 'come out' as a debutante in 1897, stunningly beautiful in virginal white. She once confided: 'When I was a girl, I said 'I am going to marry a Highlander and live by the sea'.' Her visit to Kilberry Castle with Molly in the summer of 1913 which led to Jock proposing marriage must have seemed a fulfilment of that self promise. He was 41 and she was 32, but she still wrote to her father for his permission to marry. Sir Edward was a man well respected in the diplomatic service, had served in India, was famous for his Afghan Accord and had finished his distinguished career in Washington. He sent his approval from Staines in the clipped language of the telegram: APPROVE PLAN BEST LOVE WRITING DURAND.

There was a flurry of letters and telegrams. An aunt living in Vevey said she 'wept for joy' at the announcement of Marion's engagement to 'a good soldier'. Kilberry – as Jock was called in the style of Scottish lairds – had been known to the family in India. Another Durand aunt wrote from Switzerland: 'It is delightful to me to think of you in a happy Scotch home, making your husband happy as you have made your dear father'; while from the Isle of Wight came a letter of welcome from Jock's mother, whom Marion proposed to call 'Madre.' Mrs

Campbell said Marion's communication about the engagement was 'almost the very nicest letter I have ever received' and stressed her 'perfect horror' of being 'regarded in the conventional light of mother-in-law – a person you have to be civil to and whose feelings you are bound to consider and for whom you can only be too thankful if she does not make herself disagreeable'. She added:

> A man's mother and his wife are the two women that have most to do with his life and their love for him ought to bind them together.

It was not in-law problems which were to blight Marion Durand's marriage most, but those originating still closer to home. As she tried to arrange her August wedding at Brompton Church in London, making list after characteristic list, responding to the generosity of well-wishers with charming thank-you letters and consulting her fiancé about her outfit, she was forced to face the reality of an engagement to a man not only set in his bachelor ways but whose response to even a minor crisis was to reach for a dram.

Her godfather the Duke of Northumberland gave her a ruby ring surrounded by diamonds. The Duke of Argyll, head of Clan Campbell, sent a silver gravy pot from his London address. Packages arrived daily at the Durand home – jewellery and crumb trays and coffee pots and a 'lovely hanky' from a niece in Gloucestershire addressed to 'Dear Auntie Mellon'. They went to Kilberry, too, as did letters asking the laird to make decisions when relatives proffered choices or Marion felt uncertain of the plans.

Jock was busy. July was a month for agricultural shows and wedding plans had to take second place for a member of the Highland and Agricultural Society of Scotland, a prominent cog in the machinery of the Highland Cattle Society and a colonel in the Territorial Army at a time of unrest in Europe. Miss Durand was a letter writer. She wrote so much that it became her habit to finish her letter back on the first page, fitting in a vertical line or two up the left hand side of the more conventional horizontal text, her signature sometimes written butting at right angles onto her address. Jock claimed it was a catching habit, but often his own letters needed no stealing of space to say all he had to say. He wrote from the show yard at Oban: 'My poor darling. I am treating you badly. You send such beautiful letters and I never write.'

But his letters were not always romantic and not always kind and by now she was beginning to realise the handsome soldier had his flaws. There had been warning even as Sir Edward gave his consent. Jock had suggested to his new fiancée that she ask her father 'to tell you something about the average soldier of forty, *viz* what he has probably been and done. You must not begin by thinking me good. I know that you are; that is a different matter'.

Good enough to take on a lame duck? Did Marion Durand feel her mission in life was to save Kilberry from himself? She had told him that with prayer and faith, he could change. In a letter on July 15 he claimed that he believed her.

> I am wonderfully happy. Of course I would be happier if you were here, but just think of my prospects and outlook on life a month or so ago – when I was seriously studying the ethics of suicide – it is enough to make any person happy.

But the fact that in a month he would marry the woman whose hem, he told her, he was 'not worthy to kiss', was not enough to change his irritability, his irascibility or his irresponsibility. He confessed he'd offended his sister Molly, who was 'extraordinarily sensitive' in his eyes. He told a relative he had 'no interest' in the details of his wedding (a comment which of course reached the ears of Marion when those details were causing her stress enough). Worst of all, he drank too much, wrote letters not so much of love but of lust (unacceptable in Edwardian society), and then had to write what was his first but by no means last lengthy letter pleading for forgiveness. The Territorial Army camp he attended in July was the scene of much over-indulgence and foolishly he put pen to paper after too much whisky. Not only that, but his condition after camp was so bad that in August he had to go to a spa in Harrogate to take the waters. His kidneys and liver were in a poor condition and so was his conscience. In response to what he referred to as Marion's 'terrible letter' in which she prays he can behave himself in front of the wedding guests, he pleaded that he was never 'anything like drunk' but admitted:

> I can offer venial excuses for the camp period, hard work, heat and the necessity of either entertaining or being a principal guest at big dinners every night. I am very unhappy about it, but I do honestly believe that – with you – I shall be all right. The long lonely winter days and nights at Kilberry started me again last spring after I was completely cured. One thing I would certainly never come near you unless I was absolutely all right.
>
> It's not that I get drunk for I don't but that I injure my liver and my digestion by drinking more than is good for me. . . I do honestly believe that I shall not disgrace myself or you.

She should have realised this remorse was no guarantee that her fiancé would reform under her prayerful guidance. Just three days after he had thanked her for her letter of admonition, he was sympathising with her over a bout of neuralgia and suggesting a 'table spoonful of quinine powder shaken up in a bottle of port and a glass taken thrice a day' as the only cure. She kept all of his empty promises written at what should have been such a happy time – like the letter he sent on August 16 as the wedding day came ever closer and a marriage contract which brought £4,000 from the Durand camp to Kilberry came nearer to being signed, which said:

> 'Darling, the question of drink must be mentioned. It is my curse as it is of every Highlandman but I am honestly sure that I will not cause you pain over it.'

The wedding went ahead, no doubt with Miss Durand wondeing as the reception progressed whether her bridegroom would slide from charming Highland gentleman into embarrassing society sot. Her handsome husband's charming façade hid a secret she would try to keep throughout their marriage and beyond. Victorian values were paramount: no dirty linen in public. He had myrtle planted around the castle door for her; she took on the role of Mrs Campbell of Kilberry. It was one she took seriously throughout her life and despite her demands for curtseys from the village girls and salutes from the boys she was regarded with affection by tenants and villagers for her charity work and her involvement in the local school. Kilberry might descend into drunkenness but Mrs Campbell of Kilberry would always maintain decorum.

On August 27, 1913, Colonel John Campbell and Miss Marion Isabel Durand were married at Holy Trinity Church in Brompton. After their honeymoon in Europe they returned to Kilberry on September 15 and were met at the first gate by the tenants and servants on the estate and, according to the *Argyllshire Advertiser* that week, many of the residents of the district. There were bouquets for the bride and their car was hauled down the drive to the front door preceded by pipers and an escort of boys carrying flags. The tenants and estate workers presented them with a Jacobean style silver cup and a clock and a 'sumptuous tea' was served in the barn. The new Mrs Campbell had to light a bonfire, pipers played again and there were plenty of cheers for her. The gardener Mr Simmers had created an archway of flowers at the castle door through which they slipped away from the revellers to take up their married life. By October, Mrs Campbell was ill in Glasgow while Kilberry traipsed about Oban with his cattle and councillor cronies.

'Get strong and don't expect me tomorrow night though I will come if I can', he told her in a note dashed off on Oban's Station Hotel note paper. At the New Year celebrations in 1914, the couple attended the traditional Kilberry servants' dinner and at the tenants' ball on January 8 they were joined by Campbell and Durand family members and neighbours. The new Mrs Campbell had already learned how tight money was and often the housekeeping allowance was prised from Jock with difficulty, but there was always whisky in the decanters and game birds on the table and dancing for the workers as there had been for generations.

The world and Kilberry were about to see unimaginable change, however. By the end of that year, Britain was at war and Jock was training troops to fight it. The milieu which Mrs Campbell of Kilberry dreaded most for her husband was now unavoidable. Although at first he did not volunteer and worked instead with the Territorials at a camp in Bedford, by the spring of 1915 he was in France and Marion was back at 'Rivernook', her parents' house in Wraysbury, Buckinghamshire. In May she returned to Kilberry and was receiving censored letters from somewhere in France. Jock's health was not good and he wondered if the water or the white wine was poisonous – his condition could not, he said, be put down to the red wine because it was 'nasty' and the beer 'awful'. By May 18 he was asking for a keg of whisky and it was, of course, understandable that the men were in need of something to fortify their souls. Kilberry told Marion '. . . we have to do some burying tonight – a horrid job'. On May 25, in a letter carefully numbered 20 by his wife, he received the whisky which, he said, 'is being issued carefully bottle by bottle'. It is a recurring theme throughout the summer of 1915. He told Marion on June 26: 'Don't be anxious. I am giving away bottles as I get them to the company messes – one between four or five officers, not much – and we keep a very little in common at Head Quarters.' Most wives feared death. Marion Campbell feared drunkenness. 'I've given away half what I got in the bottle and distributed the rest,' was Kilberry's written reassurance.

There was sweetness – a flower plucked from a French village garden wall and pressed between the pages of his censored letter for the anniversary of their first meeting. There were self-justifications – 'My only consolation is that though I have given you much pain and much suffering most of which was my fault, I have given you some happiness too'. But there was anger, too, expressed by each of them as the war and their separation drove a wedge between them. He demanded that she run the estate, handle the finances, and send the customary seasonal Kilberry gifts of game and seafood to friends and relatives. Unfortunately, Marion noticed that one friend who was to receive a lobster was the woman in a picture Jock had unwisely kept. She remonstrated. He saw attack as the best form of defence:

> My beloved Marion,
>
> I am very angry with you. How any female in her sound mind can write long diatribes about women, lobsters and the psychology of the human soul at this time is a marvel. If the aforesaid female expects her husband to discuss such things she is far wrong, for he is thinking far more of how to get sandbags to build up C Company's parapet and whether the Machine Gun Sergeant may survive his wounds than such details.

> . . . I am very sorry not to think more but the bullet and the shell and the sandbag and the spade make other things seem mere trifles.
>
> . . . God bless and keep you my darling and may He forgive me for marrying you and treating you as I have.
>
> Your husband John Campbell

She did not see the loss of fourteen men the morning he received this accusing letter as an extenuating circumstance. Marion wrote again about the woman in the photograph who was still on Kilberry's lobster list. His reply could hardly have mended the rift.

> I am sorry I was angry with you yesterday for I thought you were silly about the photograph. Do please let Mrs Niven alone. One time the idea of sending her a lobster brings two sheets of recriminations and then finding a photo of her makes you unhappy for days. Today I am sorry to say I am only amused by your wrath.

Other troubles were brewing. A partner in the family legal firm died in mid-July, 1915 and his demise meant that loans could be called in. Kilberry's financial situation was precarious to say the least and just days after he had brushed off Marion's concerns about his faithfulness, he was demanding that she tell his mother to find the money. He also expected her to deal with estate matters, letting shoots and farms and was surprised when instead he got a letter which threatened that she would leave him. He wrote to her on July 25:

> You said you were going on at home to look after things while the war lasted. I did not expect you to leave and hoped that by saying no more about it the affair of a photograph ten years old would be allowed to lapse.
>
> What more can I say except that I love you.

By August, he had managed to get leave and a truce was being called on the Kilberry home front. Still Jock could not get it right. Lust not love was again on the agenda and he committed the passion to paper in terms which were perhaps not wise to a wife who had threatened to 'exile' him from her bed.

> I shall arrive dead tired but if I see black knickerbockers I

> will go straight back to France. Do please, for once, think of this idiosyncrasy of mine. Some arms are very hungry and some bodies appreciate 'dessous' a great deal.

There were other demands – she was to travel to Glasgow to meet him. She was to get rid of everyone from the castle. She must understand that he could not fit in with her dates. And she must take him on trust that 'there is no drunkenness in this battalion'. On August 11 he started on leave. He didn't sail for France again until the 23rd. When he arrived back he was in trouble. There had already been difficulties over kit inspections before he left. Now he was told that the five extra days he had taken would mean another officer would have to be penalised by having his leave cut short. The colonel ostensibly accepted Jock's explanation that the dates he had requested for leave had not been questioned and therefore he had assumed they were acceptable, but in his heart, Jock knew he'd overstepped the mark. His lumbago became decidedly worse in the next few days, an ideal opportunity for the colonel to suggest his health was perhaps preventing him from working at full capacity. Jock wrote to Marion on August 28 that he was 'disgusted' with the life at the Front and 'I would do anything to get home for good'. By September 1st he was able to tell his wife that he was soon to be on his way back to Blighty. That morning he had received a letter from Major Booth enclosing a memorandum from Brigadier General Ross to the 51st Division which read:

> I need not say how sorry I am that owing to your health, it is not possible for you to continue in command of the 8th Argylls. The winter will be a severe test for all of us and will require all our energies to get through.

A post script to another communication detailing who would take over from Jock confirmed that Colonel Campbell's nerve under fire was 'excellent.' This was a very comforting crumb for Jock. His letter to Marion later that day said:

> Now for something of the greatest importance. Gen. Ross came this morning and was rather nasty about some bits of line which I had not been well enough to go round, and said that as I was always getting sick he could not feel sure

> that I would be fit at a moment of emergency and so I might give a show away. I took the hint and wrote him a letter asking if he advised me to apply to be relieved of my command owing to ill health and saying I could not stand the trenches. He had already written to the Divn. recommending I should be transferred to Home Establishment and attached my letter to it with a handsome compliment to my 'perfect nerve' under 'very heavy fire'. So I shall be turned out before long and sent home in partial disgrace. I am glad except that I fear it will make you ashamed of me. Well I have deserved disgrace for if I had drunk less my health would have been better, but in this case there is no mention of anything but lumbago, though of course many people will say otherwise.
>
> Well it is done now and I am glad for the plain truth is I have not the health and energy to command under these conditions and it is better to go now, put a brave face on it and stick it out, rather than fail really and be really disgraced.

In years to come, the official line would always be that Colonel Campbell's distinguished military career ended because of his ill health. This was a slight economy with the truth, but one thing which could not be denied Jock was the popularity he enjoyed with his men. After his death, the tributes poured in from many who had served with him and under him and he was remembered with great affection. Now, however, he could only feel that he was being sacked. His letter home added:

> Forgive me, oh forgive me my darling. I cannot write more but with shame I must say that I am glad. If I was not going back to you I don't know what I should do, but I still trust in God and you.

By 1916 he was working long hours in Dover in an Army office job, sleeping on the premises at Waterloo Crescent and frequently feeling humiliated by an inability to do the work. Quite naturally: he was a man of great intellect. He knew his classics, could speak a number of Asian languages, was musical and artistic. Here he was a square peg in a round hole as so many of his First World War contemporaries were. He had been sent to be a soldier instead of a scholar when he was a boy; at the age of 44 he was feeling the constraints of that geometric mismatch more than most.

One positive outcome of the fiasco of overstayed leave and posting home was that Marion was pregnant. She stayed in London and received sympathy from her husband, who told her in January of 1916: 'Dearest and Smallest Female, I am sorry to hear that you suffer so much. But I do pray it won't continue so bad.' He met his old nanny, Dada, and hired her for the autumn, told his mother she wouldn't be able to stay in 'her' room at Kilberry and wrote that he was in '7th heaven'. In the October, he was writing to Marion at Kilberry hoping that she 'and Isabel' were well – but such euphoria was not to last. He had gone straight to a clinic in Harrogate when he returned from France and in November 1916 he was back there, writing home that he was glad to hear baby Isabel was 'gaining weight, though slowly'. Between liver packs, douches and magnesia water he wrote to ask if his little daughter had received a rattle from him on what he called her second monthly birthday. But his liverishness prevented his offering much sympathy:

> I don't quite understand whether the usual monthly plague has come on you, or whether your milk is simply failing. Anyway, you write as if you were pretty well and Isabel also.

On November 17, the Danish masseur told him his 'lumbago' was caused 'solely by liver'. On the 20th, he was concerned that Marion could only feed Isabel once a day, 'but still I hope she is thriving for all that'. On the 25th, he decided to risk Marion's displeasure by choosing not to go straight from the Harrogate clinic to Kilberry but to travel instead to London to see his brother Archie, newly arrived from India with wife Violet and their budding family to work in the war ministry, having escaped attacks on British ships on the way. His postscript hoping that Isabel was better was in vain. The baby girl survived for just seven months and her parents were devastated – although her death did not prevent Jock from carrying out his duties or indulging in his pleasures. There were bull sales to go to in Oban, council meetings in Glasgow, meetings about possible employment – he turned down the role of Staff Captain of Volunteers – and meetings with Archie about the estate.

By November 1917, Marion had written to him to say she was again pregnant and asking that he would burn her letter. However much she wanted to keep her condition a secret, her health was again poor and must have had everyone jumping to the correct conclusion. When a son was born, both of them were overjoyed. John Edward, known as Ian, was again the subject of Jock's shopping trips. In a letter from the Central Station Hotel in Glasgow on December 17, 1918 (the usual rendezvous for members of Argyll County Council because it was more accessible than most places in the county itself) he said he had bought a chair and a crawling rug – both a little premature. The following day he went shopping again – and bought a 15 horse power Rover, despite the continuing Kilberry financial crisis. Perhaps he saw the car as a fitting accoutrement for the father of a son and heir and the recently appointed Deputy Lieutenant of Argyll.

By April, 1919, Marion was pregnant again, marking the start of a particularly unhappy nine months. By the autumn, Jock was a patient at Bowden House in Harrow on the Hill, to this day a private psychiatric clinic where people with addiction problems are treated. The doctors were proposing hypnosis, which he was adamant 'will not do'. On September 6 he wrote to Marion, now staying in London with her parents:

> I miss you and the Bubba a lot, but I am thankful that it is not you that have all the fatigues of looking after me. You will perhaps come one day if I stay long – which I don't expect.

But it was a long stay and the couple saw little of each other and wrote much in unhappy tones. He would not allow Marion to operate his bank account while he was in the clinic and when she did visit, he had to apologise for being 'cross' while she was there. On September 20, the doctor said he did not approve of Marion visiting because of her 'condition' but Jock insisted he was leaving anyway. 'I will not give up the Sales and the County Council for anything.' Oban cattle sales and his position in the County mattered above all. 'Bubba Ian' continued to be poorly and the heavily pregnant Marion was worried about her husband demanding to go back into the most difficult environments his alcoholism could confront. On September 24, Jock wrote to Marion:

> Please don't object any more to my going to Oban. It will only cause a quarrel and have no effect. After all you could not expect me to stay here more than 4 weeks and I shall have just done that. If that doesn't cure me nothing will.
>
> On the other hand if I don't go I must chuck everything in the county. There will be an election in November and we shall have to fight for our seats and I won't fight if I cannot come forward as one of the important men of the Council and if I am absent from this last meeting much will be said.
>
> ... *how do you think I will live at home out of everything County?*

He promised to go back to the clinic but insisted on at least a week at home. The doctor, he said, raised no objection and so, despite his condition and Marion's and despite being overdrawn by £259 at the bank, he left Bowden House and went off at the start of October promising the doctor to put himself into a hypnotic state if he felt the urge to drink and Marion that he would come back to London to fetch her home. Ian was suffering from a cold as he left for the Oban cattle sales. The baby was ill enough by the middle of the month for Marion to send messages to Kilberry that Jock should come to her in London. But there were the sales, the council meeting and 'a great Regimental dinner' to be attended before an anxious mother's telegrams could be dealt with. By October 14, Jock was in a mess. Of course he hoped Marion and the baby were better, but he had a bad throat and couldn't wash or dress himself. If only he had left it there, Marion might have believed that this was a bad cold. Sadly, in the erratic handwriting she had come to know meant a drinking bout, he continued to scrawl his way repetitively across the Kilberry headed note paper, lapsing into barrack room language about the servants with whom he was not pleased. Of the table maid, his most repeatable words were that '... this estate is not large enough to hold her and me'. The line which said 'I hope you are better and I do miss you' could only have served to distress his already frantic wife still further. He compounded his felony a few hours later in the cold light of October 15 by writing a second letter in the same scrawl.

> My dearest
> I wrote you a foolish letter in the early hours of this morning chiefly regarding a girl in your service who is probably extremely virtuous and admirable. So it is my fault that I say this estate is not big enough to hold both her and me.

A flurry of telegrams from London followed giving account of Ian and Marion's state of health. Marion's diary records that on October 11, Ian caught a chill. The doctors were called but at 10 pm on October 19, she writes simply 'Ian died.' He was seventeen months old.

Jock arrived on October 21 and left the following day. Marion said in her diary: 'self unable to go'. At 4 pm on the 23rd, their son was interred at the Kilberry mausoleum. The agony of it was that this was a repeat of the funeral for the infant Isabel who simply hadn't thrived. 'We began the service exactly the same as before,' Jock wrote to his grieving wife. 'Ian's coffin rested just exactly on top of Isabel's. Then I shook hands with all I could find and at this Angus played the 'Land of the Lea' well enough. . . I stood at the head and lowered the head into the grave, Wattie [his cousin Walter Campbell] the feet'. Three days later, he told Marion his 'cold' had come back. 'There is still nothing to say, is there?' he wrote. On the 29th he went to Oban bull sales and on the 31st he told his wife he'd be kept busy at Kilberry for a fortnight or so 'at least' and so 'will not come to you unless you want me'.

In London at her mother's house at 35 Ennismore Gardens, Marion grieved the loss of her baby and waited for the next child to arrive. Almost every post brought an epistle from north of the border which must have been a trial to open, wondering each time she ran the blade of the letter opener along the envelope what she could expect to read. On November 4, Jock no doubt failed to reassure her when he wrote: 'Please don't worry about me. I am not nearly so much grieved as you are, being, as you know, callous, though I admit it comes on me hard.' He certainly wasn't planning to join her, despite having spent just those few hours with her after Ian's death. The elections meant a parish council convention on November 15 and the regiment was returning to headquarters in Dunoon, another unmissable event.

When Marion Isabel Durand wrote her letter to her friend Tessa in the summer the year before the Great War broke out, she imagined happiness at Kilberry. In the year after the hostilities were over, the country was still in turmoil, strikes were bringing industry to a halt and the Communists were trying to take seats in the coming election. So many brave men had died. So many more had been deeply affected by the war. And she and John Campbell of Kilberry had lost two children and perhaps their own way in the world. In an effort to re-engage her husband, she wrote to him asking about a name for their expected third child. Neill was his choice for a boy, Marion for a girl. He told her in that bleak November of 1919:

> I will leave it absolutely to you and will not say one other single word about it except this, which I hope you will not think unfair. I gave in to you as you know much against my will to having more than one Christian name the two previous times and it did not turn out well. Do please let there be one only this next time if we are spared to see it. This is to me the most important detail.

He at last travelled to London on November 21. A nurse had been living in since Ian's death, waiting for Mrs Campbell to go into labour. On December 16, a daughter was born at 35 Ennismore Gardens, SW7, weighing 8lbs 2oz. Her mother called her by one single Christian name as her husband had superstitiously requested. This was Miss Marion Campbell of Kilberry.

CHAPTER TWO

A child out of her time

In February 1920, when the infant Marion Campbell was two months old, she was taken from her maternal grandmother's house in London to her ancestral home at Kilberry in Argyll. It was a journey which must have tortured both her parents: Jock Campbell had made the journey the previous October with a tiny white coffin from Harrods in the guard's van of the train. His wife had been ill for months. Both were still grieving the loss of two babies in their own very different ways. John Edward Campbell should have been the Kilberry heir; his dead sister had been conceived as a pledge for the future after Jock's 'retiral' from the trenches in France. Now they were understandably fearful of the threats which a long journey in bad weather could impose upon their new and precious daughter.

The emotional investment made by baby Marion's vulnerable parents was intense. When they married in 1913, he was described as a retired army officer of 41 and she was a 'spinster' of 32. He had his problem with alcohol; she had a sheltered life as a late Victorian debutante who had been presented at court in 1897. It is likely that each believed they were not destined to have partner or family and in 1913 they embarked on a marriage both knew might be difficult. If on that tiring, emotional journey north their thoughts strayed across the intervening years, each must have wondered what the future held for this precious child.

There was no need for a crystal ball to predict that life would not be easy for her. She was born at the end of a devastating war and the world had changed. Even as they embarked on this journey to Scotland, battling with striking railwaymen, socialism was in the ascendancy and around the world, people of property were no longer the automatic objects of respect and deference. Closer to home there were heavy debts owed by Kilberry which could be called in at any time. There was her father's alcohol problem, her mother's poor health, and an entail on Kilberry which meant the estate would not be this baby's but would go to her Uncle Archie or his heirs on her father's death. And although Jock was a popular laird, not everyone loved him. On February 10, 1918, Mrs Campbell had received a typed note with a Kilberry postmark which in melodramatic capital letters read:

> A WARNING
> A MANAGER RUINED YOUR FATHER. TAKE CARE HE WON'T RUIN YOUR HUSBAND.

Marion Campbell senior had a lifelong habit of keeping all her correspondence. Whether or not she showed this strange letter to her husband, she filed it away and no doubt held its dark message in her heart. In 1920 as she settled back into Kilberry after six years of disruption and grief, one of the large Durand family sent her the Australian poet Adam Lindsay Gordon's lines

> Life is mainly froth and bubble
> Two things stand like stone
> Kindness in another's trouble
> Courage in your own

There was little froth and bubble about at Kilberry that year and Marion Isabel Durand was certainly going to have to have courage in her troubles in this new decade. Her mother-in-law wrote on February 25, 1920, as the baby was introduced to Kilberry Castle:

> When I took that child in my arms, I felt such a wave of love for her come over me – may we look upon her as God's little messenger from the darlings we have lost. Not indeed to take their places in our hearts but as a sign of His infinite love and who gave and took away and has given again.

What did Kilberry think about it all? He had stayed in London until December 29 after the birth of his daughter – Marion Og (Young Marion in the Gaelic) as he called her. But he insisted on returning to

Kilberry because of the elections. Then there was New Year, when he laid on the usual hospitality for his workers – a reward he no doubt felt they deserved after the long years of disruption. The fact that he played shinty 'like a fool' to welcome in 1920 with the estate men and laid himself up (or so was his excuse in letters to London SW7 in which he denied having 'touched a drop for ten days') doesn't seem to fit the picture either of a man in mourning for his son or one celebrating the birth of a new daughter His letters to London always assured his 'dearest' wife that he would 'come any day if you send for me' but clearly from the state of his handwriting and his assurance that there was nothing in the house but cider 'so you need not think of bottles' he was still fighting his demon. A twenty first century interpretation of his behaviour might suggest a state of denial over his son's death (he wasn't even sure he'd paid the Harrods' bill for the coffin and undertaking fees) and fear that he would become attached to yet another child only to lose her.

Jock Campbell was a man of his time, however. Indeed, he and his wife seemed to remain set in their Edwardian era as the world moved on. Marion Og was not only quite understandably cosseted and protected but her childhood was to be set in the aspic of a bygone generation. But before that childhood could come under starters orders, her father had to sort out his life a little. His trip from Kilberry to London in February was not only to bring his wife and baby home but to check back into Bowden House. On January 12, 1920, the Scots 'Old New Year's Day', he was writing to Marion to sympathise with her being unable to breast feed the baby and hoping she was going well 'on the Glaxo'. On the 20th, he was at Bowden House confessing in a letter to her that he had lost 'much weight' since October. Little Ian's death and binge drinking had followed his previous visit to Bowden House, and he had lost 21lbs during that four month period. He explained to his wife: 'I had been quite teetotal for a long time except the last day.' Now he was back on the regime of physical exertion, hypnosis and healthy eating which Bowden House imposed. He was anxious to hear about the baby, still a frail mite, but also had to explain to her mother why his binge had prevented him from stopping in Glasgow to sort out the servant problem on his way south. Marion was by now on Cow and Gate and getting out in the fresh air but like her father, was still failing to gain weight. Papa also wanted to be out in the fresh air and paraded an 'important meeting' in Glasgow as a valid reason for quitting Bowden House. There is no doubt he was feeling pressured. He was being urged by all and sundry to sort out his affairs.

His brother Archie, again Jock's heir since baby Ian's demise, had written 'reminding me of the present circumstances, my having a daughter and no son, so the same settlement must be made as when Isabel was alive. That is steps must be taken to keep the estate together and for him to have the money left for paying off the mortgages'. Jock assured Marion that this situation only applied if he died before his mother and that she and little Marion would be well provided for – 'I should think about £25,000 altogether at the very least' he wrote optimistically from Bowden House. The money intended for the estate, however, was to be settled on Archie.

Promising the doctors that if he fell off the wagon while in Glasgow, he would return immediately to Bowden House, Jock told Marion that if he managed to stay off alcohol he would go home then come back to London for her if she could travel between the 15th and 20th of February. Oh yes – and when she and the baby got to Kilberry, he would have to leave straight away for the bull sales. In Glasgow at the end of January, he interviewed three men as potential servants, hiring a cook, a butler-valet and an electrician who would take charge of the Acetylene lighting, assist the cook, split wood, carry coal and possibly act as plumber when required. This gentleman, Alexander Murray, was to receive £40 a year. Alic Maclean, the 21-year-old charged with the butler-valet job, would earn £45 a year and Francis Reid, a former army and merchant navy cook, would get £60. He wrote to Marion:

> I have no doubt that you will object to them all but still it is something to have servants for you to *shikar* [hunt] when you get home and it will keep you from wearying.

The important meetings included a foot and mouth disease conference in Perth and then Jock returned to the Central Station Hotel in Glasgow on January 30, by which time he had regretted hiring the men, 'as I cannot think it possible they will agree the very stringent regulations you prescribe'. This letter to London concludes that the men must simply be sacked and 'we shall be where we were at the worst.' He went home to Kilberry and was confined there by gales and inadequate train services. Only the cook had written to say he wanted the job, influenza was spreading around Knapdale and although the news from London about Marion Og was causing concern, telegrams simply caused her father to continue to procrastinate over his return south. He wanted to buy a new Ford – a small car to save petrol. He wanted to organise a tombstone for the children and sketches went back and forth between the couple. Marion obviously wanted a full complement of servants in place when she came home but her husband, having managed to get the male cook established felt that the bull sales were enough for him to contend with.

And then the sales went well, the baby began to thrive and although Marion needed a special corset to combat the gynaecological problems she was experiencing after the birth, a few letters of humour and affection went between the pair. It couldn't last. On February 15, another of those scrawled, ink-blotted letters went south which must not only have worried Marion but hurt her deeply. Clearly written after a binge – or perhaps even during one – it ended:

> By the way I suppose that this last illness of yours and the belt etc. means that we continue to be celibate for the next year or two? I only want to know before I see you. . . I shall probably see you on Friday morning but I have asked my dentist for an appointment and so can't tell you when I shall come.

And so, the couple came together and took their baby home. Two months later, yet another sadness hit them when Jock's mother died. He went to London and took charge of the invitations, including one to the Bishop of Glasgow and another to the Duke of Argyll. The funeral service was held at Hampstead Parish Church and then there was another sad train journey with his mother's remains in the guard's van. The interment at Kilberry was all too familiar a situation. So were the death duties and settling of debts.

In times of crisis, family, tradition and Kilberry estate were the important anchors in Jock's life. He surrounded himself with those elements of the family which were perhaps less critical of him – his sister Molly and his cousin Ivy Arbuthnot – and he set about imbuing his daughter with a sense of her position, even if that position was, under the terms of the entail on Kilberry, never to be hers. He clearly fell in love with this smiling child. A year after his mother's death, when his wife Marion was in a nursing home in Glasgow, he wrote to say: 'Ivy is well and charming as usual. Bubba (the baby) is simply beaming, looking beautiful and walking splendidly.'

Later that April, with 'Bubba Marion' at home in the care of her nanny Catherine, he had cause to write to Marion in that nursing home from his own hospital bed in Stirling to explain with a certain degree of blustering bravado that he had tripped over his spurs and fallen badly during a regimental event. He had five stitches over his left eyelid and decided to go straight home as his doctors ordered rather than going to see Marion at Park Gardens in Glasgow. Then the car was lacking a part, the trains were on strike, May Day threatened to be one of demonstrations in Glasgow and again, Jock found it difficult to get his wife home. Instead, he wrote: 'Bubba grows more delightful every day. She is out all day, even after tea. . . ' As plans were made for the fragile Marion to travel home by steamer, he again wrote: 'Bubba is on the shore most of the day. She has some heat spots for which Lean [the doctor] is to send a lotion.'

Although Marion Og was just nineteen months old, these days of freedom may well have shaped her memories of childhood. This wild child playing on the Kilberry shoreline is how a much older Marion Campbell was to present her early days, yet her cousins, her contemporaries and even her second nanny retained a very different idea of the little Marion. When her protective mother was there, prim walks and even primmer clothes were the order of the day. Alone with her father, she was probably a much freer child. Perhaps she even spoke the 'kitchen Gaelic' she sometimes claimed for herself in later years – a language in which her mother dabbled only intellectually and would have felt was inappropriate for Miss Campbell of Kilberry.

Mother came back from the nursing home that summer but by the July of 1922, father was back in Bowden House. Bored, confused, he sent his 'best love to Baba and many kisses to her and you with great and deep felt gratitude for you.'

Poor Jock's problem was responsive neither to Marion's prayers nor Bowden House's most modern techniques of counselling, hypnosis and physical exertions. And as the problem grew, so did his paranoia. Brother Archie became the enemy, out to serve his own ends. There is no doubt that Archie had his own problems. Having spent a lifetime in India he now found himself about to come home to a country where property was too expensive for a man on a colonial pension trying to put his large family through public schools. His mother had had her own financial problems, her fortune having been swallowed up by Kilberry. Archie, heir to the estate if his brother didn't produce a son, didn't want to see it dissipated. He had written a lengthy letter from Dharamsala in 1920 suggesting measures Jock should take to maintain the estate in the family. He advised his brother to make a will, even if it had to be changed at a later date.

> It seems to me that it is not possible both to retain the estate in the male line and to make lavish provision for females.

he wrote in the male-oriented spirit of his generation. His main concern was to:

> . . . escape the pain of having to sell the entailed estate immediately on succeeding to it as well as the odium which I should incur from the inhabitants of the estate (who could see in my action nothing but pure selfishness) and perhaps from other members of the family.

Archie wanted to make sure his own heirs would not be made paupers by Kilberry. He wanted the mortgages to be paid off to clear the estate for the next heir and was even willing that the family silver be sold off to benefit the children.

Jock's alcohol problem was improved neither by living with the reality of constraints which gripped estates such as Kilberry after the Great War nor by letters from his brother which he increasingly saw as a threat to his autonomy, the welfare of his immediate family, and his peace of mind. Archie continued to urge Jock to make a will and attend to the future of the estate. One letter spelled it out in a particularly brutal formula:

> Should you die suddenly intestate, Coulaghailtro [one of the farms] and the undemarcated area of Baile as well as the whole £15,000 odd of mortgages on the estate would go to your daughter and the whole of the stock and furniture would go to her mother. This would create absolute deadlock. I probably couldn't raise by further mortgages of the estate sufficient money to buy the stock and furniture and to pay death duties and if I could the estate obviously could not pay the interest on these fresh mortgages as well as that on the old. I know that Hog [the family lawyer] knows and Marion knows what your intentions are but young Marion being a minor there could be no arrangement between parties concerned to carry out those intentions by surrender of rights. The estate clearly would have to be sold and in present circumstances I do not think that young Marion's guardians would consider it justified in her interest in trying to buy it. Therefore the estate would probably pass to the Birkmyre clan [a disliked branch of the family] and in such case would be lost to us.
>
> The position is much more critical than it was when my mother was alive. If she had lived and had survived you then the heir at any rate would have got the entailed estate free of mortgage.
>
> I don't feel as if I myself could possibly sell the estate, including my father and mother's graves – not to speak of your own!

Archie admitted this was 'devilish cold blooded'. Rubbing salt into Jock's wounds (no doubt with the best possible intention but certainly not read that way by his brother) he added:

> What I really wish for is for you to have another son and pass things on to him after living to a respectable old age. What I do not want is for myself to come into Kilberry as an old man and have then to see it pass out of the family.

The letters went back and forward between the brothers on the subject of mortgages and inheritance, always with an unwritten assumption that Jock was not long for this world. Archie may have been a long way away but news of Jock's lifestyle travelled fast. He was aware of Jock's fall at Stirling – that ignominious headlong sprawl when he slipped on his spurs after a military celebration – and news of Marion senior's operation in Glasgow reached him in Lahore during a Sikh uprising and agitation by Ghandi. There was a censorious tone to Archie's letters – perhaps for no other reason than because his work on the legal circuit in India informed his style – but to be fair to Jock, he was trying to sort out his affairs. Having seen to his late mother's outstanding bills, he was in touch with Mr Hog of the family's legal firm Pearson, Robertson and Maconochie at 11 St Colme Street in Edinburgh. Mr Hog suggested that by selling Achaglachgach, Jock could raise over £13,000 and be able to reduce taxation and debts.

The toddler whose future was to be profoundly affected by the outcome of this shuffling of debt was meanwhile left in a world of her own. After her operation, her mother went south to recuperate. Her father was frequently away from Kilberry, whether it was on Highland Cattle Association business or council affairs which took him to the Central Station Hotel in Glasgow or – most dangerously – at regimental reunions where he was still seen as the hero (and indeed he was awarded medals).

A nurse wrote to Mrs Campbell in London in April, 1920: 'Baby is splendid and very pleased to have her Daddy back.' Marion continued to take delight in her father, seeing him as a handsome, clever figure. A linguist, a man of undoubted intellect, a man who gave service to his kinsmen, his county and his country, a charmer with a fine moustache and a good knee for the kilt, a man of music and letters, he was indeed ostensibly worthy of hero worship. Marion Og was not exposed to his furies, or to the pathetic behaviour of a man whom neighbours eventually stopped asking to their tables because he stayed behind in the dining room to drain the dregs of other men's glasses.

Mrs Rena Sinclair, née Mackay, the nanny who came to look after Marion when she was six years old was to recall that she once was alone overnight with Kilberry and was afraid to go to bed. She said: 'I stayed in the castle alone with him once and he came home drunk. I had to sit up till two o'clock in the morning because he sat in the smoking room and the fire was on and I was terrified he would fall in the fire.' Mrs Sinclair believed Kilberry didn't bother with his daughter, yet Marion Campbell spent a lifetime singing her father's praises, giving him credit for all she knew about Highland cattle, history and much more. The man's charisma remained powerful enough to charm his daughter and keep his wife on board however distressing the situation became.

It was to become painfully so.

By September 1922, Marion senior had power of attorney over her husband's affairs and was living at Coulaghailtro – another of the five estate farms – where Archie wrote to her about the sale of Achaglachgach. The entail on the lands to be sold would have to be broken, he said. He explained that although he was heir, his permission did not have to be sought but that a legal procedure had to be followed with papers being served on him and his son Angus, which would take some time as he was in India. Disentailing Craig and Achaglachgach would not commit Jock to selling but would allow Marion to exercise her power of attorney.

> Jock ought to be made to realise that this will be the effect of disentailing, and, if my opinion is likely to weigh with him, can be told that I understand the position thoroughly, and can see no objection.

A maze of repayments would have to be made from the proceeds of any land sale. The lawyers continued to be confident it would raise £13,000 and Archie told Marion this should get rid of much of the Kilberry debt. He was, of course, against the sale of Kilberry as an entity even if this would bring in an income from the invested proceeds. He pointed out that trying to live at 'the big house' – the castle – for most of the year on Jock's current income of £1,050 per annum was not a viable proposition. And he reminded Marion that she was 'practically acting as a trustee mainly for Jock but partly for the next heir to the estate, myself at present'. As such, she would have to bring about retrenchment: the chauffeur would have to go, wages would have to be cut, one of the keepers would have to be dismissed and Jock, Marion and their child would have to live at Coulaghailtro all year round with two servants and a year-round tenant would have to be found for the castle. If these measures were not taken, the alternative according to Archie would be the 'possibility of something far more squalid in ten years time'.

Archie believed he and Marion were fighting the same battle, if from different corners. He wrote:

> Were the retention of the estate not a matter so vital to Jock's well being we might have conflicting interests, you wishing to make him as comfortable in body as possible and I wanting an effort made to save the estate. As matters are there is nothing of this sort.

Archie saw it as no exaggeration that the idea of the estate going out of the family after his death would 'embitter' Jock's life and 'react upon his health'. He assured his sister-in-law:

> As for young Marion, when she grows up she would want her father's wishes to be carried out as far as they could be . . . what I long and pray for is that Jock may be brought to realise what an asset his personality is in the object for which we are all striving and how important it is for this reason as well as for all the other many reasons that he should look after his health and keep well.

Archie warned that he was too far away to give advice quickly, but offered a letter in his handwriting 'to show to someone else' or a cable if either would be any use. His long letter, sealed with red wax, concluded with an appreciation of Marion's 'difficulties'. But as matters went down hill in the coming years, Marion came to become infected by Jock's paranoia about Archie's intentions. They were certainly shaped by self concern, but also by the same passion for Kilberry which fired Jock. Through the dispassionate language which had become a habit during those long years in the Indian civil service there does shine, however, a deep concern for the older brother whose childhood had been shared at Kilberry and at school at Harrow, where he had looked up to Jock as top scholar in his year. Jock had been, according to C.P. Wilson (known to the boys as 'Plummy'), 'one of the bonniest of boys. . . a fine specimen of British boyhood, outstanding both in physique and intellect' . . . who 'swept the boards in the Harrow Scholarships Examination' in 1886. For Archie, he had also been the brother with whom he learned about Highland cattle and with whom he wrote the famous Kilberry piping book; who shared Highland ideas of duty and tradition absorbed from their father. Now his brother was sick and Archie's concern, though perhaps ill expressed, was no doubt genuine.

The points over which the family were to disagree in later years had in fact been advised by Archie in those dark days at the beginning of the 1920s: sell the family silver, make a will, sell off the farms, break the entail. Those letters to Jock and to Marion bear silent witness to that, and his kindliness shines through his later letters to his niece when she was left alone to shoulder the same burden which had forced her father under.

The Kilberry couple swung wildly between extravagance and stringent economies. In 1921 they had a new bathroom put into the castle and for some years there were a dozen servants. Later, as Jock and Marion fought to keep their heads above water, they used tactics such as Archie had suggested, spending the winter at a farmhouse on Loch Aweside so that they didn't have to pay rates on the unoccupied castle and the summer with London relatives or one of the Kilberry farmhouses – or even in Brittany, where Marion was photographed looking forlorn. Rena Sinclair remembered the number of servants being reduced drastically and Mrs Campbell taking on the cooking herself, leaving Marion more and more in Rena's company. The walks on which Jock had taken Marion when she was a three year old and filled her head with the legends of Mid Argyll (Diarmid's Grave at Achaglachgach inspired him to tell her the legend of Diarmid, ancestor of all the Campbells who ran away with his uncle's wife and was slain by the poisoned bristle of a boar) were long finished. Rena Sinclair said: 'People used to think that the father, instead of sitting in the hall at the fire reading all day – he was a very clever man – should be taking her out rather than me. I walked her for miles. We just wandered about the grounds.'

Throughout that decade, the Campbells of Kilberry were like a family of swans, gliding elegantly as always through Argyll society while underneath the water they paddled frantically to keep up the expected unruffled appearance of paternalistic laird, elegant wife and cosseted child. On October 20, 1921, Marion Og made her first public appearance, standing up on a table to present prizes to Kilberry workers after a ploughing match and make a little speech in Gaelic. Miss Campbell of Kilberry's debut as a public speaker was reported in the *Argyllshire Advertiser*, where she was reported as saying: *Tha mi glé-thoilichte a'bhith faicinn sibh uille a'rithis* – I am very pleased to see you again. As Marion recalled many years later, this was 'totally absurd' from a two-year-old and received as such with gales of laughter. She claimed her father was 'overcome with remorse and the the fear that I might never face another audience'.

Her father intended her to inherit, to become the laird and to take on all the responsibilities which that role still then implied, but her schooling was done at home with her mother's supervision under the Parents' National Educational Union (PNEU) scheme. This, according to the Union's brochure, had been founded by Charlotte M. Mason in 1888 in response to a demand from 'thoughtful parents' who desired to know how to give intelligent supervision and guidance to the development of their children. The correspondence course young Marion followed was instituted in 1891 using PNEU methods. Marion was left-handed and found writing tiring, so she dictated her work to an anxious mother who constantly treated her as an ailing child. Rena Sinclair remembered that when she began to look after her at the age of six, Marion was a prim child whose prescribed exercise was walking with her nanny in the still well-kept gardens of Kilberry. Her mother ran the house in the manner of a *grande chatelaine*, whatever the perilous state of her budget. Morag, Anne and Betsy had a strict time-table – Mrs Campbell's room was to be 'done' at 10 am on Thursdays and Kilberry's at 9.30 am on Wednesdays. Breakfast was at 8 am, dinner at 12.25 pm, tea at 6 pm and supper at 9 pm. At 9.45 pm, water had to be put in the bedrooms. Mrs Campbell dressed in her own room but to accommodate the cleaning, on Thursdays she dressed in Kilberry's room. Rena looked after her clever, pretty little charge with devotion.

Lessons were perhaps less than academic but from her mother Marion also learned about wild birds and plants and how to draw them and from her father she absorbed a love of language. She famously recalled that when she went to him in his study to ask him to read to her, he would simply read out loud the book he was engrossed in, whether it was Homer in the original Ancient Greek, some Latin text or a book in English far from suitable for an under-five. She loved the 'noise' those languages made and perhaps it was then that words became her passion. She dictated stories and poems to her mother before she could write herself and her mother willingly nurtured her talent by dutifully taking down her daughter's imaginings. Often they were about children becoming involved in the affairs of the kings and princes, and perhaps significantly they also involved families with three children.

Just as he made no concession to the age of his daughter when she asked for a story, so too must Jock have prattled on about his own interests when they talked together. Highland cattle was his specialist subject and she must often have been told that Daddy was away at the bull sales. In October 1926, she sent him a postcard which reflects the gypsy life they were already leading. She first addressed it to Kilberry, crossed that out and wrote 'Station Hotel Oban', and then put 'Castle Sweyne Cottage Achnamara'. It read: 'I hope you like this PC I have sent you. love from Marion.' Kilberry Castle may have defined her life but as a child she was frequently living with one or both parents in a farm house, with Argyll friends, or with London relatives. She developed a nice, teasing relationship with her mother's brother Morty (Mortimer Henry Marion Durand, youngest of Sir Henry Durand's brood of seven and later to be a naval commander), who encouraged her imagination with funny letters about Russian spies and daring agents, all written in nonsense French or silly rhymes.

Rena Sinclair described her charge was 'very mannerly and very old fashioned. . . she was a beautiful looking wee girl.' Almost eight decades after his death she ruefully said of the laird: 'They said if he had kept off the drink he would have been a Field Marshall.' Rena called his little daughter with the long fair hair 'prim'. Betty Durie, née Learoyd, who knew Marion from the age of about seven or eight, described her as 'perjink' – a Scottish word which imbues primness with a pejorative quality her affectionate nanny would never have implied. Betty, was the only daughter of an Indian Army grandee whose widow had set up home in Ardrishaig. She was a year older than Marion and much more in the Mid Argyll social loop than Marion ever was. She recalled 'Kilberry' as a strong presence but Mrs Campbell as a much more shadowy (and 'perjink') figure. Helen Kenneth, Uncle Archie's daughter, who was three years older than Marion and first met her when her little cousin was four, said:

> I was taken with my brothers to stay at the castle with our oldest nanny and one can see looking back that Uncle Jock and Aunt Marion seemed rather elderly parents for this little tiny girl and were also rather crushed by the death of their little boy. Marion was the only survivor – and she would of course be a girl. My impression was that it was a rather austere, dignified atmosphere – very kind and very hospitable but Marion was really rather repressed as a little girl. My first sight of her was standing on the steps looking at these unusual things – my brothers and me, all rather well made. She hardly saw anyone in that very remote place.

Archie's family were 'parked', as Helen put it, with a variety of relatives while their father was in India and had a 'completely English' upbringing. When Archie came home on leave, the children and nanny were sent on ahead to Kilberry, the last part of the journey being made by steamer to Tarbert. 'We all lined up on the deck and the captain knew who we were and told us that Kilberry was waiting for us. Our nanny broke down because she hadn't seen a tall, elderly, grey haired man wearing a kilt before. Kilts were for little boys at dancing classes.' The children thought they were never going to reach Kilberry as Uncle Jock stopped at every farm and introduced Archie's offspring. When they did arrive, there was their cousin standing at the front door to welcome them. Helen, who had been advised to wear her convent school gym slip for the journey, said:

> She was an apparition, like a Victorian child from an old Scottish painting. The most striking thing about her was her hair, which reached to the back of her knees. It was like a

> golden cloak all round her little form, and a pure white silk dress down to her ankles.
>
> Marion was speechless with joy. She had never seen boys before and she took to them at once. The impression was that she was being very strictly brought up. Quite affectionally, but Aunt Marion was very aristocratic, rigid, shy and retiring and never gave way to any kind of emotion and Marion never had any outlet. It was all very stiff at first but then she relaxed and enjoyed our company. When my father said to her that she seemed to be fond of books, she told him rather pathetically 'I live in books'.

Jock was grand but less stiff than her mother. When Marion was bridesmaid to Catherine, her first nanny, she wasn't allowed flowers in her hair. Instead, a hat was ordered from London. Because she had very little social life with other children and was so stiffly brought up, Helen confessed that some saw her cousin as 'a little toffee nosed'. She said:

> Poor Marion was longing to romp and run about but with that long hair she couldn't climb trees or crawl under bushes or play hide and seek on the shore hiding behind rocks like we did because her hair always tripped her up. She said to me once 'I suppose now I have to go in and change for tea.' I asked 'What will you wear?' and she said 'Oh, I suppose a tea gown'.

Even her mother saw her as 'an odd little creature with a personality of her own', so it was little wonder that outsiders saw Marion as something of an oddity. She didn't play games as others did, although she derived a great deal of amusement from her 'huge family of dolls', according to her mother, and took Princess Carnation with her everywhere. She dressed like a child from the ancestral portraits on the walls of Kilberry Castle. Her manner was grand and probably inappropriate. Because her parents were experiencing economic (not to mention emotional) problems, she did not take her place in the social milieu of local lairds and their offspring. Her life seems to have been lived through her imaginings and her stories while her future was juggled by adults scarcely capable of buying the weekly groceries.

A year before she was introduced to her more robust and worldly cousins, her father had actually been following Archie's advice. Sadly for her, his instructions meant little because trustees other than those Jock nominated were put in charge of the estate. On February 23, 1923, when Marion was little more than three years old, a petition was lodged by Lt Col John Campbell of Kilberry 'for authority to record Instrument of Disentail'. Three days later, Jock received a letter from Alan Hog the lawyer, in which he enclosed a print of the Petition. He told him:

> . . . the entail of Kilberry is what is called an old entail. That being so and as you were born after 1848 you are entitled to disentail without consent and without paying compensation to the next heirs. In other words after the formal procedure of this Petition is carried through there is no restriction upon you as to the destination of the property.
>
> In view of the disentail and in the further view of the prospective sale of stock at Coulaghailtro, I would suggest that your existing Will ought to be reconsidered.

And on April 16, 1923, Kilberry did in fact make a new Will. His daughter did not open the copy in its sealed envelope, witnessed by two other people, until February 2, 1989 – a little late for Kilberry estate's history to be rewritten. That letter read:

> Dear Hog
> I am just going to Tarbert to get the deed of Disentail witnessed. In case of accident I tell you now that it is my wish that all my property whatsoever shall, in the event of my death, go to my daughter and to my wife as sole trustee for her until her majority. And this I declare as my last will and testament and revoke all other wills made by me.
> Signed at Kilberry this sixteenth day of April 1923.

It was signed John Campbell of Kilberry and witnessed by A. McNeill and W. Linners. It was a document legal under Scottish law and in line with Archie's advice to make a will, although the idea of breaking the male entail on the property was not what Archie had in mind.

Five years later, after an increasingly difficult period for both of Marion's parents, Jock was dead. It was not expected but it can hardly have come as a surprise to his wife, his doctor, his brother or even his neighbours and workers. Mrs Campbell had experienced embarrassment over the non-payment of bills in local shops. The family silver was sold off by Dowell's, a George Street auctioneers in Edinburgh – presented anonymously in the catalogue of a sale to take place from July 7 to 9, 1927, as 'rare and valuable antique silver including that from a West Highland Castle'. Some of Marion's personal property went into this auction but most items were Campbell heirlooms, including Georgian silver sauce tureens, salvers, candlesticks, decanter stands, a brandy saucepan and other items, as well as some modern silver and Sheffield plate. The lot fetched £1,020.17s after the expenses of Col Henderson, Jock's old army crony and now the estate factor, were deducted – scarcely enough to meet the estate's debt but at least that Christmas a party was held at Kilberry according to tradition on December 27, a couple of weeks after Marion's eighth birthday. Kilberry and his wife were at home on the estate for the shinty on January 12, the 'old New Year', although Marion senior remarked in her diary that it was too wet for her daughter. They had been living at Ford in the modest Finchairn farmhouse and were driven over to Kilberry from Ford Hotel by 'Young Gray' a local driver. It had taken just five minutes short of two hours to cover the thirty or so miles with just one stop. On a fair day, the journey could be done in an hour and a half but now it was wet and the road was bad.

By the end of January, Dr McCall Smith, the family doctor, was called in to see Jock. He sounded his heart and said his blood pressure was that 'of a young man' but he told Jock he wasn't taking enough exercise. On February 1, Marion was having to poultice him because he felt 'seedy' and had had a very bad night. On Thursday, February 2, the doctor was called back at 6.30 am. At 9.30 am, he called for a second opinion. Marion wrote in her diary:

> Terrible day of increasing pain and thirst. So patient and uncomplaining. Mr Russell and Nurse came at last. Stopped by snow on the Rest [Rest and Be thankful – the pass on the military Croe Road from Loch Lomond to Inveraray].

Operation 9 pm – successful but revealed extent of illness. Surgeon and Doctor both very grave about the case.

On February 3, Canon Moir from the Episcopal Church was called although the doctor was pronounced 'pleased' with Jock's progress. The next day, the doctor was 'disappointed' and Marion contacted Archie and other relatives. Colonel Henderson called and took little Marion to his home on February 4 when the doctor again had to be sent for after Jock had a bad night. Brother Archie was just one of a succession of visitors throughout the Sunday. On the Monday, Jock was declared 'desperately ill'. Mrs Campbell's diary recorded that on Tuesday, February 7, 1928, at 9.30 am, John Campbell of Kilberry died. On the Friday, he was buried at Kilberry at 3 pm with military honours. Some relatives stayed and went back to the Ford Hotel with Marion, where her daughter was brought back from the Hendersons on Monday, February 13.

On February 17, the heavy luggage was taken from Kilberry on William Bell's lorry. Marion, her sister Beryl Haviland, her eight-year-old daughter and Colonel Henderson went over to Kilberry where she saw 'the wreaths still beautiful in the tomb'. She wrote in her diary: 'Home by Achaglachgach very late' – but where WAS home now? Since Marion had been born in 1919, the Campbells of Kilberry had lived a precarious and unsettled life. Now Kilberry was in his grave and his widow was told she hadn't a roof over her head. After taking Holy Communion at Christ Church in Lochgilphead, she, Beryl, Rena and young Marion left for Glasgow via Dalmally and on Monday, February 21, eight years almost to the day since she and Jock had brought their baby daughter home to Kilberry, the return journey was made to Euston on the 10.15 am train.

CHAPTER THREE

Exile

It was a strange widowhood; perhaps an even stranger childhood. Rena Sinclair, Marion's nanny, remembered going south to Durand relatives after Kilberry's death. She said:

> . . . after her father died, her aunt, her mother's sister, took them to Staffordshire and we were there for a month to let the mother get a rest. She stayed in bed for a week and wrote a hundred letters thanking folk for sympathy.

Some of the sympathy letters went to Archie. He told Marion the line had to be drawn somewhere and that these had probably been written to him to save her from the pain of response. Mrs Campbell as always drew up her lists and did it 'properly'. But while the letters may have been written with a degree of obsession, in other ways, life went on. By February 24, she was taking her daughter to a dancing class in London which she said 'Marion joined after some shy hesitation'. There was shopping, a children's drawing lesson, more dancing classes. Marion had a cold and the doctor was called, but then Campbell cousin Ivy Arbuthnot came to dine, Granny Durand took the two Marions to the zoo and little Marion had her photograph taken.

Mrs Campbell's diary began to bristle with accounts. Every small purchase was recorded there with its price, and even the money put into the collection at Brompton Church was written down. The budget, however, seemed to run to little Marion's first ever trip to the theatre on Easter Monday and at the end of that week, the child was mounted on a pony called Daylight to her 'great joy'. Rena Sinclair was with them (her wages were £2.12s 4d, recorded in the diary with all other outgoings). She said: 'I loved it. The housekeeper was a very knowledgeable woman and a most interesting person. We hired bikes and went round all over the place. I didn't know the Durands so much but any I met were very nice.'

But in effect, Marion and her mother were locked out of Kilberry while trustees decided what was the best course of action. Keeping Mrs Campbell's hands off the property seemed part of that master plan. Eventually, mother, daughter and nanny went back to Argyll on June 12. Mrs Campbell had pleaded with trustee George Robertson in May for his consent to return to Kilberry and stay there until 'about July 20'. She told George:

> It is necessary for me to return. Practically all Marion's and my possessions, including clothes, are locked away at home. It is not possible to travel about as I have been doing, with such luggage.

There was worse. Mrs Campbell added:

> I am hurt beyond all expression to receive . . . a cutting from the *Glasgow Herald* advertising my house for sale.
> I will not tell Marion until she is quite herself again. It will be a most terrible shock to her.

To learn that their home was to be sold through the medium of a newspaper advertisement – and told by the lawyers that Colonel Henderson, Archie and her brother knew of the advert, and that it was 'impossible' to inform her of 'everything' – must have been devastating. It must also have been humiliating in the extreme to have been escorted back there from the south by 'Mr and Mrs Archibald Campbell' as Marion now referred very coolly to her brother and sister-in-law. She had written to Mr Hog that although Jock expressly left his brother's name out of his will, Archie had been 'very kind to me personally'. Even so, she was puzzled and annoyed that it was Archie who was being consulted on all her affairs – the brother Jock had to be persuaded to allow at his bedside at the end.

However, Ivy Arbuthnot also went to Kilberry and young Marion seems to have been protected from both the bereavement and the proposed sale of her home. There were picnics and walks and her mother said she climbed up Dundubh, a local hill, 'like a deer', but she was prone to chills all that year and her mother took no chances, calling in the doctor at every opportunity.

And Dr Bryce McCall Smith of The Corran, Lochgilphead, had another role to play in little Marion's life. She was never to accept that her father was an alcoholic – or indeed, anything less than a towering giant deserving the utmost respect and affection. What little girl who has experienced a loving relationship with her father could be convinced otherwise? But all the circumstances surrounding his death must have impinged on her childhood. Rena Sinclair recalled:

> He wasn't very ill before he died. It was just drink. His brother Mr Archie Campbell and his wife thought it would be nice if he could lie in Kilberry in the hall until he was buried. They had to carry him down the stairs at the farmhouse on planks. Marion was sent to a friend and I went to the castle where Kilberry was. After that they had to get out.

Yet Marion was helped in maintaining her hero worship for her father by a mother determined to keep up appearances and by Dr McCall Smith two weeks after Jock's death. He sent medicine for little Marion and enclosed a note which read:

> I think you should know that Kilberry died of malignant disease of some abdominal organ – probably stomach or bowel – the cause of which is unknown and which can in no way be attributed to Alcoholism. It grew silently and by the time it made itself manifest was inoperable.

He referred to Jock's exceptional mind, as did so many of the letters of sympathy received, then urged Mrs Campbell to take time to get fit before she started work 'or even housekeeping' again.

> I would suggest that you do nothing for two or three months – if possible not even worry about the future.

But there was no option but to worry about the future. Jock may, as Margaret Bonham-Carter suggested in her letter of condolence, have gone to his glory and 'his troubled soul... at last found the peace which passeth all understanding', but for his widow and daughter there was no home to go to and his widow was ill herself. In July of 1928, while she and Marion were back living at Ford Hotel on Loch Awe, she thought that she, too, might not survive. She wrote to Ivy, who had gone home to 6 Burton Court, London SW, confiding her wishes for her daughter were she not to be there to care for her. In the 1970s, her daughter read that letter for the first time and wrote on the envelope: 'MIC re her (and my Father's) ideas for me – alas never communicated to me later on. MC'.

Her mother's letter revealed the state of her mind as much as her physical state. She had spent fifteen years on a knife edge, emotionally and economically. She had lost two children, her husband and her health and she had no home to which she could retreat with her daughter in her period of mourning. She told Jock's sympathetic cousin: 'I am more and more anxious – desperately so.' The financial worries were only part of the problem. She had a cyst of which she evidently thought the worst and confided in Ivy with much underscored emphasis:

> Whilst I can I wish to tell you that if anything should happen to me and Rena Mackay [later Sinclair] is free I wish her to be sent for to attend to Marion. She loves the child devotedly and is devotedly loved by Marion. No-one could help my darling so well if I were not there.
>
> I should not wish her to be brought up with Beryl's children – one is too old, the other too young – is reason enough.
>
> You know that I have made my cousin Reginald Monckton her guardian because as he has now retired and inherited his property so far as one can forsee he is settled. You and Mother are Trustees. Both Jock and I wish Marion to be brought up on low church principles, and at present she is inclined to follow architecture. This gives much scope for many talents and all her schooling will come in usefully. We all 3 discussed this and Jock was quite of the same opinion. He thought my grandfather's engineering genius

and my father's artistic sense showed in Marion's character and that as an architect she would have scope for these. Also and this is a most important point – it is a profession which can improve conditions of life – of real service to others.

I don't feel ill but I have had such a lesson this winter in other people's muddles and want of preparedness that I wish to try to avoid such myself.

. . . More and more I feel that George [trustee George Robertson] and Archie have some definite end in view and more and more do I resent the consultation of Archie. Jock very expressly – and as I see now, tho' I did not agree with him at the time – very wisely left Archie out of the trusteeship. Archie is warped – he has thought for years of himself as 'Kilberry'. All his thoughts have worked round that and now he is unable to see truly. Jock was quite right. He had a very uncanny insight into people's motives. You will say, 'But how sad for Archie to be disappointed'. Is it not just as sad for Jock? He wished his daughter to succeed, as his son was dead. Had he been able to leave her well-off he would very probably have acted against his own wishes – he was not selfish and he perhaps more than any of those others grieved that there would be no 'Kilberry'. They have done what they could to make the loss of my husband a bitter bitter loss.

Yours lovingly
Marion Campbell

Was it paranoia or were there forces conspiring against her and her daughter? It was all such a muddle that it is difficult to sort out whether Jock had simply left a mess behind him or if the lawyers – and his brother – were working for their own ends. The fact that mother and daughter had to live in hotels – first at Lochgair, then Ford then back to Lochgair – was not conducive to either's peace of mind or physical health. The year was punctuated by finalities – the sale of the Kilberry fold at the Highland Cattle sale in October; the death of a Durand sister – so when Marion's dolls' house was liberated from Kilberry and brought to the hotel at Lochgair, some small fragment of stability must have been restored. Even so, the child suffered a succession of sore throats and chills, treated by Dr McCall Smith.

They had left Ford in September without paying the bill. The trustees were advising that the estate should be 'nursed' through the current economic depression then sold. A committee of creditors, meanwhile, were ever present like spectres at the feast and Mrs Campbell was told that she, too, was a creditor of the estate to the tune of her £4,000 marriage contract money, but that she would have to wait like the rest until the estate was sold. It is impossible to conjecture what she thought about her £4,000 being balanced against possession of her home. Penniless, she needed the former and could not afford to live in the latter, but her heart was in her marital home. In November, Mrs Campbell was notified she would receive a pension – a lump sum of £25 plus £6.1s 4d for herself and £18.6s 7d for Marion, a total of £49.7s 11d, which was a godsend. There was an early birthday party for Marion on December 15, attended by adults only, while the child was still in bed five weeks after contracting laryngitis, which was accompanied by an erratic pulse. Little Marion struggled to Christ Church in Lochgilphead on Christmas Day. On January 4, her mother took her to Glasgow.

During her father's lifetime, her parents had led a gypsy life to economise on rates and other household expenses. Now her mother was locked out of Kilberry and could not take her daughter home. Once her father had been master of all he surveyed, leading family prayers with his coterie of servants in the dining room and taking his place in local society. Now her mother's wedding presents were listed for the lawyers and they and all her personal possessions locked in rooms in the castle while she sought a roof with family and friends. The Will Jock had written, the entail he had broken in favour of the female line seemed to serve for nothing. The marriage contract which had been signed back in 1913 was in limbo and the trustees were offering Mrs Campbell of Kilberry not one crumb of comfort in her darkest days.

On November 11, 1928, she wrote to Mr Hog the lawyer explaining that the bill for Lochgair Hotel was £264 per annum. She also had to meet bills for journeys, clothes, school books and other expenses and she had no money. While she was nursing a very sick child at Lochgair Hotel, she decided to take things into her own hands. A draft of the letter she wrote to the family lawyers reveals her annoyance and frustration at delays over pensions, allowances and tax settlements which she simply could not afford to tolerate. Writing to Mr Hog she said:

> I will send you the particulars of the small investment. I am quite sure you knew all about it at the time (September 1927) as it was money from the sale of my personal silver which Kilberry insisted must be set aside from his and he directed Col. Henderson to invest it. I will get the particulars from his office.

This salvo was the start of a decades-long struggle with those supposed to be looking after her affairs. The woman who still styled herself Mrs Campbell of Kilberry had to fight to even catch sight of the place or to receive any annuity which would keep her and her daughter – all at a time when she was at her most vulnerable. A note dated 10.11.28 accompanying her list of possessions at the castle read:

> My wedding presents and my own possessions are scattered through the castle and it would be impossible to gather them into one room. I consider it would be really better in the matter of linen and blankets to reserve all that is locked up and possibly to sign an agreement to hand over any there is superfluous should need arise to remove any of it with the reservations.
>
> My list of wedding presents exists, locked away in the castle. The present list is from memory and as accurate as I can make it without the list to refer to. I do not guarantee there are no omissions but I do guarantee that I have not claimed other than my own.

This was the painful and muddled backdrop to the next phase in Marion's life. In 1929, Rena was dismissed because there was no money to pay her and the two Marions moved to Edinburgh where little Marion went to the PNEU school, St Margaret's. Rena remembered: 'I left school at 16 and was with her until they went to live in Edinburgh and couldn't afford to have a nanny. Mrs Campbell was a very educated woman. She taught Marion and she taught the children in the Sunday school.' However messy her parents' lives had been, Rena believed that Marion had been happy if 'very lonely' in her early years. 'Mrs Campbell kept her out of anything,' she said of the protection Marion's mother built round her to shield her from Kilberry problems. Rena insisted, too, that Jock had been 'very fond' of his daughter. Had he lived, that love may have served to give her confidence. But now his love was gone, her nanny's dependable affection was denied her and she found herself in a school full of confident young ladies who were not slow to criticise her old fashioned clothes, her excessively long hair or to mock her insistence on signing her name 'Marion Campbell of Kilberry'. MCK became her nickname – not always used kindly. Rena said her charge was 'very very clever'. She said: 'When she was little, if she came across a big word she would know the meaning right away.' Indeed, her father had written of her in the year before his death just a month after her seventh birthday:

> Marion – who is not yet a classical scholar – said today 'It is funny how much better one remembers things one has seen, than things one has heard. . .'

and referred to an appropriate Latin quotation to confirm her erudition. But she was a child who had rarely played with others and didn't know the rules of formal school rooms.

She had not been exposed to any childhood illnesses and now she was open to them all – much to her anxious mother's consternation. Almost the first task which faced Marion senior in Edinburgh was to get medication for her daughter. Among the condolences she had received listing Jock's many qualities and kindnesses, there were those like Catherine Livingstone's written from Achaglachgach, which said what a blessing Marion must be.

> Dear Madam,
> Your sorrow cup has been full a few times since we have known you but thank God you have your little daughter to fill your arms.

Mrs Campbell certainly did thank God and she did hold her young daughter very tightly in her arms, wondering all the while how long either of them was destined for this life.

But there was a certain robustness about young Marion even in these dark times. Betty Durie, then Learoyd, was sent to play with Marion on the beach at Ardrishaig with their friend Archie Kenneth when Marion was about 10 years old. Betty and Archie liked to turn up stones and find crabs. Marion didn't enjoy that at all. Betty said:

> We very reluctantly got a tennis ball and went into the field nearby and proceeded rather demurely to play ball. There we probably baulked at something she wanted to do – and she said – 'I shall kick you in the face!'

Betty was staggered at this display from the normally demure little girl. Betty had no truck with twenty first century psychology, but there can be little doubt that this crude and uncharacteristic display of temper in the ten year old Marion was an outward sign of inner turmoil following her father's death. Her cousin Helen admitted from the distance of some seventy years that the bereaved child would have been treated more kindly in a modern climate. A great aunt had written that it was always better if a child didn't see the reality of death because 'it frightens them so', but there seems to have been no release for her grief in all this activity. It could be suggested that it manifested itself in poor health, bad temper and prickliness.

This, then, was the child who went to school in Edinburgh as the family fought ever so discreetly over the estate she had already added to her name in the style of all Scottish lairds. Marion Campbell of Kilberry – was she or wasn't she? However much her mother kept things from her, as Rena suggested, Marion must have been aware that all was not well with her beloved Kilberry. A verse which survived from those days read:

> Kilberry, Kilberry, O far away place
> Kilberry Kilberry, the home of my race.
> Kilberry, Kilberry, my own dearest home
> So near the wide ocean, so near the white foam.

CHAPTER FOUR

The learning curve

From the earliest days, Marion's Uncle Morty was to encourage his sister to show the child's literary ventures to a publisher, but more pressing things faced Mrs Campbell at the start of the 1930s. The truth was that no-one actually wanted to buy an estate in a remote area of Argyll with a draughty castle and a clutch of non-too-productive farms. While she played a waiting game to see if a potential buyer would appear on the scene, she had school fees of eight guineas to pay (which would go up to fourteen guineas as Marion went up through the school) and a roof to find for herself and her daughter. Marion boarded at St Margaret's in Darnaway Street, Edinburgh, but Mrs Campbell stayed nearby at first and invited Marion's classmates over for tea from time to time.

Marion's transition from home learner to the classroom was not easy. Headmistress Christian Strachan wrote to her mother on October 10, 1931:

> I have questioned my staff about Marion's work and they tell me that Arithmetic is not up to the term's work but that Marion is quite a good worker and is very accurate. For Latin and English grammar Marion is in the lower division but is quite good. She is doing Form IIa work in Geometry and has just begun Algebra.
> Marion is very good at Scripture and narrates well but does not narrate enough in other subjects.

For most of her classmates, St Margaret's was a springboard to other, more recognised boarding schools with reputations equal to those attended by their brothers, even if the emphasis would still be on a less academic outcome. MCK was to spend her whole school career at St Margaret's, in keeping with her mother's ever more straitened circumstances. In the September before he died, Jock had signed a Trust deed in favour of George Alan Robertson (of the family legal firm) 'for behoof of creditors'. It intended to keep Marion's £4,000 from the marriage contract intact in lieu of the furniture and stock she would have been left through her husband's estate. This was eventually confirmed as legally correct by Sir Matthew P. Fraser KC, Sheriff of Chancery, and the £4,000 was given to her in 1935 as her 'absolute property' rather than being swallowed up by creditors. But these deliberations and others surrounding that marriage contract dragged on throughout the 1930s and as Mrs Campbell learned, deliberations do not pay rent.

In 1932, a little girl called Mary Sandeman came to St Margaret's. Her home was in Jura, the island across the Sound from Kilberry, where her father was the doctor. He was a member of the Sandeman port family and quite comfortably off. He had been the doctor in Islay but when war broke out he was mobilised and sent first to the Somme and then to India. He fell ill there and his wife went to look after him, leaving two older children at home. Mary Louise Stewart Sandeman was born on December 9, 1917 in Muttra, Uttaar Pradesh, and celebrated her second birthday by arriving with her parents at Southampton. Once established in the Jura practice, the Sandemans sent their youngest child off to the PNEU school at Ambleside and then its newer sister school in Edinburgh.

Despite the two year age gap the two girls struck up a friendship which was to last throughout their lives. The fact that they were boarders at a school where most pupils were day girls explains how the friendship might have begun, even though Marion was extremely wary of new people in her life.

Daphne Tullis, one of the girls who went off to another boarding school, says the emphasis was on English and history with less expertise in the maths department. Examination answers were dictated, as was the norm at the time, and there was great store put in Guides, music and singing rather than the social graces. That was a pity in the eyes of Aunt Violet, Uncle Archie's wife. Marion may have been considered polite by her nanny but Aunt Violet's rather grander expectations meant she saw Marion as lacking in gracious manners. No-one, Helen Kenneth remembered, seemed to have told Marion not to express her displeasure quite so audibly as she did. 'My mother thought she lacked a guiding hand,' Helen said. But then, Aunt Violet expected no more from a child raised in a household where the butler left the table between courses to play the pipes in the hall.

During what Helen Kenneth described as her aunt and uncle's 'tempestuous' marriage ('I suppose they were not really well suited to each other,' she said), there had been no money for the kind of governess who could have given the objective guidance Aunt Violet felt was missing. Jock, according to Helen Kenneth, would never have allowed boarding school but she added: 'I dare say the school tidied up the manners.'

Despite the emphasis on extras at St Margaret's, most of Marion's talents stemmed from a combination of inherited skills and talents. Sir Edward Durand was not only a successful diplomat but a delightful water colourist and her Campbell grandfather had written charming diaries. St Margaret's could not claim to have developed those talents and her immense natural history knowledge came more from her mother than from school. Helen Kenneth, who liked her aunt very much despite her parents' antipathy, remembered that during the holidays, the Lithgow girls from the neighbouring Ormsary estate came over on bicycles with their governess to learn about birds from Mrs Campbell. Perhaps because she had received the wisdom, spoken or implied, that she should have been a boy, Marion interested herself in those days more in regimental histories and according to her cousin Helen developed tomboyish behaviour whenever she could escape from the strictures of tea gowns.

While Marion struggled on through her studies, her weekly letters home occasionally reflecting misery inflicted by the pernicious bullying in which 'young ladies' can be so expert, her mother continued her struggles to sort out her financial situation. Helen Kenneth's version of the story naturally comes from her parents' perspective. Jock, she said, hadn't been very financially adept or worldly. Her father didn't quite get along with Aunt Marion. 'I think he tried to advise but she got some bee in her bonnet.' It has been suggested that Mrs Campbell asked if Archie would take on the estate to stave off bankruptcy and further antipathy developed when it became clear she had no intention of selling up if she could prevent the trustees from doing so. A different perspective says that it wasn't a question of intention but of inability to sell. The early 1930s were a time of economic depression and few wanted to take on an estate as economically unviable as Kilberry. Then in 1933, cousin Ivy Arbuthnot bought it from the estate trustees and as Helen said, 'kept it afloat'.

Miss Arbuthnot had recently come into funds and it seemed the ideal solution to everyone's problems that she would buy the estate and take her cousin Jock's widow on as a companion, thereby giving her and the 14-year-old Marion a home – their true home. Miss Arbuthnot took possession on May 15, 1933 and it seems that her Campbell relatives were not as against the plan as she had feared. Marion's letters home were addressed to Mrs Campbell of Kilberry, a title which Cousin Ivy must have agreed to, and whatever Aunt Violet thought about young Marion and her lack of manners, Cousin Ivy had already developed a great affection for her. Marion's mother's personal finances continued to be the cause of legal scrutiny and great concern and Ivy was neither a wealthy woman nor skilled in running an estate, but between them they muddled through the rest of the decade.

The trustees rarely gave Mrs Campbell peace of mind. Pearson and Company hung onto deeds she believed they had no right to. Mr Hog's advice often seemed questionable to her and there was always a question mark hanging over who owned the furniture and silver and whether Mrs Campbell's marriage contract money should pay death duties. In 1934, she was sent an Army warrant for signature, at which tardiness Colonel Henderson the estate factor expressed outrage. Marion's brother paid for the King's Counsel to fight out the marriage contract problems but the lawyers got their revenge by charging £3500 in fees. Little wonder that eventually Marion clawed back control of her own affairs and told them she would even fill in her own tax forms.

In a parallel existence, she was almost mistress of her own domain again and little Marion could feel confident she had a home to go to.

When school closed on July 26, 1933, she travelled back to Kilberry via Glasgow, Rothesay and the SS *Columba* to Tarbert. When a trip south was made for the summer holidays, there was no longer the fear that her fairytale castle would have disappeared by the time they got back. When Ivy went to London, Marion senior could feel that her marital home still was hers. There were holidays and dances and when she went to Oban to organise a function her late husband had initiated, she may have had to write to Colonel Henderson to release funds to pay for her guests, but Cousin Ivy was indulging young Marion with the hire of a boat which she handled, according to her mother, like a true sailor.

Ivy's health, however, deteriorated in the summer of 1938 and a nurse was installed at Kilberry in August. In December, Dr Cameron was being called in on a daily basis until on Thursday, December 15, she died at 4.45 am. Archie Campbell was there before the day was out, as was young Marion – thoughts of her birthday the following day no doubt very far from her mind. Her mother's diary records that Colonel Henderson also arrived that day and Ivy's will was read while she still lay on her death bed.

The will named Marion as her heir. She was inheriting Kilberry estate for a second time and as Ivy was coffined on her birthday, she must have wondered whether there would be as much sorrow and confusion over the inheritance this time around as there had been a decade before. Whether she knew that she was Ivy's third choice is another matter, Helen Kenneth's recollection is that Ivy's preferred successor was Archie, who turned down the offer on the ground that he had four children to educate and couldn't afford it. He was by then lecturing in law at Pembroke College and was settled at his Cambridge base. Ivy's second choice was her first cousin, Billy Fox, a Kilberry descendant. He turned it down because he enjoyed hunting, of which there was none in Mid Argyll, and he was also in line to inherit a large and prosperous estate in Hampshire. He didn't need a struggling estate in Scotland. Marion Campbell was third choice to inherit the home she loved and had been left by her father.

Ivy's funeral was held at Christ Church in Lochgilphead at 2.30 pm on Saturday, December 17, 1938. Archie left on the Monday and on the Friday, the two Marions made another trip to London. This time there was no question about being locked out of the castle when they returned to Scotland. The key was in their hands and they enjoyed a dinner party on Christmas Day at 37 Egerton Gardens, went to see Red Riding Hood on the 28th and went shopping together on December 30. As the year closed, Marion Campbell realised she could once more add 'of Kilberry' to her name with some justification.

CHAPTER FIVE

Disappointments and aspirations

Her new status as a laird did not, however, change life much for Marion. Her father's cousin had taken over Kilberry on May 15, 1933, and on March 24 that year Ivy had written to her mother:

> My dear Marion
> It would be so nice if we (you and I) could be there together, but as she [young Marion] is not there, there is is no use thinking of that but of course you know that you could have free board and lodging there when you want it.
> I shall have to economise considerably so I thought the cheapest thing would be to go there together.
> . . . I am truly sorry for you. It is a relief for you in one way but horrid in another, but I am really only a 'trustee'. . . you must work with me or it will be no fun.
> I hope Marion is not taking it badly
> Much love, Your loving Ivy

There was obviously some contention in the family. Jock's sister Molly had said to Ivy on the telephone:

> Of course it is not the buying of it – we could have managed that but there is the keeping of it up. How are you going to do that?

Sharing with Jock's widow was, to a degree, the answer, but it was certainly a struggle. Having agreed to Ivy's coaxing invitation, Marion senior set about trying to make some kind of income at Kilberry. In the August of 1933, she wrote off for advice on bee keeping, poultry rearing and a herb garden 'as a remunerative business'. She explained that she was considering setting up a co-operative scheme and had a small amount of capital. This doesn't fit the aristocratic and perjink image which persisted in the minds of Betty Durie and Helen Kenneth but necessity is a great leveller. Or was it simply that without Jock to worry about, Marion was able to become a person in her own right?

On June 19, 1933, she made her debut as a speaker for the PNEU Group at a meeting in Glasgow's Hillhead. She was so nervous about speaking in public that, according to one of the parents who attended, she read her long address but she was seen to be 'an extremely charming lady' and was 'so helpful afterwards talking to parents'. Once she'd found her confidence, there was no stopping her – she spoke to the Scottish Mothers Union, the Red Cross and in time became a vocal campaigner for the war effort. Her speech to the Mother's Union in Clachan in 1936 about teaching children to pray perhaps gives an insight into the way she raised her daughter. She told her audience:

> I do believe a child learns to pray more naturally and easily if its parents pray with it. . . Fold the tiny hands, they are never too small, take the small person on your knee and very quietly, very reverently, ask 'What do you want to thank God for? What shall we ask our Father in heaven to do'?

A perfect role model for her daughter? Or an overpowering force who made her own 'little person' feel inadequate? Reading the letters between the two Marions during the years at St Margaret's and then cramming for Oxford at a college in London, Marion senior's liberation did not seem to give her daughter the self confidence she so lacked when she went off to Edinburgh.

Miss Arbuthnot and Mrs Campbell were two women to survive the 1930s by pushing pieces of paper around a Monopoly board and Marion junior was already developing her mother's habit of recording every purchase, repaying every 10 shilling note she borrowed from her mother for necessities like stockings and toiletries. Ivy borrowed £3,000 from Mrs Campbell's Marriage Trustees knowing that under the Marriage Trust the funds in the Trust would not pass to Marion until after the death of her mother – and also knowing that a K.C. was still fighting to let Mrs Campbell get her hands on that Marriage Trust money. Ivy took over the castle on the understanding that the furniture would be there for her unless the Trustees found it necessary to sell it to pay off creditors. There wasn't enough insurance to cover the furniture which as Mrs Campbell pointed out was irreplaceable in any case. Estate duties had still not been paid at the beginning of 1934 and at the end of that year the lawyers were still blundering on through Mrs Campbell's finances without making any headway (or perhaps making enough headway for their own benefit but certainly not hers).

But as always, this was genteel poverty rather than the deprivation suffered by Britain's workers in the early 1930s. Mrs Campbell had a black lace evening frock made by Hélène Chambers, a dressmaker and ladies' tailor at 22a Bucchleuch Place, Edinburgh. Her bill on August 1, 1933, also included a dark blue day dress and other items. However it was managed, she, Ivy and Marion enjoyed barn dances at Kilberry – young Marion dancing the Petronella to Willie MacMillan's accordion, partnered by local boys. Her letters suggest such socialising wasn't easy, but Marion loved to have Mary Sandeman to stay.

All too often, Marion's school reports from Edinburgh recorded that her work had been interrupted by illness and as she had been told she had a weak heart she had to avoid exertion. Her marks veered from 35 for Algebra to 100 for composition. She was strong in sciences but languages were weak. At Christmas 1935, her geometry paper was not given in on time. By Christmas 1936, she was leaving at the age of 17 to go to stay with her grandmother in London to study for Oxford. Christian Strachan, her head mistress, wrote:

> Looking back over the period that Marion has been at school I feel that she has made very good use of her opportunities. She came already knowing how to work and that has been a great asset. I hope she will continue to work hard and she has my best wishes for her future success.

She had always been a child who read voraciously – as she had told her Uncle Archie, she lived in her books. Her reports said that she was 'familiar' with her books and that she worked 'excellently' when she was interested. Before she went off to Edinburgh, of course, there were many letters from Marion's mother to the PNEU explaining lack of work – illness and domestic disruption being the two destructive elements. Her mother had written in December 1930:

> A very much disrupted term – as we were obliged to leave Home and travel about, making visits; we took books with us, but in several subjects work had to cease or be curtailed. Whenever we had the chance to work Marion did her best and she read several of her set books alone. I am much disappointed with her written answers but writing is still so laborious and her hand (left) becomes so stiff I am sure this interferes greatly with her output.

A few months later, Mrs Campbell was on the receiving end of much more positive letters. Marion's papers impressed the PNEU examiners even if her high standards meant she was anxious about her daughter's progress. 'She is doing most excellent and intelligent work.' Her standards were perhaps too demanding. An examiner wrote:

> I know that you are anxious about the work, and anxious that Marion should get on, and I sometimes wonder if this militates against a feeling of leisure in some of the subjects.

Going to London at 17 did not mean she escaped her mother's supervisory attentions. By then, however, there seemed to be an exchange of ideas between the two and Marion wrote almost daily letters from Lady Durand's home at 37 Egerton Gardens. Marion listened to schools broadcasts on topics such as 'History in the Making: The Highlands and Islands of Scotland' by Professor A.D. Gib and her explanation of the programme – 'economic distress therein and what can be done to alleviate it' was punctuated by three ironic exclamation marks. This was a topic about which both mother and daughter knew as much as the good professor.

By January 1939, she had joined the Auxiliary Territorial Service (ATS) and was doing rifle practice as well as studying for her Oxford entrance exams which were to be held in the March. She was also receiving an education in the broadest sense – concerts, operas, choral performances and the very latest plays and stage shows were her entertainment, even though the budget was as ever very tight. She had worked out a plan for her future – knowing nothing of those plans her mother and father had discussed for her more than a decade previously. She wrote to her mother:

> a) Should I fail this exam, I propose to work up mathematics, try to enter a ship-builder's office and work up from the bottom.
>
> b) Should I pass, I shall work at Maths; and ship construction in spare time; on leaving Oxford, either get a job on the technical (ie design) side of some firm such as Harland and Woolf or John Brown, or else to go into the secretarial side and transfer when better (languages etc.) qualified.
>
> In the present state of British shipbuilding there must of necessity be a big increase in output soon, if the Merchant Marine is to go on – already there is a shortage of technicians in the trade – therefore there will be good openings in that job for a long time. Also, this will mean working in Glasgow and there are Sir James Lithgow and Mr Campbell. . . I may as well have a shot at this job.

There was no doubt in her mind that she would have a career of some sort and was looking for one which would pay. Her twenty years had witnessed nothing but cheese paring and penny pinching. She took ongoing arguments about the ownership of Kilberry furniture and drawings in her stride and unlike her mother, she was all for presenting a case for a scholarship rather than hiding the Kilberry poverty. 'Let us by all means give them all the facts they want – after all, lots of hard up girls are trying for Oxford, and we're no better off than most of them,' she told her mother bluntly.

Meanwhile, she was studying English, French, German and Italian. She had perhaps been distracted from her Oxford cramming by her enrolment in the ATS (in which her number was W/409). She had applied for membership on Wednesday, September 28, 1938, while war was still just a nasty suggestion the general populace hoped would go away. She enrolled as a member of the ATS on Thursday, November 3 that year, determined to join the 'Terries' because her father had served with them in the Great War. She wrote a note to her mother asking : 'Do you think my Daddy is glad I'm a Terrier too? Perhaps he's pleased – I hope so.' What seemed much more pressing than war, however, was a three hour general paper for the Lady Margaret Hall Scholarship and Entrance Examination and a three hour Italian translation for the Lady Margaret Hall and Somerville College Joint Scholarship and Entrance Examination in March, 1939. As she waited for the results of her exams, she sent a Mothering Sunday card home for March 12, when she and Mary Sandeman went to church in the Guards' Chapel. She had been told on the Friday night she would have got promotion at the ATS if she had not been going home to Scotland. 'Rather sad,' she said – but a more devastating disappointment was to come. On March 16, she wrote to her mother:

> Today is, I suppose, the last hope I have of hearing about an interview as tomorrow is the last day for that. 6 pm and no news, so I am dreadfully afraid I have failed you once again.

If Oxford had turned her down, a break at Kilberry was a glimmer of brightness in her gloom, but even before she left London she knew that war was inevitable. She told her mother:

> In my humble opinion Europe is nearer a war now than she ever was last year. It is rather terrifying to feel the utter calm and lack of interest here in London – none of the emotion of last year. . . Have you got any extra provisions laid in?
>
> I am volunteering to serve under Betty Learoyd for the summer if she'll have me as I've finished my training. The commander says, very nicely, a) I'm fully qualified to help any officer with a new company and b) she'd have made me an NCO if I hadn't been going away for so long. Still no uniform.

And then she had to send the confirmatory telegram to Kilberry on March 20 which read: FAILURE CERTAIN RETURNING THURSDAY MARION. There she tried to put her disappointments behind her by heading off to

Jura to the Sandemans, reporting back on the minutiae of life – a swallow in April, geese flying overhead – and put life on hold for a while.

She had wanted so much to go to Oxford and perhaps her 'I've let you down yet again' indicates a mother pushing her daughter rather than supporting her. Marion turned therefore to doing her best in another field where she thought she could please her mother – the army in which her father had spent his life and the 'Terries' to which he had retired after his Indian career. Marion asked to be seconded to Argyll and spent the summer doing drill under the eye of Betty Learoyd, Commander in Campbeltown. Betty put aside her memories of the ill-tempered child who had threatened to kick her and Archie Kenneth in the face and agreed to take Marion under her wing. Mrs Learoyd had moved out of her home in Ardrishaig temporarily, as so many families did at the start of the war, and was living in Tarbert. The two young women used to travel the length of Kintyre to Campbeltown, do drill with the 11th Argyll Company, have supper in one of the hotels and travel home in the dark late at night. Betty recalled that although her mother kept her on a tight rein in most areas of her life at that age, she didn't seem to think that this traipsing around Kintyre in the cause of duty was anything that should concern her.

Marion recalled later:

> Lord, how I loved those first drills! I looked forward to them all week and I used to go shaking with eagerness and straining to back up my officers as far as I could.

Once, Betty and Marion had driven home with a flat tyre, too tired to notice it. Marion stayed with Betty rather than at Kilberry, because it was just too far out of the way.

There were other distractions, too. Before the Oxford fiasco, she had planned to go to camp in England and there was a place arranged for her there – albeit with a warning that she would have to pay her own fare from Scotland. Jeanne Ling, her English commanding officer, tactfully suggested that if Marion was already coming up to town for a dance at the end of May, she might not want to face the expense of another trip soon afterwards. She didn't and the Argyll camp won out.

Her mother, as always, had grand aspirations and got it into her head that Marion, like Mrs Learoyd's daughter, was an officer. Marion put her straight: 'And For the 999th Time' she wrote with emphatic capital letters, 'I'm not an officer, whatever her nice little daughter may be.'

Between her stay at Craighouse on Jura with the Sandemans and the ATS drills at Campbeltown, Marion did go to the Ball mentioned by Jeanne Ling – the Caledonian Ball run then as now for charity. Pre war it was a highlight of the year for Scotland's bright young things in search of a life partner. It was formal, regimentally organised and rigorously rehearsed. Marion wrote home from Egerton Gardens at the end of May, 1939 that her shoes blistered her feet during the reel practices. Two of her friends, Vicky Erskine and Hopie Maitland, were unable to attend the Ball, but nothing stopped Marion's enjoyment. She told her mother that the party at the Grosvenor consisted of:

> Rob Durie (you remember the boy who used to stay at Erines?) and his sister Maimie who is very charming – rather older than the rest of us – then Hugh Campbell, two nieces and nephews of Mrs L's [Learoyd] and sundry others. All very nice 14 in all.

Rob Durie was to marry Betty Learoyd, a love match which involved much Scottish country dancing during the decades it endured.

For once, Marion went on a spending spree. Her dress came from Langworthy's and she declared it 'a great success'. The shoes, white and silver, came from Raul in Regent Street and cost 38 shillings. They were very pretty but were the ones which blistered her big toes, despite wearing them at granny's first. It turned out to be a night like few others in her life. Her dance programme, written in pencil, showed that she danced a number of foxtrots with young men called Desmond, Charlie, Edmund and Hugh to tunes like 'Jeepers Creepers' and 'Two Sleepy People'. But it was the Scottish dancing she found most exhilarating. She wrote home:

> The Set Reels went very well I think. I had one of the tallest men in the room as my partner – a lad of the name of Ramsay. We had a good set, but someone went wild in the

> last chain so odd things happened suddenly! We danced all night until 4 am and then the Learoyds left – the Duries, Hugh and we were game however so collecting up two more members of the party we left for Hyde Park where we found a crowd from the Ball and a piper! So needless to say we set off at more Reels – an enormous man – Capt. MacKerrol of that strange blue tartan – seemed to manage the arrangements and danced in our set – most beautifully. It really was lovely dancing under the bright early sky. A crowd stood and cheered!!! One cabby said, near me – 'The 'eadlines termorrer'll be 'Orrible Riots in Royal Park!' Lovely idea. From there we went to Lyon's at the Marble Arch and had some coffee, and some of us . . . had eggs and bacon (not for me at 5.30 am thank you). Then we sat there and talked madly for ages.

She got back to her grandmother's house at around 6.45 am. It was never her style to be a 'bright young thing' but that night must surely have made up for all the missed Mid Argyll tennis parties and dances of her isolated, peripatetic young life. The disappointments of the early spring, the fears for the future, the responsibilities which her mother never let her forget were hers as Miss Campbell of Kilberry, disappeared in a blur of tartan and white dresses and reality had not returned when she went to her bed at seven in the morning.

One Ball does not make a flibbertigibbet, however, and when her mother, ever anxious about her daughter's welfare, had warned Marion that university life might hold its dangers, Marion had written back to her in no uncertain terms:

> Don't worry about me at Oxford my darling, I can 'look after myself' quite satisfactorily if need be – and I don't think I'm the sort that gets into 'that sort' of difficulty much. As far as I've seen, the girls who do get into difficulties are the ones who behave as if they wanted to. I don't know if people think I'm stand-offish or anything at dances etc., but any fooling about of the so-called 'petting' sort not only disgusts me but bores me, so now! I think I have a fairly good sense of proportion which is really the mainspring, and I try to be friendly with everyone and silly with no-one and wait for the right

> person 'to fall in love' with – so please worry not!! but all the same I do see your point about judging for myself and I'm grateful to you for thinking of it. After all, if you think back for the last six years, I have had to depend very largely on my own judgement in a lot of things for some time! How lovely it must have been for you to have 'your own house'. How I shall love mine, if it comes. and (unlike the declared intentions of many of my contemporaries . . .) I want lots of babies! – the more the merrier perhaps!

Marion was a young woman who wanted to share her life with someone. She said: 'I suppose a really good Christian would never be lonely – I am not alone, but I want a human too sometimes'. And she wanted the things other girls liked, even if she did have aspirations to work in shipbuilding. She asked for pretty French knickers for Christmas and saw no conflict between that and her intention to stay pure until the right man came along. Times were changing for young women but Marion Campbell of Kilberry had no intention of changing her own moral code instilled by family and church.

Her mother's letters, like those she had sent to Jock at the Front, demanded instructions about the estate and made suggestions about her way of life. Once she said Marion should take the Board of Trade Examination for Second Mate's Certificate and got short shrift from her daughter. Another time she insisted she had to sell Marion's bicycle and Marion ferociously defended her right to keep it. Her letters could show some of that lack of graciousness which her Aunt Violet had so criticised in her childhood. Yet at other times she appealed to her mother for help – would SHE ask granny if Mary Sandeman could stay during her momentous exams for Oxford? She was a young woman finding her feet and while sometimes she could treat her mother in a woman-to-woman way, on other occasions she spat the feathers of any difficult teenager and at still others she could slip into the language of childhood – 'darling mummie. . . B'ess 'oo'. She recognised the transition she was making. When a piece of work she did was praised she wrote home:

> This is such a pleasant change from the 'inferiority

> complex' of the last few month or even years! I suppose I'm growing up.

She was growing up with ideas ahead of her time. Other young women were still following gender stereotypes. Marion turned down the opportunity to work at the British Museum for a decent salary with a pension because 'I do want so terribly to have something to do with ships and engineering.' But what did the future hold for her? Her finances were as slender as ever, her failure to get into Oxford closed an academic door and now Hitler was threatening ever more loudly to make reels in Hyde Park at dawn a thing of the past. Drills with Betty Learoyd in Campbeltown and a return to an uneasy peace in London brought the reality of war ever closer. She had seen submarines off Prestwick, destroyers near the Isle of May and travelling by steamer down to London from Leith she was shocked by the obvious preparations for defence and conflict. The skies may have been washed blue over Edinburgh as she left Scotland but that £2.10s steamer ticket was with hindsight taking her to war.

CHAPTER SIX

A frustrating war

Kilberry would never stop picking at the elbow of Marion Campbell. It wasn't just that her mother and Colonel Henderson the estate factor constantly sent her estate business to deal with in the manner of a minister receiving red government boxes wherever she travelled. Marion's mind's eye was set on the castle, the woods, the fish ponds, the family mausoleum, the shore, the view of Jura, the farms and the stock. She wrote home: 'I don't like to think of my 'calf country' these days. I want to be there too badly.'

Just occasionally, a confident young woman emerged from the overweight, self-conscious, isolated teenager. She'd been told by the doctor in 1938 that she was overweight for her age. She was advised to stop eating milk puddings and to have potatoes or bread for lunch – but not both. She was told to exercise, as long as she didn't put a strain on her heart – the 'weak' heart her mother had always told her daughter she possessed after some childhood illness. As she lost weight and went to a gym, she developed an energy which gave the lie to this 'delicate' disposition – confirmed by her general practitioner in later life, Dr Neil MacDonald, who saw evidence of an anxious mother rather than a history of early heart strain in his patient.

It wasn't only her physical health and body image which was shaping her emerging persona: her religion grounded her. Her first memory was learning the 23rd Psalm and linking it with the 'Good Shepherd' picture in the nursery. Now she went to church whenever possible, but even hymns transported her back to Kilberry, visualising childhood images and prayers with Rena. 'Dear Daddie' had sat beside her and told her a favourite hymn was 'The Church's one foundation'.

Away from home, sleeplessness was always a problem but Marion was now beginning to move on from the tiredness and depression she suffered around the time of her Oxford exams. She had 'come out' – despite her protestations that she didn't want to go to any Courts. Her mother had been a beauty when she made her debut in 1897. Marion could be an attractive, vivacious girl in the right company, but she had admitted in 1938 that the boredom she suffered at school had followed her into her young adulthood and while she rather missed having any young people around, she didn't 'want to meet any strange ones'. Her menstrual cycle – not something to be discussed then – caused her pain and depression and Granny's cocktail parties were often a nightmare because of this. Much more to her taste were concerts, plays and ceilidhs which reminded her of home. To go to a 'ripping' harping ceilidh in London at which the Kilberry Pipers played in public for the first time was almost a thrill too much.

Kilberry and Craighouse were like magnets to her. Ironically, while Margie Fletcher, née Brown, grew to feel that Marion was overly possessive of their joint friend Mary Sandeman, Marion was trying to field her mother's jealousy of the time she spent at Craighouse – jealousy no doubt fired by letters describing fun times with the Sandemans and the 'most amusing and quite mad' Browns. Margie, whose own family were lairds of Jura, saw Marion as stand-offish; Marion felt she was fully participating in the walks and picnics and parties with the young people on the island. They were what kept her so long on Jura – yet the impression she gave to all but the understanding Mary was that she was a figure apart She was Miss Campbell of Kilberry – even to those whose status far outstripped that of laird of a struggling west coast property. This persona had so much more to do with having been raised by parents rooted in the past and time spent with Lady Durand, her grand grannie in London, than with any feeling of superiority and sadly, Marion's innate shyness and an old fashioned manner did little to project her into the mainstream of contemporary social life.

That Caledonian Ball when she relaxed into spontaneous enjoyment of the evening seems to have been an exception: a formality beyond her years were her more usual manner, witnessed in this snippet from a teenage anecdote written to her mother about an encounter with an aunt on the pier at Tarbert: 'I was thrilled . . . so I rushed to the side and conversed with her ad lib'. The same letter described a couple on the boat as 'rather amusing old birds' and records that she took tea at the Ca'doro in Glasgow. Still out of sync with her contemporaries, it was a difficult time for her. It was to be come more difficult as she pursued her career in the forces.

At school she had suffered bullying – or 'ragging' as she termed it – to the extent that she was 'simply terrified' she would, to her shame, cry. She had wanted to leave as soon as possible to get away from it all. In London, cramming for Oxford, she had not been exposed to that cruelty but in the ATS and the WRNS she would antagonise her peers and irritate her officers, who in truth must have found it difficult to deal with a young woman who had such an air of being in charge. She was born to be a laird. She took her responsibilities seriously. She had 5,000 acres to control, wages to pay, decisions to make about buying and selling produce and stock. Her mother passed on every query and although Colonel Henderson's rather supercilious correspondence implied he was allowing a child to play with a toy which he would put away at bedtime, he nonetheless deferred to her. Throughout her service career she tried to get a posting which would allow her access to run Kilberry properly. Some officers were sympathetic; others (and many of those of her own rank and below) displayed the same attitude at those 'kids' who did the 'ragging' at school. Marion Campbell of Kilberry? Who does she think she is?

When Rosa Margaret Ivy Florence Arbuthnot's Will was finally processed in the spring of 1939, it gave Marion the title to the lands and estate of Kilberry in the Parish of South Knapdale. It coincided with a letter written by Mrs Campbell to Brindixen's, the Baker Street college where Marion had studied for the Oxford scholarship for the sum of £29. 3s. Her mother told the college that the first failure would not divert her daughter from her ambition. The college pointed out that should she resume her studies, 'she should realise that they demand her first and keenest attention and that other activities must be subsidiary and only such as are desirable from a mental and physical health point of view'. The hint was that the ATS, the Sloane School of Swedish Gymnastics and possibly the responsibilities of Kilberry itself should be put on hold if Marion was ever to get a place at Oxford.

When Marion 'came out' at the Oban Gathering in September 1937, she was still three months short of 18. Her mother spared no expense, although there was no spare cash in the kitty. She had to ask Colonel Henderson to extend her overdraft with Lloyds Bank so that she could pay for tickets to the Oban Ball and a number of hotel rooms, dinners, drinks and a car. Because 'Old Kilberry' – Marion's grandfather – had been an originator of the Oban event Mrs Campbell felt it was 'all rather unkind' that she should have to pay for any of this, but her main concern was that her cheque should be honoured. The £4,000 which had eventually been received from her marriage contract on June 10, 1935 had obviously not gone far.

The following year Mrs Campbell received the special invitations which allowed her daughter to be presented at Court. The invitation from the Lord Chamberlain read that he was commanded by 'their Majesties' to summon Mrs Campbell of Kilberry and Miss Marion Campbell to a Court at Buckingham Palace on Wednesday, May 16, 1938 at 9.30 pm. Ladies were required to wear court dresses with feathers and trains and gentlemen 'full court dress'. Then 'Mrs John Campbell and Miss Marion Campbell' were also invited to an afternoon party in the garden of Buckingham Palace on July 21st, 1938, from 4 pm to 6.30 pm.

But balls and gowns were not really Marion's idea of fun. She liked clothes but no doubt felt she did not compare well with her mother or her even more beautiful aunt, who had become Mrs Everild Lucas Tooth, whose presentations at court were recorded in enviably glamorous photographs from the last decades of the previous century. Marion had far preferred being out in the boat Aunt Ivy hired for her at Oban to the dancing, the dinners and the young men for whom Mrs Campbell had bought tickets; and the Buckingham Palace events were duties not pleasures. Sadly, her grandmother's house in London was bombed, so any record of her appearance at her debut was lost –

only a portrait photograph remains from the year, showing an attractive, smiling young woman.

The war brought an end to any aspirations she had to resit her Oxford entrance exam. Mary Sandeman joined the Royal Naval Reserve and that swung Marion's loyalties away from the Terries towards the WRNS. Having trained in London and served with Betty Learoyd in Kintyre she was embodied for service in the ATS on September 16, 1939 and served at Blackdown near Aldershot until June, 1940. She had applied to join the WRNS in December, 1939, and the day after she was discharged from the ATS she reported to the WRNS for duty. On July 5, 1940, she was sent to the naval depot HMS *Pembroke.*

By July 11, however, she was suffering from German Measles and was on sick leave for a whole month. This was not the first of a series of illnesses which interrupted her war career. While she was still with the ATS, her mother had sent a letter to Jeanne Ling, Marion's boss at the Blackdown Barracks, to say she couldn't report for duty in January 1940 and was given short shrift. After the German Measles, she rejoined the *Pembroke* on August 11th, then moved around from one centre to another – HMS *Bachante,* HMS *Orlando,* HMS *Spartiate,* HMS *President* and HMS *Boscwen.* She was promoted to Third Officer in September 1941.

The wartime journey was not smooth and perhaps her mother and the spectre of Kilberry proved to be the biggest barrier between Marion and comradeship. When Miss Ling of the ATS replied to Mrs Campbell about Marion's illness in the January of 1940, she asked that her thanks be passed on to Lady Durand for her 'very kind invitation' to visit her when next in London. Miss Ling rather pointedly added that 'being without a Company Assistant at the moment, I find that my time is fairly fully occupied, and on my infrequent and short trips to London I find that every moment is booked up'. Having an aristocratic grandmother in this instance was far from being an asset. But then, nor was having the responsibilities of lairdship when there was a war to be fought.

Just as she had during the Great War, Mrs Campbell wrote letters about every little estate detail which worried her. Her husband, a seasoned soldier, was unable to take the minutiae of the estate on board while his men were falling in the trenches and when his inhibitions were diminished by temper or alcohol was not above telling his darling wife he did not wish to be bothered by it all. Her daughter was at first happy to receive dispatches from the home front but her comments in return reflected divided loyalties.

In March, 1940, she told her mother she was sorry the men at Kilberry should have 'nothing better to do than grouse and make a nuisance of themselves'. She added: 'If they only knew how the men here envy them!'

She had not enjoyed the ATS, however proud she felt her father might have been for her to be in its ranks. Relaying the bad news that she was not to get leave, she told her mother: 'Sometimes I would give almost anything to get out of this,' an echo of one of her father's First World War letters. Being given a new job as 'dogsbody' to a Sergeant Drakely, she was more concerned that her mother was having 'trouble about maids'. When she went for her interview for the WRNS in London in April, 1940, she was sent to the wrong address and arrived late. If she allowed her thoughts to show, she was laying in trouble for herself: 'The underlings tried to freeze me out,' she said. And even on that very first day when she was sent for a signalling test and told she could be sent on a course then be posted to the coast as a Chief Wren, she was planning that she would do her best 'to be posted to Scotland'. She wrote to her mother: 'Oh, wouldn't it be lovely if I were sent to the West Coast? But don't let's hope for too much.'

The normality of pre-war civilian life was at this point not too unattainable. After the WRNS interview, Marion went off to the cinema with Lady Durand where they watched a documentary about Zulus and the *Wizard of Oz* – Marion described the latter as 'a delightful fantasy'. And perhaps imagining the rustle of a Wren's fat pay packet containing 43 shillings a week with 1s 3d living allowance, she indulged herself by buying a water colour sketch with a vaguely Scottish or Norwegian feel to it. Anything which reminded her of home was welcome and the idea of sixteen days home leave in May put all else out of her mind.

'Is Willie's bus running now?' she asked. 'If not, how does one get luggage etc. to Kilberry?' Her superior, Captain Davis, told her that she had been 'very unsettled' for the previous six months since she had applied to the WRNS and 'that it was time to pull myself together and begin to work hard'. Sadly she was working hard – but as laird of Kilberry rather than ATS subordinate.

Her punishment for apparently not pulling her weight was to index cards, and not having heard from the Admiralty about her acceptance into the WRNS asked instead if she could have a transfer within the ATS to a Scottish unit. Captain Davis told her this was impossible. It was a strange, unsettling environment in which one minute she had the luxury of worrying about dyeing a cream taffeta dress in 'suitable browns' while the next she was completely rattled by colleagues ghoulishly picking over the horror of war. On one particularly trying day in May she sent a postcard to her mother saying (in French, the code used by the Campbell women for this public form of correspondence) she was nervous and how much she wanted to be home. Next day she wrote an apologetic letter: there were too many around her harping on the worst. But while letters to her mother showed Marion's vulnerable side, her colleagues obviously saw something different. 'People come and pour out their worries to me, which doesn't help,' she said, adding that her mother shouldn't worry about her: 'You know what a moody animal I am at times.'

Whatever her colleagues and superiors in the ATS may have thought, Marion Campbell was never a malingerer. The 'curse' as she termed her menstrual cycle still caused her problems, emotional and physical, but she also suffered very badly from sore throats. She told her mother she'd wait to get her tonsils out until she was in the WRNS. In fact, they weren't removed until 1966 and continued to trouble her throughout the next quarter of a century. Meanwhile she was given yet another new job, this time sorting out the platoon office for 'an appreciative officer'. On May 29, she was sensible enough to report to the sick bay with a high temperature, swollen glands and another bad throat. This time it was mumps. Her early isolation meant that all the childhood illnesses were now attacking with a vengeance as she was exposed to so many new people.

All of this was played out against the continued Kilberry uncertainty. Yes, she had inherited the estate from Ivy Arbuthnot. Yes, she was now Miss Campbell of Kilberry thanks to Cousin Ivy's Will. But Ivy's Will was no cornucopia of good things. Jock's cousin had left a whole series of legacies to estate workers and servants. Her estate was unable to pay them and in time, Marion paid them herself from her own meagre assets. There were those on the estate who felt hard done by and even suggested through Colonel Henderson that the stock from Tiretigan and Keppoch farms should be sold off to meet the sums left. Henderson told Marion in October 1939 that he had set one worker straight, explaining that the legacies were to be met 'solely out of Miss Arbuthnot's invested capital under the terms of her Will'.

None of this was sorted out until 1942 and meanwhile, Kilberry was yet again on the market. One Durand relative wrote to Mrs Campbell in February 1939 that a sale was inevitable but that 'it would be fatal to attempt it at the moment'. War did not make Kilberry any more attractive than it had been during the Great Depression. As Colonel Henderson pointed out, 'Kilberry is not an easy place to sell and it might take a long time to find a purchaser.'

The place was let out in August and September of 1939 while Mrs Campbell went to West Kilbride and then to Ripon in Wales. When Marion eventually was given leave in November, she was relieved to find there were no evacuees. But when it was evident that war was a long term situation and the Clyde conurbation came under fire, evacuees were regularly housed on the estate farms – some presenting greater problems than others.

Marion obviously saw no need to conceal from her comrades at arms that she was in command of a 5,000 acre estate. She revealed nothing of the troubles at home, however, but she did consistently seek to be posted nearer home by citing her responsibilities. She had the trappings of wealth, like the amber pendant left to her by her Durand Aunt Marion and other family jewels, but in reality this young WREN was starting her adult life with a £20,000 overdraft and an ailing estate parked in the hands of the rather negative Colonel Henderson while she did her bit for king and country. On the one hand she had a burden of responsibility few of her peers would share; on the other,

her lack of exposure to the real world meant she was often destructively naive. Having been posted to Peterhead with the WRNS in 1940, she wrote to her superior:

> Sir, I respectfully beg to request that I may be posted to Greenock, on the grounds that I shall then be within reach of my home and able to supervise my personal affairs, and also that I shall be able to serve with a friend, Wren M. Sandeman, now serving there.

Not surprisingly, this did not elicit the desired response. Instead, she faced the tensions of any small office magnified by the fears of war. In her digs – sharing rooms in private houses – she often found it difficult to maintain friendships. She had lived too long in the company of her mother, her grandmother and Cousin Ivy. She was cosseted by them and isolated by them. Typically, her mother had written in 1935 on the eve of an operation:

> Sweetheart, my own darling little daughter. I am writing this just in case anything goes wrong this evening. You must always think that Daddie and I are waiting for you with those other darlings Isabel and Ian. Always my love will be around you. But remember well. It is God's love you must rely upon. Live your minutes hours days weeks and years in the light of this wonderful love. . . ever your most devoted loving Mummie.

Those young women of a certain social status who went into the armed forces as officers could maintain the same distance from their subordinates as they had done in civilian life. Marion Campbell was an ordinary rating and therefore exposed to what some may have told her was the real world. The experience coloured her life. Despite the difficulties she encountered, the illnesses she suffered and the injury she endured, she would always refer to her period in the WRNS as a highlight of her life. It certainly changed much for her, and perhaps symbolic of those changes was the fact that she stopped the Kilberry village children curtseying and saluting her as they had her mother.

Her mother wanted so much for her but so often Marion felt she was letting her mother down. How difficult to achieve her mother's desire: 'I do want you to make such a lovely, beautiful thing of your life – a clear shining jewel.' In digs in Peterhead, Helensburgh, Edinburgh and Glasgow with women she could not always get on with, working in jobs which must have seemed less than heroic, burdened with responsibility and debt, Marion must frequently have felt her life was a tawdry bauble rather than a clear shining jewel. Yet she took her mother's advice to use her 'undoubted talents', to 'always keep on educating yourself' and never to 'fail to do small kindnesses as well as big ones'.

One such intended small kindness was recorded in a Will she had made on September 9, 1939. The estate was to go to her mother in the event of her losing her life during the war. Her trustees were also to look in the lining of her uniform jacket at the right side near the breast pocket. There they would find the £5 given her by her grandmother, Maude, Lady Durand. If grannie would not take the money, it was to go to any charity named by her or to the Children's Union Funds. Marion never left the country during her time in the ATS or the WRNS, but there were dangerous occasions when someone could have been faced with the task of cutting into the lining of her jacket.

In the summer of 1940, however, her state of health kept her from service duties but did not prevent her running the estate from her hospital bed. At last she left hospital towards the end of June, returned to Blackdown to get her discharge papers from the ATS and went to the Admiralty to finalise her admission to the WRNS before going home to Kilberry for ten days sick leave. In August she spent time at the WRNS Training and Drafting Depot at Greenwich, admitting: 'I am just getting out of the most abysmal depression I've had in years, the result of 'too much home', I'm afraid. I can't tell you how I hated coming back here, especially when I found how bad my work was.'

She settled down to a routine of training, Kilberry estate work and air raids. Sometimes the shelters were so crowded she simply sat under trees listening to bombs drop and exchanges of gunfire. She found there was no prospect of being transferred to the Clyde if she continued training in signals and she decided instead to go on with clerical work in the hope that this would take her north of the border. It did – but to Peterhead on the north east coast rather than the Firth of Clyde on which she had set her sights. Her commanding officer had advised her that this at least was in the right command to apply for a transfer to the Clyde. There were again echoes of her father's letters from the Great War when she wrote home:

> I'm afraid a lot of people will think I've chucked the job because I can't do it but actually I'm only a class behind Attfield and among the better ones of the class – so that doesn't arise. The CO says that if there's ever a chance of a W/T [wireless/telegraph] Operator being wanted in the west I shall be able to retrain, which won't after all take long. . . Thank goodness I've done it, anyway, at least that's settled now. I've had a sort of mental fox gnawing me for ages. You do understand, don't you?

The fox would go on gnawing for some time, because the transfer to Greenock would not be easy or quick to achieve. Increasing air raids postponed her journey to Peterhead for around a week and the WRNS were crammed seven to a cellar as a makeshift shelter. At least she finally went north with a crumb of hope – she had inadvertently seen a letter about herself which was 'very flattering' and implied that promotion was not out of the question. But she still did not have a complete uniform and had only been paid eight shillings in the month since she had returned to duty. She and a Wren named Fletcher were billeted together in one of the last houses on the way out of Peterhead owned by a Miss Shewan, described by Marion as 'an old dear – very clean and tidy and a good cook and ready to do everything for us'. The young women had a sitting room to themselves and were twenty minutes from the base where she was given 'confidential' work to do. She explained to her mother that it was 'not unlike what Daddy may have dealt with at times (e.g. at Simla)', and she found her training at Greenwich useful. The work was going to be interesting – but even in her first days at Peterhead, she was discussing the chances of a move to the Clyde. And of course, her letters home were concerned with the letting of farmhouses on the estate, what progress Colonel Henderson was making with the instructions she had sent him and even the setting of the gamekeeper's wages.

She sought out the local Episcopal Church, asked for honey and wool from home and set about knitting in whatever spare time was left her. On her days off, she went fishing, usually without success. She found it an overwhelming experience to represent the WRNS at a sea funeral for five young men whose Merchant Navy vessel had been attacked. She was angered at the loss of life but found that this was an area where air raids were far less frequent than she had become used to at Greenwich. She was glad to be away from the nightly dive into the air raid shelters, where the dust made her nose bleed and gave her hay fever.

Nothing, however, was settled. When Miss Shewan's sister and brother-in-law arrived from London with their own tales of bombings and raids, WRNS Campbell and Fletcher were asked to find new digs. Wren Campbell was planning further ahead than a change of quarters in Peterhead: Mary Sandeman was to ask her commanding officer if Marion could join the Greenock operation and already Marion was asking her mother if there might be a chance of accommodation with Campbell relatives or Lady Lithgow, their generous neighbour at Ormsary, north of Kilberry, whose family seat was at Langbank. Meanwhile, the present move from Miss Shewan's was delayed because of a lack of other digs in the town.

Plans were already in motion for her twenty first birthday, but Marion warned her mother: 'I don't know if anyone will want to give 'twenty first' presents this year.' Her suggestions for those who did were:

> 1) Cigarette case and 'flapjack' matching
> 2) Suitcase and dressing case, really light!!
> 3) A small 'evening' wristwatch
> 4) A light warm travelling rug
> 5) A light portable gramophone (a thing I'm always wishing I had these days)
> and NOT a brush-and-comb set or another jewel case!

Marion was far from insensitive to the impression this list might give. 'What an extravagant-minded child!' she wrote. 'This life does make one appreciate pleasant things, and look out for beauty in odd places!'

Because of her supposed delicate heart, Marion had never been inoculated. Now the doctor at the base said there was no risk of complications and the deed was done. It got her a day off work, when she sat by the fire with a jigsaw, cards and books and her friend Fletcher and slept all day. They both roused themselves to have the grouse which Mrs Campbell had sent from Kilberry and they enjoyed apple jelly, raspberry jam and heather honey from the estate. Fletcher sent a message to Mrs Campbell saying what a useful person Marion was to lodge with. By the end of September, the pair had moved to Craigemachie, a house owned by a Miss Buchan in Links Terrace, where they shared a downstairs front room as a bed sitting room and ate with the family in a warm, pretty kitchen. There were other lodgers sharing, one a teacher, and Miss Buchan served a high tea when her paying guests came home from work. With more space and a view of the bay, life was looking up on the domestic front.

Meanwhile, the gnawing fox reminded Marion that she now faced a circular problem in relation to her much desired transfer to the west: without lodgings, she could have no job, but she couldn't apply for lodgings without having a job. There was nothing for it but to apply her mind to birthday celebrations. December 16, 1940 was a Monday. Marion suggested to her mother that they could meet in Glasgow for her birthday weekend and save her leave for Christmas or New Year.

There was quite a social life in Peterhead. She had already attended a dinner with the Captain in the local hotel. Now he hosted a dance to inaugurate the Navy's social club and Marion found it good fun, especially as there was no drinking – 'which is such a pleasant change from the Army dances'. Perhaps she was giving the idea that she had time on her hands, because her mother suggested that she concentrate on brushing up her languages. Yet another letter echoing her father's correspondence to her mother was sent to Kilberry: 'I'm afraid that if I can't find the time to write to my own mother, I'm hardly likely to find much for Languages!' Even so, she asked for her French, German, Italian and Latin dictionaries to be sent along with her Gaelic Testament, saying she'd long wanted to make some comparison of French and Gaelic as she was convinced that a lot of French derived from Gaelic roots and that the Bible offered her a 'fairly easy' approach to this line of study. She refused to waste money on a correspondence course as she felt she would have too little time to study. Her spare time was for Kilberry work, and she was angry that Colonel Henderson was not carrying out her instructions despite several verbal and written statements.

In October 1940, her longed-for move to the Clyde was approved, but that went for little in that chaotic year. Factory workers and dockers were needed on this vital artery as well as armed forces, so the lodgings problem was still to be overcome. Marion's mother, however, had other worries about the transfer: was her daughter at risk of getting into the 'wrong set'? Marion's robust riposte was a letter which asked that she think about the 'set' she was working with in Peterhead – 'Bank clerks and trawler hands!' she wrote with a flourish, adding: 'I do not fancy the YMCA – see under 'factory hands' above!'

Mrs Campbell also had worries about this constant movement, describing it as 'shuffling about', a charge her daughter hotly denied. She was following a master plan and had never seen Peterhead as anything but temporary en route to the Clyde. A truce between mother and daughter was called when another gift of game arrived in Peterhead and the Misses Buchan, who had never been confronted by pheasant or blackcock before, nevertheless produced delightful meals one chilly October weekend. And all the while there were instructions to be sent to Kilberry about cattle sales and disputes on the estate. Marion also had to remind her mother not to tell anyone about her work in Peterhead or to put into letters any detail about the ships she saw passing in the Sound of Jura. Considering the personal secrets which Mrs Campbell had kept during the previous three decades, these officious instructions from her daughter must have elicited a wry smile.

Although she had been dismissive about the possibility of continuing her studies, the reading which Marion managed to cram in during these war years provided her with a far wider education than any correspondence course could have given her. She and Fletcher shared interests and library books. Like Marion, Fletcher had Indian and Italian connections, although Fletcher's were first rather than second hand. They read *The Living India* by Sir George MacMinn, which

Marion said filled in 'many of the gaps left by the Sykes *History*' and inspired her to want to 'learn Sanskrit and/or Arabic at once'.

She may not have learned Sanskrit or Arabic, but this was the start of a lifetime pattern of sucking subjects dry. 'Research' was to become the middle name her father didn't want her to have and she had the ability to assimilate and analyse any of the myriad issues she would seize like a Poltalloch terrier throughout her life. A more formal education would perhaps have saved her the endless lists she would make as she wrapped her mind around a language, a medieval religious order, a prehistoric travel pattern or her own complex family tree. But as a friend in later years, Queen's Counsel Ian Hamilton pointed out, a university degree would probably have locked her into a narrow academic field rather than allowing her to roam enthusiastically across so many areas of interest. There is no doubt that her mother, considered less than intellectual by some, 'very clever' by others, gifted Marion a broad church of interest; and that her relationship with her father, however short, was intensely influential in her determination to conquer intellectual mountains.

The quiet days of Peterhead, with their opportunities for reading, were soon over. Her move to Greenock was confirmed on October 22 and by November 1 she was ensconced in a house called Woodburn at Kilcreggan, having been told that her work would in fact be across the Clyde from Greenock at Helensburgh. Her work was to be technical and involved the protection of merchant shipping and her digs were in the house of two middle aged sisters and their brother who were 'charming' and had soft Highland voices which pleased her and made her feel at home. She was working in an old fort at the water's edge and the sirens warning against raids were to be a regular punctuation of each day. Like her father before her, she asked for gifts of game to be sent to those who had been kind to her or given her hospitality, including Captain Hewitt RN at the Palace Hotel, Peterhead, her friend Fletcher and the Misses Buchan. She enlivened her letters home, however, with sharp comment about those around her – one young woman was described as 'a little bourgeoisie but pretty, brunette, vivacious and gay'. This individual criticised Marion's work, an unwelcome additional pressure at a time when Tarbert had witnessed enemy activity and she need to know if her insurance policies covered air raid damage to stock or property. By the beginning of December she was angling again for a job in Gourock.

Damage to property on the Clyde was becoming commonplace and Marion wasn't settled in digs until well into December when she went to stay with the Teachers in Lower Sutherland Crescent – a Helensburgh family with Jura connections and a grand piano, elements which pleased Marion as much as the cosy sitting room and big bedroom she was allotted. She had plans for both Mary Sandeman's birthday on December 9 and her own twenty first on the 16th. She telegrammed her mother that the Central Hotel was booked for her birthday weekend from the Saturday to the Tuesday and she was to go home to Kilberry for Christmas. Her birthday celebrations took in a Sunday afternoon concert by the Choral and Orchestral Union of Glasgow, the Glasgow Choral Union and the Scottish Orchestra at the Paramount Theatre. It wasn't too much of an extravagance at twopence a ticket and the music included Mendelssohn's Fingal's Cave, Puccini's *One Fine Day* and Elgar's *Enigma Opus 36.* Marion, Mary and Mrs Campbell went back to the Central Hotel afterwards and toasted Marion's majority. She was toasted again in January, 1941, when she went home to a presentation by the Kilberry tenants and estate workers. Her thank you speech on that chilly January 10 was in English, not the Gaelic of her debut speech as a toddler. She had been given a signet ring and she told the Kilberry folk who had contributed to it:

> I wish I could tell you what an encouragement it is when I'm a long way from home and on my own to feel that you are all with me in your thoughts. . . I remember a story about a magic ring. If the person who had it was in trouble, he only had to give the ring a little twist and there was an army coming to help him. This ring is going to do the same magic for me. Whenever I turn it on my finger I'll see all of you as I see you now and I'll know I have your friendship and love to go with me wherever I go.

In 1941, her personal battles were fought on the Clyde, where the work increased and interested her. She said that the harder she worked the faster her brain worked and 'I enjoy the feeling of being an engine running at full speed'. For the first time, she commented in a letter home: 'I'm enjoying myself very much.' She found time for concerts in Glasgow with Mary, and took it upon herself to take fellow WRNS under her wing. There were now bereaved women, women who found the discipline of the WRNS difficult, women who had not developed other interests in life and found it difficult being away from home. Her work moved to Glasgow, involving freezing train journeys from Helensburgh while her future was debated. Those journeys, when her fingers sometimes became so cold she could no longer write, gave her time to keep up with the estate business and to indulge in bird spotting along the river – oyster catchers , curlew, redshanks, shelduck and ringplovers could all be seen from the grubby carriage windows. Occasionally her letters became less businesslike as a scene from the train caught her imagination. Passing Dumbarton one February evening she wrote: '. . . the Rock is so opalescent in the early morning and most lovely at sunset!'

Then on February 27 she was able to write home: 'I can hardly believe it, but I am really going to stay in the Glasgow job!' She was billeted temporarily in a service women's hostel in Lynedoch Place, former home of the Girl Guides, but as always there was a mix up and no-one expected her there. She eschewed the proffered dirty linen and found a 2s 6d-a-night bed and breakfast instead. Then, as she was on permanent loan to Glasgow from Greenock, she found digs in Hyndland, the city's upmarket west end suburb which Marion reassured her mother 'roughly equals Kensington'. The muddled move was made no easier by requests from home about the feasibility of buying an engine for the mill: her opinion was that this was no time to start new ventures but that if the old watermill at Coulaghailtro still worked it might be worth making an agreement to share costs with the Kilberry neighbours. There were difficulties with renovations to the gardener's cottage, too, and eating in the naval offices canteen in St Enoch's Hotel after a tough day manning the telephones, the demands from home must have seemed quite surreal – but then, life for everyone was becoming ever more so as the months went by.

The digs in Hyndland were ten shillings a week for bed and breakfast only, although Marion had an electric fire in her room and full use of the sitting and bathrooms. At Mrs Gimson's in Turnberry Road, she was just a minute from the tram stop and she wrote reassuringly to her mother about the place's good points. Then there was a bomb and the Gimson residence was no more and Marion moved to 11 Victoria Park Gardens to live with a Mrs MacMillan, which she wrote in French on a postcard home was highly preferable to her original digs and she got tea with the family as well as breakfast.

Marion, as always, made light of the major events and a drama out of petty squabbles at work – so her account of the raid in which the Turnberry Road flat was damaged had more to do with how tired she felt after a sleepless night than with the incident itself. On March 15, 1941, she wrote home to say how lucky she was to escape with just 'one tiny scratch' on her finger. She had taken charge of directing local residents as the damage all around became apparent. She was able to rescue some of her belongings and went off to Greenock to stay with Mary for the weekend, planning to return later for her things. She wrote laconically: 'How does one get plaster out of one's hair? I had no hat and my hair is almost grey with it.' She joked that she didn't want to risk washing it and turning it into plaster of Paris. When she went back for her things, she said she found her Bible in the debris open at the psalms, 'Lift up your heads' and 'He will be our Guide', commenting to her mother, 'He certainly guided me all that night.' It prompted her to make her Will – the one in which she left her Grannie's five pound note to charity.

The Hyndland bombing was the tail end of the Clydebank Blitz and there were refugees from that devastation trying to find shelter all around Glasgow. The MacMillans were friends of the Gimsons and in that sense, Marion landed lucky. Less fortunate was the fact that on the night of the bombing, the truth was that she had received rather more than a scratch on her finger. The brave face she initially wore slipped some ten days later when she felt more able to describe the scene. Ostensibly she wrote home to complain about a fellow WREN who had spent the night of the Blitz in a first aid post with nothing to do and moaned about the fact to Marion when she arrived at work straight from the scene of the west end bombing. Marion had found only a tin of lint, no scissors, no water, no pins and not enough bandages to deal with the injuries she encountered. The colleague was also loud in her complaint about being hit on the back by an ambulance door; Marion was playing down the fact that she, too, had a more severe injury. 'I twisted my back lifting a pram out over debris, but it's all right again,' she told her mother.

It was not all right. In later years, the outcome of this act of humanity was to come back and haunt her. She had damaged a disc and suffered increasing back pain throughout her life. At the time, she dismissed her injury, saying at the end of her letter: 'She [the annoying WREN in question] is about 10 days older than I, and a little trying to work with! I'm afraid I always have a grouse, don't I?'

Marion did not get home for Easter that year and she was again homeless because Mrs MacMillan had become ill. She had a poisoned leg, her husband was a semi-invalid and her 16-year-old son had just come home from hospital after diphtheria. Marion simply left with her bags to give the family its space and in time found a room in a ground floor flat near the university where she had to cook in a shared kitchen. She and Mary had fantasised about renting somewhere in the country halfway between Glasgow and Greenock so they could meet half way and spend weekends together. The irony of all their efforts to get postings near each other was that just as Marion was settling into Glasgow, Mary was to be moved from Greenock. She went before the Board in London for a Commission, prompting Marion to ask for one in the hope that they would land together in Greenwich for the same cadets' course. Marion hoped this commitment would please her mother and they must have talked about such a move at great length when Mrs Campbell came and stayed in Havelock Street, where the landlady Mrs Ryder was delighted to play hostess to a lady she had feared would be very grand but whom she found 'a darling', as she whispered deferentially when Mrs Campbell left after the weekend. Mrs Ryder proved to be something of a surrogate mother to Marion and she enjoyed the homely pleasures of making oatcakes and being scolded for 'too much tasting'.

But there was little enjoyment in the nightly retreats to the shelter away from the bombs and while Marion sometimes went with a fearful

Mrs Ryder for company, there were times when work and the noisy, sleepless nights left her too weary to budge. She had plans to buy a blow-up mattress, finding that sitting on a narrow bench in a shelter made her back sore. Her plans also included a proposed trip home on leave when she intended to 'have it out' with Colonel Henderson on a number of estate matters which she found impossible to deal with at a distance.

It was difficult during that dangerous spring of 1941 not to think profoundly about life and love. In May, 1941, one of Marion's letters home revealed some of her real feelings under the sometimes glib, sometimes tetchy, sometimes downright bossy façade.

> I sometimes feel I must be a very unsatisfactory child – Do I seem terribly engrossed and wrapped up in myself? It's only a mask to hide rather a sentimental little ass! I do so love you and I want to get every ounce out of life so that people will admire your daughter and Daddy's. Nothing makes me happier than when people, like Mrs Birkinyre on Sunday, say how wonderfully you taught me – because though I know it's true, and I do thank you with all my heart and mind, it gives me a glow of joy to know other people know it too. And just as, when I found myself automatically put in charge (as that night in Turnberry Avenue) I am proud to come of such a father that these things are my right and duty; so when I find myself able to enjoy music or art or learning, and get the kernel of delight out of it, I'm proud and thankful to have been your child. It makes me sorry for others when I see their minds half-developed and under exercised. You used to think I had no 'passion for perfection'. Perhaps I have it too much – so that imperfection, and failures to try one's best, sicken me. The attempt, not the result, is what redeems a thing from disaster. To do one's best should be the good – to be as true as possible to whatever values one accepts – to run the course which is set us (to quote Tagore again) 'Let me light my lamp,' says the star, 'And never debate if it will help to remove the darkness'.
>
> It's more value to do moderate work by a bad light that indifferent work by an excellent one surely?
>
> I am morally certain that something enormous is in the

> wind but have no inkling what. . . begin to suspect that I'm fervently patriotic, which used to be thought old fashioned – but if so, then I am old fashioned and drat these 'ere new fangled notions.

Perhaps she surprised herself at being able to put this all down on paper, because she ended: 'What a weird letter'. But she sent it all the same and her mother kept it along with the telegrams reassuring her that her daughter was surviving the raids and the much more mundane letters about digs and duties and inter-office strife.

Mrs Campbell shared her own innermost feelings in a letter to Marion that same month which was typically suffocating and oppressive in its tone:

> My own darling Marion
> I often think what a different life we should lead, you and I, if our darlings were here – Isabel and Ian and darling Daddy. But you and I have each other still thank God. What do you think? I like to think they know something about us . . . I want them so much. It is better of course when you are with me, but you must never feel tied to me to such an extent that it is irksome. I want you to lead as full a life as possible but there are things so precious between you and me – and I do think we can 'bridge the generations' and 'spirit within spirit meet'. I am sometimes afraid you may feel I want to intrude my life and thoughts into yours. To a Mother, who is a Mother, her child matters so very much, and it is difficult to withhold and keep away, and not to show how much we yearn to know and understand and it gives us a little pang to be shut out and to lose touch in any way or any thing – can you appreciate that?
> Perhaps living the 'apart life' I do, I have become too introspective and too sensitive. . . An entirely selfless life is impossible but it should be one's aim.

By June, Marion had been ordered into WRNS quarter at 6 Clairmont Gardens where she had to share a room with five other women, at least one of whom she decided was nice. Sharing was not her forte, but she persevered, possibly empowered by the knowledge that her papers had gone up for the Commission. At home, evacuees were staying on the estate, some welcome, others more difficult, and Marion tried to keep her mind and body on an even keel by walking with Mary in the hills above Greenock whenever there were free days. She borrowed money from her mother to meet her bills, explaining: 'Perhaps it's wrong in war time to spend money on oneself but this perpetual herding-together does make one stale and tired.'

By the time she was due leave in July, she had to confess she hadn't been well for some time. Invigorated by Kilberry she went back into the fray only to have to write from Ward 6 West, Belvedere Hospital in Glasgow that she was suffering from chickenpox and was the only adult in the two chickenpox wards which were bursting at the seams with children aged between six months and thirteen years old. Some of the older boys were Channel Island evacuees, who must have wondered how 'safe' Glasgow was as the raids continued. Others were from what Marion described as 'poor homes' and in a 'disgusting state' when they arrived in the infectious diseases ward. She was distressed by these 'horribly skinny, poor little mites' but had to get on as usual with Ministry of Agriculture business, the prospects for the Kilberry harvest and requests to her mother to keep an ever closer eye on Colonel Henderson. Back in harness towards the end of August, she watched Mary play hockey and decided to start a team in her own unit.

At last the word came for her to have an interview in London about her Commission and she found the English capital less damaged than she had imagined. She took a sleeper down, fitted in visits to family and the cinema to allay her nerves and depression, went up before a woman Rear Admiral, two women captains and a woman Lieutenant Commander. There was a late tea with family before dashing back to Euston for the sleeper back to Glasgow feeling a little more cheerful. On September 23, she sent a telegram home to say she was heading for the Royal Naval College at Greenwich and the estate trade in rabbits and evacuee problems at Kilberry had to go on hold. 'It's really thrilling to be here' she said. 'The whole atmosphere is so lovely.' Letters became infrequent because of the pressure of studying, but Kilberry business was always dealt with at some time in the week. The hard work paid off and she passed as a Third Officer and was appointed to operational duties at Portland for a few weeks with more training at Greenwich planned. Her new uniform was ordered from Gieves in London on Mummie's account and she stocked up on underwear while she was in spending mood. No sooner had she arrived at Portland, of course, than she put in for a transfer to Scotland and the director of operations promised to send her north if there was a vacancy. Billeted in WRNS quarters in Weymouth, Dorset, she was set to do classified work which she at least found interesting.

Her health, however, was to prove a difficulty. She had been suffering from bouts of intestinal pain for some time and was putting off seeing a doctor. After she had collapsed in pain in Glasgow, the medical officer had suggested an inflammation causing a reaction in her appendix but she knew an X-ray was the only way her problem could be properly identified.

At the end of October, she was back at Greenwich, feeling very excited that she was training alongside university graduates. She worked out a code to inform her mother where she had been posted, and it would be the word 'breakfast' if the much longed for West of Scotland was her secret destination. After leave in November, however, she was sent to Cardiff. She stayed with Mrs Wideman at 7 Westbourne Road, Penarth, just outside the city, which was not a happy experience, but within days was told she be working as secretary to the chief of staff of the Commander in Chief in Liverpool – but first she had to go to Bristol to have her back examined. She was told it was 'the finest hospital for service women in the country' and already she was able to pass judgement, having experienced a number of other hospital wards already in her short service career. As always, she was financially embarrassed. So much moving about meant, as for so many service men and women, that her pay rarely caught up with her. She wondered if she could justifiably borrow £50 from the farm and pay it back with interest at the end of the war so that she wasn't always running so close to the wind. She booked into the WRNS sick quarters in Apsley Road, Bristol, at the end of November with £20 in her personal bank account.

Looking on the bright side, she decided that if the period of observation meant she lost the Liverpool job, she'd apply for one in

Scotland instead. By December 7, the doctors had identified a stone in the right kidney which had to be operated on because it would be a danger if left. It was to be the first one three operations to remove stones from that kidney by 1960. In 1941, it was a difficult procedure. Before she went for surgery, she offered to lend her mother money for Home Farm from the estate, for which Mrs Campbell held the tenancy, as a more economical option than borrowing from the bank. She was expecting over £1500 from the sale of sheep on Tiretigan and didn't want outside debt. There can have been few service women in those wards running an estate from their hospital beds as well as worrying about their service careers.

In December, butter, cheese and game were delivered to Bristol from Kilberry. Marion advised her mother against coming to see her because the accommodation was so difficult to find – whole streets had disappeared under enemy raids. She reassured her that Mr Oldham the surgeon was very well known and an expert in removing renal calculus. Even so, Mrs Campbell descended from the north in time for Marion's birthday. After the operation she went home and it was a long haul back to health. It wasn't until March, 1942, that Marion was passed fit and she was hoping her superiors would allow her to work in Helensburgh, but instead, she was immediately sent to Liverpool, where she found herself living in a warm, comfortable house in Birkenhead. There were nine WRNS and a baby grand sharing this house of Chippendale and mahogany, fine linen, good china and silver. She was working for a Lt Kerr from Ayrshire who struck her as a nice man at the outset. They were plotting the course of convoys to keep them safe and she frequently slept in the office, rousing herself quickly to respond to incoming messages. It was responsible work and despite its intensity she found time to start up a country dancing club with an introductory reel party. She bought a gramophone and records of her choice – *Fledermaus,* Franck's *Symphonie Variations* and *Jesu, joy of man's desiring* – confident in the knowledge that her legacy share in 1942 would be £100.

She was senior watch keeper in the Liverpool posting, the youngest member of staff and the first WREN to do the job. Rather than being pleased with this state of affairs, she was again pushing for a move north, still worrying about what was going on at Kilberry as the Rent Restrictions Act compromised decisions on who would get particular contracts. Perhaps it was the external worry which made her make mistakes at work and engender the resentment of colleagues over her assumption of authority. She wrote home:

> This is a lonely business. You can trust none of them. They all talk too much. Besides, one can't talk about this job, there are too many lives involved. . . I am very tired and rather harried by the office situation – full of touchiness and grievances and so forth – besides the work which is rather heavy at the moment. . . I'm enjoying it a lot but it is rather tiring! The worst is coming back to a lot of WREN cadets talking about the importance of their jobs!! They all have such raucous voices.

On May 1, 1942, she moved to new quarters in Alexandra Drive, Liverpool, and she was sharing with a WREN called Horrobin with whom she could at least rub along. At work, it was the busiest week in memory and one task was to land an acute appendix case safely from a vessel at sea. The excitement, she said, meant she was sick on night duty. 'I am beginning to 'desire' my hills very much,' she wrote home. She was desiring them even more later in the month when she was blamed for what she claimed were the mistakes of others. She felt her chances of promotion were finished: 'Still, who cares,' she said defiantly, but she obviously did and spent a miserable weekend brooding on her situation. She was angry with the aggressive woman in her shared 'cabin' (Horrobin had left) and angry at the 'general snappiness' of the men in the office.

> Just at the moment all my self-confidence has gone (this frequently happens!) and I feel flat, stale and unprofitable and absolutely inefficient. Apparently I can do nothing right which is most inconvenient for the others. . . I'm sure a lot of it has to do with my own health and the irritation of wanting to do more than I can.

This was an irritation which would stay with her for the rest of her life. Dr Neil MacDonald, her physician at the end of her life, would have recognised the psychological make-up of that young frustrated woman trying to do her best against the odds. She refused to report sick because it would have made her feel 'more depressed and useless' and it culminated in an explosion from Lt Kerr to the Captain, who saw Marion at the heart of all the office's problems and immediately moved her to an office where she was required to do a lot of standing. The doctor said the job was too much for her ('I'd come to the same conclusion first!!' she said) and she was expecting to be moved at any moment.

She was sent off home, advised by the doctor to play gentle tennis, and some six weeks later in July was sent to Somerset where she claimed to be in excellent health. There were eight RNS and 200 men and her work was 'experimental and to do with training pilots'. No sooner was she through the door than the old question of a transfer to Scotland was again proposed. She had been in a state about this transfer before she left home, but admitted it was 'not as bad as I feared'. Her job involved analysing and commenting on photographic records made during training. It was demanding work but she was looking forward to lecturing on the theory to lieutenants – although she admitted that she was 'prickly' about the prospect of working with a 'Highly Intelligent Woman'.

Her mood was much more influenced by the fact that living at Kilberry was becoming – yet again – an impossible option and – yet again – it was to go up for sale. Colonel Henderson had instructions not to allow anyone to view while Mrs Campbell was absent, but the two women had to console themselves that their loss was not as great as that of others. It was a building, not a loved one, that they were to lose. Marion wrote home on June 14, 1942:

> The time has come when we must face the question of where else to live, I'm afraid. Is there anywhere you would like? I feel myself I'd like a quiet country, and a small, handy, but not ultramodern house with a good small garden and a view of some sort. Where do you suggest – I could house hunt in a vague way. . . I've now got to the state of not daring to minimalize Kilberry at all and trying to believe I live somewhere else instead. I don't like the thought of Angus perhaps thinking of coming back to it.

Angus was one of Uncle Archie's sons and as such, still the enemy. To lose her home a third time would be destruction enough without it going to this branch of the family. The Kilberry problem hung heavily but there was little sympathy to be had from the officer in whom she confided. She was, he told her, taking too serious a view of 'just moving house'.

CHAPTER SEVEN
The Homecoming

It seemed impossible for Marion Campbell to engage in the kind of life most young women in the services experienced. Her attempts to separate herself from home were subverted by her mother's dependency and by the millstone of Kilberry. There seemed little option now but to sell Kilberry and her mother was seriously ill. Granted compassionate leave, she spent a frustrating and distressing two weeks at home. Returning south she wrote to her mother on August 1 saying: 'Oh my dear, what can I say? You must be feeling so empty if you feel like me, and even I have Mary coming.'

A sympathetic first officer discussed Marion's personal situation and a transfer to the Clyde was requested. Her mother was still ill but sending Marion the Kilberry garden produce by the box load – plums, eggs and gooseberries arrived regularly, some travelling better than others. Lady Lithgow was – as she frequently had been in the past – a practical help to the Kilberry women and refusing all thanks. A tractor was being sent over from Ormsary and the harvest would be possible after all. And other factors meant the black cloud was not so heavy: a letter from Marion's cousin Walter Campbell was forwarded to her by her mother. She promised to write to him when she had a chance. He was a Lt Commander on the HMS *Delhi* and his address was c/o GPO London. Her letters got through.

It was a brief respite from negativity. In October, word began to circulate that Mary Sandeman's sister-in-law was dead, leaving two little sons. More detail suggested this was not an accident. The newspapers got hold of the story and it was sensationalised to Marion's deep distress and disgust in the *Daily Mirror.* A 16-year-old girl who helped with the children had taken the boys to the police station and said it was she who had killed Eva. It became clear that Mary would have to leave the WRNS and go to her brother to look after the children.

It was now that Marion got her much longed for transfer north, too late to serve with her friend. The transfer was to Leith, the only post likely to be vacant for the foreseeable future. The Navy, as usual, wasn't expecting her and when they learned she was in Edinburgh, decided she had arranged her own digs. She hadn't and went to the North British Hotel, hoping the Admiralty would pay for it. In the long term, it became something of a homecoming for her as she was welcomed by staff from St Margaret's school and moved into lodgings fixed through 'a very kind dame at the tram stop', but the three men in the office were, according to Marion, anti-WREN and 'furious' at her arrival. It was cheaper to live in Edinburgh than Yeovilton, where mess bills leeched £3 from the monthly £10 allowance, 'however little one smoked or drank – not that I do either so you'd notice'. Here, Mrs Ross was charging 35 shillings a week all found and Marion could get lunch across the road from the office at Crawford's tea room for 1s 9d. She became involved with the Sea Rangers in her spare time, met up with old Edinburgh acquaintances and was using the Swedish she had learned for pre-war holidays in Scandinavia to have a stab at translating Norwegian merchant navy documents in the office. She said she needed these distractions to take her out of herself, 'otherwise I'd sink into a dreadful bog of inertia'.

It was becoming evident as the year came to a close that no-one wanted the castle and that with all the produce there, Marion and her mother couldn't hope to live as cheaply anywhere else. Although they felt they were on the breadline, they were at least sharing pheasant while Scotland's city dwellers were approaching malnutrition levels. On the other hand, the Inland Revenue was demanding large sums relating to Mrs Campbell's legacy and Marion and Colonel Henderson were trying to pay off a compromise figure by selling Kilberry's remaining Jamaica Bonds from the bygone days when the family was making its money there. Colonel Henderson was in Edinburgh rather than at *The Hollies*, his Ardrishaig home, which meant that Marion's involvement with estate business became even more intense, but the

Royal Navy's demands did not diminish. Indeed, the strain they put on Marion was added to by a superior officer who lunched too well then complained about her work. She couldn't tolerate such behaviour and set about asking yet again for the transfer to the west. A more immediate antidote was to go to the theatre with Miss Strachan, her former teacher from St Margaret's, to see a pre-London try-out of Noel Coward's *This Happy Breed*, and in the face of Mary's problems, she perhaps thought she was lucky despite it all. Mary was to move her brother Stewart's four and one-year-old sons to somewhere more accessible than Jura in the New Year and Marion asked her mother to offer them hospitality in transit. It wasn't, after all, a feasible option for Mrs Campbell to come to Edinburgh over the festive period – if festivities there would be – because the city was packed. Mary had told Marion she'd had no-one to talk to since the tragedy happened and said: 'I don't know if I'm the same or quite different'. The young woman who had confessed to the killing was sentenced to five years in prison but it wasn't all plain sailing for Mary to get her discharge, and more than one attempt had to be made to achieve the freedom she needed to look after her little nephews.

Marion's life became an odd mixture of society teas and suppers with well-connected family friends and cosy nights in at her digs where she made friends with a soap saleswoman who insisted on sending sample packets of Oxydol to Kilberry for her mother. She got leave in early January and arrived back in Edinburgh after a journey of slush and snow on January 10. Mother and daughter were light hearted enough for written banter – a Chinese style poem from Mrs Campbell to Marion, an arch comment in very bad Gaelic about ready cash from Marion to her mother. Marion saw the film *Mrs Miniver* and saw it as 'excellent propaganda'; and she practised rifle shooting on the range at Granton. Reading for the first time Neil Gunn's *The Silver Darlings* in the chilly February of 1943, she felt Gunn captured 'the deep and ancient heart of Scotland'.

In the office, she was simultaneously typist, tea maker and officer. Her pay went up to £160 a year and she could afford to ask Mary for a weekend visit to her digs in Dudley Gardens. The weekend went by in a flash and served only to make Marion realise how lonely she was.

She'd had a run in with the office commander and letters from home were occasionally censored: life seemed to be bearable only if lived through promises of future experiences, such as sharing her Easter leave with her mother and Mary. But yet again, with news of a fire at Kilberry, the gifted tractor causing difficulties and the usual office dog fights, came psychological ill health and a Navy doctor advised sick leave. She said: 'I think myself that I'm thoroughly worn out by all the unpleasantness and strain here. I feel I'd give anything to get a few days of idleness.'

She was given a week off and decided to spend it in Edinburgh, telling her anxious mother by postcard on March 17, 1943 that there was no room for her to visit her at Mrs Ross's. She worked on her recovery by catching up on letters, finishing a Liberty dressing gown she was making for her mother, sleeping – and plotting future tenancies for Kilberry's farms. The best medicine, however, was the ballet with a former WREN colleague. They went on from Les Ballets Jouss to a naval officers' club, danced all evening to a 'very good band of naval ratings' and Marion was given a lift home on the back of a naval lorry, and loudly wished goodnight by this jolly crew.

Was it shyness or her mother's warnings which normally kept her away from the fun other young people were determined to have during the war? She always enjoyed herself so much when she partied but always talked of partying with disdain. Perhaps she knew too well the snide gossip which circulated about young women in the forces. She had been on the receiving end of it in 1942 when she had her kidney stone operation. 'You know that many people asked me pointed questions about my long time off duty last year, don't you?' she asked her mother. 'Particularly when they knew that I hadn't been able to do very much for some time before! It all goes to show, doesn't it?' Proper to within an inch of her life, such title-tattle must have hurt her more than most.

Now, going back to the office at the end of March anaemic and edgy, she was told there'd be no leave for her at Easter because her new commander was going to a wedding and had not had leave for six months. Then the Navy dropped its own bombshell: all WREN officers would be liable to serve overseas unless they claimed exemption on compassionate grounds within a month. Marion immediately had a private interview with her Superintendent in Rosyth and explained her circumstances: she had a sick mother and an even sicker estate to look after. Her letter of March 3 explained:

> I have a 5,000 acre estate in the West of Argyll, now on maximum food production. My Estate Factor is too busy with work for the Ministry of Agriculture and the Government Departments to devote much time to private business and he has in any case the care of several other estates whose owners are away. Consequently it remains for me to supervise the five farms of the estate as much as possible during leave and by post, and to make most of the executive decisions about rents, wages and so on.
>
> My mother, who is widowed, lives there alone at present, but she suffers increasingly from rheumatoid arthritis and is not strong. . . I am an only child. . . I have not been able to find anyone who would be free to look after her in case of further illness.
>
> I feel bound, therefore, to apply for exemption for these reasons.

It was certainly a better letter than her previous plea about being near home and working with her friend. For good measure, she asked for a posting in the west and had further discussions with the chief officer. The sense of the request, however, did not impress her senior officers. Neither could understand why a move west was preferable to a discharge from the WRNS and signing up with the Women's Land Army. The best she could hope for was a post in Oban, where she said at least she could see 'my beasts in the ring perhaps' and could keep a better eye on Colonel Henderson.

By now she and Mrs Ross were taking Sanatogen tonic wine and advising Mrs Campbell to do the same because she was having to deal with the moral issue of a single parent teacher at Kilberry: should she be sent packing or not? Illegitimacy was a shocking thing in 1943. For Marion, the Sanatogen put her troublesome new boss out of her consciousness for a few hours while for the nervy Mrs Ross, it took the edge off her fear of the air raids.

And Marion's judgement of people was not as sharp as it would become. Time and again she told her mother of a nice new colleague or boss; time and again she discovered how wrong she had been. The office boss in Leith who had seemed so pleasant on arrival was soon 'so rude' that she almost asked to be relieved of her duties. However, at the end of April after much wartime muddle, a posting westwards seemed at last on the cards. It couldn't come a day too soon as the office in Leith was becoming a hotbed of dissent. She refused to be 'snubbed by a shipping clerk, however many stripes he has' and told the commander so in no uncertain terms. It was almost a blessing to have Colonel Henderson's dictatorial behaviour towards her mother to deal with and certainly a delight to have letters from Mary Sandeman's nephew Charles, who had fallen under the spell of 'Malon' and wanted to see her on Jura soon.

In June she was still in Edinburgh when Colonel Henderson informed her of an offer for the estate but only if it was split up. She was beginning to feel that rather than selling, the estate would have to be her place of work after the war and that they should therefore proceed with developments whenever possible. Because she had no formal training, she saw little chance of a job elsewhere in the longed-for peace, but she was torn – she had seen some of the world, knew its promise, and instead of her usual passion for Kilberry, she actually articulated the thought that 'interesting though it would be to work the place up, there are other things in the world to do'.

Meanwhile, the war dragged on and so did Marion's placement in Leith. Her mother was to visit in July and Mrs Ross the landlady was anxious: 'What'll she think, coming from a castle to my wee but and ben!' she demanded of Marion. It was a happy visit, but by the 19th of August after feeling unwell for some days, Marion was again in hospital. Writing from Ward 5C, Bangour Hospital, Broxburn, West Lothian, Marion told her mother how isolated the place was and how difficult to get there. It was a fifteen mile bus ride from Edinburgh and the hospital grounds were enormous – not the place for an older lady with her own health problems to visit, especially when Marion believed she would only be there for a few days for X-rays. A month later, she was thanking her mother for struggling up to the hospital with her radio because she was enjoying listening to it in the aftermath of having her stitches out. Another kidney stone operation had been performed. Two months sick leave was on the cards for a full recovery. By September 24, she was able to stand for a few seconds and then with the help of a nurse walked around the ward. It was time to make plans about getting home, but Mary was in Jura with two little boys and Mrs Ross didn't know the ropes of trains and steamers and Marion feared she would get flustered. Although she was struggling to get to the bathroom on her own and knitting in bed was too uncomfortable, she was still conducting a dialogue with Colonel Henderson about the estate and approving lets for the winter shooting at Kilberry.

On October 2 she was told she could go home and a room was booked at the Central Hotel in Glasgow as a staging post for mother and daughter. They shared a few short weeks at home, then Marion was left in charge of Kilberry while her mother took her own turn in hospital, travelling to Glasgow where Dr McCall Smith was now a hospital consultant. Her old gynaecological problems meant an operation, the details of which she was still far too modest to share even with her daughter.

Marion was only too happy to send her vivid word pictures of the world she had left behind – 50 geese 'beating against the strong south east wind and creaking and gaggling as they flew' – as well as keeping her up-to-date about the Leith office to which she was still unable to return. In early November, she promised to demand three months leave to look after her, despite her own frail state of health. As Mrs Campbell went off to stay with Lady Lithgow in Renfrewhsire to recuperate, Marion went to Jura to stay with Mary. First, however, there was the matter of damage caused by evacuees to be dealt with. Back in 1939 she had generously offered toys and books for evacuees from her childhood store. Now she found one family had abused trust and caused damage to an estate property. After a visit by the Provost of Lochgilphead, it was confirmed that the council, which had allocated the evacuees to Kilberry, would pay up.

On Jura, Marion was exposed to influenza. A maid and the boys, Charles and Sim (James) all had temperatures of well over 100. While Mary nursed the patients, Marion took on cleaning duties and made

Welsh Rarebit from a recipe book for supper. She of course caught 'flu and couldn't travel home but nonetheless, at the end of November, Marion was told she had to report to a medical board as soon as she was fit to travel. She told them her mother was seriously ill and requested a month's compassionate leave. Along with this correspondence came word that there was a vacancy in Oban for which she was considered suitable and 'it is proposed to appoint you there on expiration of your sick leave'. In the stiff and unyielding language of the Royal Navy, Marion's superiors wished information 'as to what date you anticipate being medically fit to take up this new work'. Instead of the Oban appointment, however, she was granted compassionate leave and then a further month's unpaid leave starting on January 2, 1944. Her emergency ration cards were posted on to Kilberry. It was the beginning of the end of Marion's life in His Majesty's armed forces. On January 27 she asked for a discharge from the service. On February 15, that request was acknowledged and a further month's unpaid leave was granted pending an Admiralty decision.

Interestingly, throughout much of the time of her compassionate leave, Marion was staying on Jura with Mary Sandeman and the boys rather than at Kilberry looking after her mother. On February 2, she wrote to her mother from Craighouse saying she couldn't go home on the coming Saturday because that was Simmie's third birthday.

> He seems to take it for granted that I'm staying and is displaying a most fascinating affection for me this time! So do you think you can manage on your own till Tuesday? If you don't do as you really feel inclined, I'll never dare go away again I think!

She had been beating for snipe, cock pheasant and the 'odd woodcock' the previous day – perhaps not the way the Admiralty envisaged their Third Officer Campbell spending her sick/compassionate leave.

Her discharge came through on March 16, 1944 and she spent much of the rest of 1944 looking after the estate, interspersed with visits to Jura or visits by Mary to Kilberry. She became immersed in potato census returns, wool control forms and form machinery returns. She had turned up her nose at the idea of becoming a Land

Girl, but now she was one in her own right and enjoying the freedom – even if the estate was still in its perpetual perilous state and there was little future in it as a business. In December, she went to Craighouse for Mary's birthday and young Charles, Mary's older nephew, manfully struggled to keep up with the adults as they went beating for a couple of hours over heather and bog on a bitter windy day. The visits to Jura continued in 1945 and Marion enjoyed her role as surrogate aunt, reading to the children at bedtime and taking a pride in their childish pronouncements. Motherhood was something she had long yearned for. On October 2, 1939, when she was stationed at Blackdown Barracks in the south of England, she wrote home telling her mother about a young room mate.

> I feel I want to 'mother' her, in case I never have anyone of my own. I'm afraid of one thing now, above everything – that I may never have that now. It's all I want, you know! We must lay aside our womanhood these days, or the greater part, and who knows when we shall take it again? This is a new fear and one I had not thought of before these weeks. No doubt it will pass.

But it didn't pass for many years. Her neighbour Lady Fiona Byatt recalled visiting Marion at the castle after the war and seeing a beautiful recently-decorated cot in the nursery all ready for an infant.

Every time she went to Craighouse, she stayed longer than she intended – or certainly longer than she ever indicated to her mother. There were always postcards, letters and telegrams asking for patience and fortitude until she caught a ferry in another few days' time. She revelled in the domesticity she experienced at Craighouse, baking for the children, cleaning the kitchen and taking on other housewifely duties which her upbringing had certainly never encompassed even if her service billetings had. But it wasn't all gingerbread men and bedtime stories. In April, 1945, she used the kind of salty language which would continue to shock those who saw her as a sheltered spinster lady when she discovered that arrangements with the Stag garage in Lochgilphead to transport her 'd——d heifers' had gone awry. She was also looking for a shepherd and she went to the Oban cattle sales with the same enthusiasm as her father and grandfather before her. She became known in Highland Cattle circles as something of an expert, though like Jane Nelson, who with her husband was a major Highland Cattle breeder, few realised that her father had died when she was eight because she constantly quoted his expertise 'as if she had been talking with him yesterday', as Mrs Nelson said.

Marion celebrated the peace at Craighouse, telegraphing her mother on August 17: PROPOSE CELEBRATING PEACE TILL TUESDAY, LOVE MARION. And then, not surprisingly, on August 21 she had to send another telegram saying SORRY TOO STORMY LOVE MARION. In later years, she often cited her naval career as one of the best times of her life. It had started with a letter to her mother begging: 'When you write to me on service, you won't put 'of Kilberry' unless and until I'm made an officer, will you?' and ended without glory in sick leave and compassionate leave. Throughout the war she had wanted to be at Kilberry, had found office relationships difficult, and sharing quarters with such a broad mix of women had tried her sensitivities. But for the first time in her life she had experienced independence, had a taste of a very different kind of life and got some measure of herself. Despite her ill health, her personal worries, the put downs and the frustrations, war for Marion Campbell of Kilberry had been a defining time and in retrospect she could see she was capable of meeting a challenge.

CHAPTER EIGHT

Life and love for a Renaissance woman

Whatever else her discharge from the armed services brought, financial security in Marion Campbell's life was not part of the package. Emergency ration books may have kept food on the table for a couple of months after she went home to Kilberry, but once she was cast adrift from the WRNS there was no pay packet, no living allowance, only the reality of the Kilberry situation.

Never a favourite with her mother, the factor Colonel Henderson was now increasingly seen by Marion as liability rather than a help. He questioned her decisions and challenged her authority. He tried to impose tenants and timetables on both Marion and her mother. More significantly in Marion's eyes, he was not running the estate efficiently and there were shades of her mother's deep distrust of the old family lawyers. She decided to take matters into her own hands and run Kilberry without him. Almost her first task in 1944 was to tell Colonel Henderson his services were no longer required and that she wanted all the title deeds and paperwork relating to the estate.

She received a somewhat patronising response – such documents were too numerous and bulky for posting or even picking up in a car. Eventually she managed to master the correct terminology, ask the right questions and was rewarded with access to the papers she needed. They were not, it seems, in order. Tax returns and valuations were not up to date, and nor were they signed or certified. When Marion wrote to the Inland Revenue in October, 1944, she explained that she had taken over the factorship of Kilberry Home Farm from Colonel Henderson at the beginning of that year along with factorship of the Kilberry Estate and Tiretigan Farm, still her property.

She had evidently sugared the pill when she told Colonel Henderson his services were no longer wanted. So much so that he wrote to thank her for her kind words. There was, however, a barb in his obsequious response:

> . . . my one and sole objective since I took over the management of Kilberry was to keep things going until you were personally able to consider the position from all angles. I quite agree that the course you have adopted was in the circumstances the only one possible especially as you could not ultimately adopt the course which I advised. By taking over the management of the property and farms you will get a thorough insight into the whole position, which, to you, is bound to be much more satisfactory than any explanation given by another. I very much hope that things will improve both from the point of view of the farms and of the estate, to enable you to steer the ship through the troubled seas.

Marion had told him there was 'a mass of questions to ask' but on March 9, 1944, the day that he handed over factorship to Marion, he warned that everything would now be on 'a business footing' – the factor's fee ended but the bills for any single piece of advice would begin. It had been his modus operandi to advance money to cover estate business. As the war progressed the banks were jumpy and Colonel Henderson himself was financially challenged. Marion had an overdraft of £2500 to repay him and in what must have sounded to Marion like a warning from the Cawdor witches he told her:

> You will certainly require a considerable sum of free working capital because there will be very little income except from seed corn and barley from the Home Farm until the May sales. . . If you have any difficulty with the work I shall still be very glad to give you any help I can but I can assure you that you will find it pretty exacting. . .
> From my records in the office I find that I wrote no less than 925 letters in connection with the Farms and Estate in 1943. The Farm records and accounts will, of course, require to be carefully kept, made up and balanced and

> reconciled with the previous year for the Inspector of Taxes . . . The £2,500 will need £2,000 to repay me.

By the middle of 1945, the tax repayments were made and Marion was beginning to get the books in some sort of order, even if the financial situation continued to teeter on the brink of collapse. There was little free time: she was book keeper, hay maker, cattle dealer and general dogsbody. There are those who question that she had a 'hands on' involvement with the farm at this time, but much had to be done by the two women because there were fewer staff than there had ever been in Kilberry's history and less money to pay wages than ever before.

The Department of Health looked at the hours and wages at Kilberry and suggested 'improvements'. Marion had already approved a raise in pay for the gamekeeper George Young, who at the beginning of the war was paid 40s a week with a free house, four tons of coal, a yearly allowance of six hundredweight of potatoes and 2s 6d a week to feed his working dog. The gardener had been paid 42 shillings a week from 1941, with a free house, four tons of coal a year and two pints of milk a day. Archie Sinclair the ploughman, paid 36 shillings a week, with a free house, two tons of coals a year and extra payments to look after the gas plant at the castle, told the Department of Health he wanted to work 50 hours a week all year round as he had done before the Agricultural Committee made 'improvements' to his conditions. 'The hours laid down. . . are unsuitable for any every day work at home such as gardening,' he said. All these details and the meetings and paperwork which went with them were part and parcel of Marion's new life after the WRNS. Little wonder she took the opportunity to escape to Jura for the peace celebrations, leaving the estate workers and tenants to have their own ball at Kilberry.

When she received her discharge from the WRNS she had written to the National Service Officer at the Stag Annexe in Lochgilphead explaining that she had been allowed to leave on compassionate grounds to look after her mother, who had been seriously ill following her operation the previous November. Dr McCall Smith at the Victoria Infirmary had said Marion was required at home. She explained that she planned to cultivate an acre of vegetables and administrate the two farms under her own control and the three which were let. She could see no work locally of 'any greater importance' and she asked if this was enough work 'to enable me to remain at home'. She signed this letter 'Marion Campbell of Kilberry' – the styling she had begged her mother not to use while she was in the forces.

She seemed to be taking charge of her own destiny, but despite this apparent display of confidence in her own status she was not above seeking (as her mother had done on many occasions as a young woman) the advice of an astrologer. A Sagittarian, she was told that the Sun was 'badly placed' at the time of her birth. The restriction of her early life had made her 'inclined to live in a world entirely of your own, which very few people realise exists'. She was short tempered and irritable. She would have kidney trouble at various times and severe strain on her nervous system. And under the house of Venus, Marion was advised: 'If you marry, as I think you will, be careful to find out whether there is any tendency to alcoholism in the partner's family, as you might have to endure the results of such a fault.'

The sceptic might suggest that this astrologer had inside information about her subject. Whatever store Marion put in this reading of the planets based on her December 16 birthday, there could be no doubt that she wanted marriage and a family – and that she had a fear of the effects of alcohol, even if she would never admit to her father's problems. When she was in the WRNS, she said:

> I'm sick of these dances where everyone swigs beer (except me!) and everyone points out their 'best boy' to you.

There had to date been no 'best boy' in her life, although people played guessing games as to who might be a candidate. The Scandinavian holidays before the war had provoked rumours of a love interest there. Archie Kenneth, who had as a child been on the receiving end of little Marion's violently expressed wrath in an Ardrishaig field, was a favourite in the eyes of Mrs Campbell and Mrs Kenneth and when they stood at a window of the Kenneth home at Stronachullin and saw Archie kneel at Marion's feet, they were convinced he had proposed. Marion always maintained this was a piece of mischief on the part of the young ones and that Archie had in fact stooped to retrieve something from the garden path.

Now as she struggled to run her property and was far from the boozy dances and service parties, she had to admit to herself that she was more than fond of Walter John Campbell, the cousin whose career in the Royal Navy was taking off. There had been letters and meetings. Walter John was handsome and charismatic. When in the right company, Marion was vivacious, charming and witty with a pleasant tone of voice. At 5 ft 5 ins tall, her fair hair cropped (to the horror of her family) when she joined the WRNS, she was a striking young woman. Walter John was happy to flirt with her and to spend time in her company, although when Marion invited him to a Kilberry ball in 1945, Lady Fiona Byatt – a daughter of the Coats of Paisley family who was then a romantic 16-year-old – said there was never any thought of him as a boyfriend. 'I don't remember a look between them or a dance', she said. 'Nothing to fire my romantic imagination.'

The Coats were seasonal neighbours of Kilberry in those days and Fiona and her younger sister Jilly, who would grow up to be Mrs Mackie-Campbell, became close friends of Marion despite the age difference. Lady Byatt felt that like so many women of her generation, Marion had lost her chance of finding a life partner. She remembered three Kilberry balls in those immediate post war years. At one of them in 1947, when electricity had just come to Kilberry, the lights failed and the old candelabra had to be lit. Even in that romantic light, the young Fiona was oblivious to the fact that a spark had ignited between Marion and Walter. Yet in her last months, Marion was to admit to her heir's wife Charmian that the photograph of the handsome naval officer at her bedside was Walter John Campbell, 'the love of my life'.

Marion would never be demonstrative in the company of a man she liked: she had seen too much 'silly' behaviour during her years in the WRNS. But yet another great sadness in her life would also have prevented her from making any show of affection. Her mother's health did not recover, and on November 19, 1945, she died in the Victoria Infirmary in Glasgow. Marion was alone. The funds from her parents' marriage contract, which had been so long in coming to her mother after her father's death, now came to Marion in 1946. They made little difference to her existence and she was to spend the next few years desperately clinging to her home as laws changed and taxation stiffened to make her fiscal state even leaner.

These were the years when the Labour Government legislated to improve the lot of the ordinary man. Rented properties were to be made habitable by the landlords and many of Marion's neighbours who were far wealthier than she found it more equitable to sell houses and farms to sitting tenants at negligible prices than to install water closets, bathrooms and other modern necessities. Rates on large properties went so high that instead of taking measures like the Campbells of Kilberry in the 1920s to live elsewhere for several months of the year, landowners lifted the roofs from their luxurious mansions and destroyed them in order to avoid crippling payments.

Any efforts on Marion Campbell's part to make Kilberry an attractive proposition to potential buyers were doomed to fail because such properties had become even larger white elephants than ever. By the post war years, without her mother's domestic influence, without an income and with debt mounting, it wasn't simply Government rulings which made Kilberry an unsaleable property. Always seen as remote, never particularly profitable as an agricultural venture, and now increasingly cold, damp and unwelcoming, Kilberry was even turned down by monks as being 'too uncomfortable'.

Marion was under huge pressure and there was no Mary Sandeman to support her; no Jura to escape to. After his wife was murdered, Mary's brother left the Royal Navy as she had done to look after the boys. A doctor like his father, he returned to his medical practice in Durness in the far north west of Scotland and Mary had gone with him. When Dr Sandeman senior died suddenly in 1950, Mrs Sandeman also went to Durness and Marion felt increasingly isolated.

Lady Fiona Byatt recalled her coming to her parents' house in deep distress having spent a sleepless night (possible many more than one) because 'all her ancestors' had been tramping up and down the stairs of the castle all night. Although Marion would claim the second sight on occasion, this was more the evidence of someone overworked, emotionally stressed and distressingly isolated.

There were many plans in Marion's head to change Kilberry's and her own lot. Her loyalty to the family, to tradition and to the father and aunt who had both left her this millstone made her determined to hang onto her home and of course, she had to admit that she loved the place to the core of her being. She knew, however, that hanging on a farm gate was not how she wanted to spend the rest of her life. She was proud of her ability to produce saleable Highland cattle, get the harvest in on time and grow produce in the market garden but she was increasingly aware that there were other things she wanted to do in life. She had failed to get into Oxford and now was not the time to try again. But she knew she wanted to write.

She was aware that there was much about Kilberry, Argyll, Scottish culture and heritage of which she knew too little. She wanted marriage and a family. She could take none of these any further as long as she had 5,000 acres to oversee. Day after day she exhausted herself physically and mentally with the tasks and responsibilities of the estate. Lady Lithgow had continued to be her mentor and sometime fairy godmother. Her advice not to overdo things was wise but sometimes completely impractical. She had advised registering a market garden. She had reassured Marion that by going home from the WRNS to look after her land and her mother was 'not the easy way out'. If Marion had suspected it was, it was a self-indulgence she was soon to grow out of. She perhaps clung to Lady Lithgow's hope for her that she could hang onto Kilberry until she chose to leave, rather than because the choice was made for her – but when could she choose to turn her back on home? A further horoscope told her to develop her mental and literary powers as much as she possibly could. There were those who thought it a tragedy that Marion sold the farms off after the war, but at the time they were nothing more than an economic drain on her bank balance and a physical drain on her health. They had to go.

The farms actually sold. Then in the early 1950s the castle was put on the market yet again and Marion went house hunting, visualising a new life in more hospitable surroundings. There was a house near Oban, others nearer home. She was wasting her time. Only the

Cistercians made a firm enquiry and they were looking for a new monastery. As Marion would tell a rates appeal tribunal almost thirty years later, this gothic pile with its forty nine rooms on four floors, its crumbling conservatory, rising and descending damp and encroaching garden had no appeal even for these ascetics.

From her earliest childhood, rooms were filled with personal property and locked against the invasion of either tenants renting the castle for a shooting season or Uncle Archie and Aunt Violet's apparently predatory eyes. Now in the post war year, half of the basement and the top floor were furnished as holiday flats but could only be let to people Marion knew because both areas were exposed to the rest of the house. As regulations became ever more strict, even these sources of income were closed off to her because the installation of fire doors and other safety precautions would not only have ruined the layout of the castle but her bank balance as well. Dampness in the basement – its source believed to be an ancient well which once was the salvation of the female inhabitants of the earlier castle during a siege – eventually meant that part of the house could not be let either. Marion was living in negative equity, farming at a time when prices were falling, and was desperately seeking a way out.

One avenue was to sell off the historic and prehistoric treasures which were to be found in the castle and its grounds. There were – as there are throughout Argyll – the cairns, henges and standing stones of prehistoric times. Flints, spears and other artefacts had regularly been turned up at Kilberry and cottages and walls had been built of once-sacred stones. Monks in the early Christian era had meditated, cultivated and been buried here, content with much less than the latter-day Cistercians were willing to put up with.

Marion began a correspondence with Uncle Archie to learn what she could about Kilberry, although he confessed that as a youth his mind had been more on piping, cattle and shooting than history. Her eyes were opened to the landscape around her at a time when most cared little for such heritage. She sent flints off to the National Museum of Antiquities in Edinburgh which sparked a correspondence with Robert B.L. Stevenson. She wrote to him on April 3, 1949, that she had been studying the map carefully to see what sites were in the area which she had never visited and was 'amazed to find a great number quite near here'. She was already planning to visit some of those sites so that she would be able to guide Professor Piggott, a respected prehistorian who was planning to visit Kilberry to see more of the artefacts stashed in the castle in the autumn of that year, to the more obvious prehistorical features of Argyll. This was the start of a whole new 'career' for Marion.

She had by now burned much midnight oil writing the children's books which created in her a passion for Scottish history. Her vision allowed her to see history and prehistory as one continuous landscape. She was never to 'specialise' in a particular period as the academically trained historian would but embraced all time as part of her own heritage and as the heritage of Scotland. She admitted that when she began to write *The Wide Blue Road*, she had little knowledge of Scottish history, having been fed the Wars of the Roses and Henry VIII's wives at St Margaret's in Edinburgh. She said she had a vague recollection that a battle had been fought at Largs – something to do with the Vikings.

It was perhaps a trait inherited from her mother, the list maker, that when she decided to research these two strands – history and prehistory – Marion did it with a methodical intensity. She tapped into the network of Campbells and Durands, of distant kinsmen and women who could supply her with information, tell her what books to read, which museums to contact, what data was available and where. She devoured research, but she did not then simply regurgitate it. Professionals like Argyll archivist Murdo MacDonald and historians Michael Davis and Joanna Gordon agree that she had the intellect to process her research and reach conclusions which were of great value. Murdo MacDonald admitted that sometimes her wild cards were horribly off course. But frequently her spark of intuition made sense of the jumble of information which has come down the millennia to us.

When Mr Stevenson returned Marion's flints, axe and paw to Kilberry, he told her that a Glasgow antique dealer had brought some Argyll artefacts to the Museum of Antiquities which he had been told came from Loup, near Clachan on West Loch Tarbert. This was

Marion's own stamping ground – could she make inquiries about these bronze age food vessels? Marion made contact with the Kintyre Antiquarian Society, which had been founded in 1921. This series of contacts were Damascenian in their effect. By the end of that year she had been accepted as a member of the Society of Antiquaries and was stirring up the beginnings of a storm of interest in Argyll's heritage and history.

She began on her own front door with the Kilberry stones – carved medieval stones which included a cross of the Loch Sween school of carving, several grave slabs depicting Kilberry inhabitants in battle dress, including one with the inscription *Hic jacet Johannes Mauritii et eius filius* (here lies John MacMurachie and his son). Marion's research led her to believe this was the grave slab of a descendant of the eleventh century Murchaidh bards of the Lords of the Isles who in the fourteenth century built the first Kilberry castle. Argyll in post-World War II Britain was no different in its attitude towards its natural heritage than the minister of Kilmartin had been when he wrote his contribution to the *First Statistical Account* of the county in 1790. This man of the cloth wrote without a qualm that there was nothing in the parish of Kilmartin of interest – this of a glen now seen as one of the most archaeologically important in the UK. Five enormous chambered burial cairns seem to have skipped his notice; fifteen foot high standing stones were not worthy of mention. At Kilberry and elsewhere, the story was the same. Medieval carved crosses had been vandalised at the Reformation and cannibalised for door lintels; cairns were utilised for new enclosure walls; the treasures of prehistoric cists were either pocketed or sent off to distant museums and never seen again. As Marion's eyes were opened to an almost embarrassing wealth of artefacts by her own family's treasure trove and the large scale Ordinance Survey maps she acquired, she set herself the task of recording that wealth and protecting it.

A letter went off to the Royal Commission for Ancient and Historical Monuments asking for assistance to protect the grave slab of John MacMurachie and all those of other Kilberry heritors whose memorial stones were crumbling after centuries of exposure to the winds and rain driving in from the west. This would take several years to bear fruit, but in the meantime, her links to the Royal Commission would grow until she, with Mary Sandeman, would be finally credited with laying the foundations of the Commission's volumes on Argyll.

Marion began her quest to shelter the Kilberry stones by suggesting to the Secretary of Ancient Monuments for Scotland at Parliament House in Edinburgh that a small museum would be a good idea. Mr Cruden, Inspector of Ancient Monuments, agreed, but pointed out that the financial stringencies of the post war era would not stretch to that. In the end, an attractive wooden shelter was built at the end of the shared drive to the castle and Home Farm: an unfortunate siting when Marion eventually sold off the farm and its new owners were far from keen on the steady stream of pilgrims who came to inspect the stones. Fortunately for those still inspired by Marion's evocative writings about the Argyll heritage, that era has long past.

Natural history was another string to Marion's bow. Much more evidently inherited from her mother was her love and knowledge of birds. Spotting redshanks from a grimy wartime train had been a poor substitute for watching the year-round theatre of woodland and sea birds which inhabited or visited Kilberry. In the late 1940s, she became an official contributor to a publication which recorded numbers and locations of birds throughout Scotland and eventually in 1960 was to publish a booklet of Mid Argyll birds.

The seeds of her future were being sown in these austere years after the war. She had seen it as her duty to be the caretaker of Kilberry but now much more beckoned and she grew weary of the long hours of estate work which drained her physically and buried her under a mountain of paper which even wartime clerical work had not prepared her for. When Lady Lithgow wrote to her in February, 1946 to say: 'I do hope things aren't too difficult on the land. You are a brick to stick to it and I do hope you aren't too weary with it all,' she was aware that things were already weighing heavily on Marion's shoulders.

As the decade came to a close and the 1950s stretched bleakly ahead with no national improvement in the financial situation (and certainly none for Marion personally), being a brick seemed like a bad option. In 1952, Uncle Archie wrote hoping that she would 'manage to get some money at Oban for the heifers' and that his pessimism about bull breeding at Kilberry would be overcome. Colonel Henderson, now retiring from his career in estate management, wrote that same year thanking Marion for her gift of a Kilberry crest and complimenting her on her 'courage and ability' to 'keep the Kilberry flag flying' at a time when most of the estates with which he had been associated in Argyll were being sold or broken up. 'I marvel at your ability to hold the old home together. Even the Argyll Estates are now disintegrating,' he told her.

In 1953, she had put the castle and the farms up for sale yet again. Already there were new owners in Coulaghailtro and Tiretigan and she was relieved to know that the new people at Tiretigan would probably take on the Highland herd. The one bright spot for her was selling a bull at Oban. She told Mary Sandeman:

> There was a flap about the wee bull because all the men went off for 'their dinners' (like hell they were having dinner!) after the heifers – and there was nobody there when the bull's turn came. One of the mart men offered to lead him for me but Wee Wully thought not – so I took him myself and he behaved angelically and sold for 48 guineas – nearly double what I'd expected! However he turned skittish in the pen when I was fastening him up again and I'm black and blue all down one thigh! never mind, it was fun to do and a good finish.
> Some day I suspect I'll have a Highland herd again – 3rd time lucky etc.!

This witty narrative hid the pain of laying down the mantle of a Highland Cattle breeder of renown but it revealed the writing skill which she was developing in the wee small hours at Kilberry. By October 1954 she had finished *The Wide Blue Road*, her first children's book, and was negotiating with Dent the publisher over its publication. She was still working the home farm, still attending Oban sales, but the other facets of her life were taking over. One of her stories was broadcast by the BBC. She had meetings at the Museum of Antiquities in Edinburgh, meetings in London with Dent – and very occasionally, meetings with Walter John Campbell.

It was the latter which caused her the most joy and the most pain. Walter – who in later life dropped that name in favour of John Campbell – had come to figure largely in her life since the war years. Whether she figured largely in his life was another matter. His nephew Jonathan Howard described him as a handsome man used to the attentions of attractive women. Jonathan, who didn't meet Marion until her last decade, was smitten by her wit and intellect but instinctively felt she perhaps had never had the glamour Uncle Walter John was seeking. Marion's knowledge of naval commitments meant she was very patient when Walter sailed in and out of her life, sometimes inviting her to top brass occasions on board ship, sometimes coming to see her at Kilberry. Sometimes he said he was coming to Kilberry and didn't and Marion was clearly upset by his thoughtlessness. She confided in Mary:

> W's leave was fixed for 24th September and he wanted to come here... and then he went on a NATO exercise (which he must have known about, or so you'd think!). As it ended yesterday, presumably he may appear now. Blast the man, I've had the house full of food twice and I'm DD and double D'd if I bother again! He'll probably turn up tomorrow as I've been asked out to dinner at Barnlongart by the shooting tenants!...
> ... W. has just wired he wants to come Fri-Sun. Oban calf sale Sat!! Hell and Damn. MEN!!!

Sometimes Walter turned up with his sister Rosemary and her racy boyfriends. Sometimes he was the instigator of boozy parties. She must have thought he saw her as someone special when he invited her to join the big brass on board his ship. She certainly enjoyed the party, describing it as 'the best... I have ever been to' and the day as 'heavenly'. She was sympathetic when he was depressed at a missed promotion in early 1954 but then came the brush off. She was making marmalade in Kilberry's basement kitchen. About 100 barnacle geese had landed that morning and the noise was deafening. The postman arrived with a registered parcel and she knew it was from Walter. She told Mary with great understatement and not a little irony:

> I was a bit miserable because I never had so much as a card from him this Xmas, and. . . a rgd. parcel arrived from Gieves with a very nice little naval crown brooch, not the usual design at all, and my name engraved on the back – no note or anything of course but that's the answer – wasn't it a kind cousinly thought? It's most useful because I can wear it any time – neat but not gaudy etc.

In the April of 1954, he sent a postcard from Gibraltar. He renewed their correspondence in the late 1970s when his days were numbered, sending her a complimentary letter from Malta about her newly published controversial book *Dark Twin*, which sparked in him memories of a 'vile and vivid dream' she had told him of in war years which foresaw the sinking of a ship. The *Twin* landscape reminded him of the shore at Kilberry. He had a hundred questions about the book, 'whenever (if ever) we see each other again'. He ended with 'much love' and after his death before the end of the decade, she learned he had left her £100.

This then was the 'love of her life'. And if ever a girl needed to wash that man right out of her hair, it was Marion. In the end, she told Charmian in her last months, a decision had been taken not to marry because of the madness in Walter's family which they feared could be passed on to any children they may have had. From a twenty first century perspective, that seems a spurious reason: it would have been very possible in the 1950s simply not to have had children. This was said to have been Walter's way out of the relationship. Perhaps that is true – but then, despite Marion's denial of her father's problems, the last thing she would have wanted was to perpetuate the miseries of the Campbells of Kilberry. The beautiful crib with its frilled trimmings which young Fiona Coats saw in the Kilberry nursery was not created by someone prepared to forego having children. And yet that was to be Marion's future. No-one else matched Walter's charm. Miss Campbell of Kilberry was to remain so.

CHAPTER NINE
Miss Somebody

The two world wars of the twentieth century denied so many women personal happiness. Marion Campbell and Mary Sandeman each had to come to terms in the post war years that a future which was then conventionally expected had been denied them by the circumstances of their service and sacrifice. Each had volunteered to serve their country. Each had to withdraw from that service on compassionate grounds: Marion's mother was too ill to manage on her own, while Mary found herself in bizarre and tragic circumstances looking after her two nephews. Each had commitments from which it would have been difficult to extricate themselves even had the perfect partnership presented itself on a plate. After the death of Mary's father, her mother moved to Durness, her son Stuart's home, and the two women remained there until Stuart's remarriage. Marion's cross was Kilberry – a financial and emotional burden which she simultaneously struggled to keep and to be free from.

Her interest in antiquities and history, her love of writing and her ability to communicate were not really able to come together until she freed herself of the major part of the estate and perhaps from the spectre of Walter Campbell. At the start of the 1950s, house hunting and packing dominated her spare time. It wasn't only a cattle herd she had to dispose of. If she had to leave Kilberry, what was she to do with the mass of correspondence which her mother, father, grandfather, great-grandfather and many of her Kilberry ancestors had left behind? What, if she were to move to a small house somewhere after the sale of the estate, was she to do with the heirlooms, the priceless treasures and the assorted useless bric-a-brac which four centuries of Campbells had accumulated? Some items went for sale. Some went to the museums. Some were thrown out. But Marion had inherited an excess of the collector's gene which compelled her not only to hang onto her heritage but to put it to use. Her interest in her heritage and that of Argyll led quickly to a letter from the National Museum of Antiquities of Scotland in Queen Street, Edinburgh, which formally said:

> We have the honour to inform you that at a General Meeting of the Society of Antiquaries of Scotland held here this day [December 12, 1949] you were elected a Fellow of the Society.

Signed by Lord Haddington, the Society's president, it was an honour which meant so much more in Marion's own eyes because of her lack of academic status.

Despite the problem back, the menstrual depressions, the recurring kidney stones and the constant stress of her precarious financial situation, Marion threw herself into a dozen diverse projects.

The sorting out of her belongings with a view to moving led to an historical exhibition in the drawing room of the castle – the exhibits including fashion, objects from the nursery and the archaeological treasures about which she was already developing expert knowledge. She began to lecture on historical subjects for Glasgow University's extra mural department, travelling the length and breadth of Argyll for a couple of pounds a lecture plus travelling expenses. Those journeys perhaps allowed her to examine more closely the archaeological sites which were becoming something of a passion and laid the ground work for the all encompassing report done by Marion and Mary which informed the Commission for Ancient Monuments' Volumes on Argyll.

The history led her to politics and more specifically to the Scottish National Party, for whom she became an outspoken voice in Argyll. Professor Sir Neil MacCormick, who campaigned in Argyll in the heady days of the 1960s and 70s when the SNP was gathering ground not only in Argyll but throughout Scotland, said that support from a respected laird like Marion gave an emotional 'permission' to the people of Argyll to cast their vote and return an SNP candidate to Westminster. She chaired meetings with dignity and wit (sometimes acerbic) as she did when she became a member (later chairman – none of that chairperson nonsense for Miss Campbell of Kilberry) of her local community council, following in the footsteps of her father and grandfather.

Argyll and Bute Councillor Donnie MacMillan said she was always courteous in her public roles – but many admit privately that she did not suffer fools gladly and the tetchiness she had displayed as a child occasionally spilled over into her adult life. Her private letters to those in her inner circle reveal that she retained a naval saltiness in calling a spade a spade and acquaintances 'foolish' or worse if the mood took her. The minister who is alleged to have been told by Madam Chairman Campbell to sit down because he was wasting the time of the meeting would not have been the only one to experience her forthrightness. But for her, this work was a serious duty and commitment and she fought for the underdog, campaigning for better rural bus services and risking censure to give deserving marginalised people council houses.

And however acerbic her tongue, she could be kindness itself. In 1954, Mrs Sandeman wasn't well and Marion invited Mary and her mother to Kilberry so that Mrs Sandeman could recuperate. The weeks turned into months and eventually a decision was taken that this would be their permanent home. With the Sandeman financial input to the upkeep of the castle, it meant Marion could at last decide to take it off the market and this stability gave her breathing space to research her children's books.

Marion would later say that her life was 'endlessly enhanced' by the presence of Mary and although many – including Charles Sandeman, one of the nephews Mary had left the WRNS to care for – agree that Mary was 'put upon', this was a relationship which strengthened Marion. A pillar of the Church of Scotland, a moving force in the South Knapdale Sheepdog Trials Society and co-author with Marion of the famous archaeological survey of Mid Argyll, Mary may have found herself sometimes cast in the role of chief cook and bottle washer, but the two women laughed together, cried together, dug up archaeological sites together (sometimes measuring burial cists with a dressmaker's tape measure until they acquired more professional tools) and smoked like chimneys together. They had bonded at school, taken every opportunity to be together during the war, picnicking on the hills above Greenock and walking on Loch Lomondside. They had confided in each other, become part of each other's families – and now they were to be family for each other.

The modern interpretation of two women living together is that there must have been a sexual element to the relationship. Those who knew them best believe that instead, this was the kind of companionship which women of previous generations had enjoyed (or suffered) and was entirely in keeping with the outlook with which Marion was instilled by her late Victorian parents. It is clear that both women would have preferred a marriage and children and that war and family commitments denied them that. This companionship was mutually beneficial, even if it sometimes appeared – and in reality was – weighted in favour of Marion Campbell.

Marion's mother had begun a number of projects at Kilberry to keep herself afloat. Marion and Mary were to continue or develop some of them. Mary took on an acre of garden at the castle and developed it as a market garden. For many years they ran a craft co-operative, selling goods not only from Mid-Argyll but all over Scotland. It was never an entirely successful organisation and Marion perhaps bullied her producers when they weren't coming up with the goods quickly enough or the quality of their products fell below her high standards. It was to become, however, one of Marion's famous excuses. She was overstretched and would use the co-operative as a reason for not fulfilling deadlines for her books, the deadlines for her books for not having written up an archaeological project, an archaeological dig for not being able to send out orders for the co-operative. There was a circularity about her chaos, but she muddled through – and she was able to do that because Mary Sandeman was there to run the house, rustle up a meal, soothe a fraying temper.

Some saw Mary as the watchdog who kept people away from Marion. Others saw her as the friendly face of Kilberry. In those early years, when the Sandeman boys came for holidays and the two friends went off to examine yet another find up in the hills, there must have been an immense feeling of throwing off the chains for Marion. She finally stopped farming in 1957 and the liberation allowed the Renaissance woman to come into her own. Argyll historian Michael Davis, one of the many bright young men who were attracted to the flame of Marion's wit and intellect, said that it was only when he got to know her that he understood she continued to feel restricted by her lack of 'paper qualifications'. His admiration of the breadth and variety of her work and her contribution to Argyll's heritage is shared by amateur and professional historians, archaeologists and writers alike. She was only able to make that contribution, however, by making demands on anyone and everyone who might be able to add to her store of knowledge.

Uncle Archie now became an ally, sharing his store of family knowledge, language, and animal husbandry expertise. Notebooks in his possession yielded up information about Lord Berness, a late eighteenth century ancestor who produced an heir with a 12-year-old taken from a relative's household in London to Kilberry. He was able to tell her of name changes – Asknish had become Arduaine, for instance, and Castleton had been Shirvan – which helped her track down historical and prehistorical sites. it was perhaps Archie's suggestion that she publish 'Knockbuy's letters' – his grandfather's correspondence – which prompted her to look at her grandfather's diaries and the eighteenth century letters from Jamaica with a view to publication and in later years to take on tasks such as translating the accounts for the building of Tarbert Castle in Bruce's day from the Latin and digging out the documents about the Depredations of the Campbells in the bloody 1600s.

The children's books – *The Wide Blue Road,* finally published in 1957, *Lances and Longships* (1963), *Young Hugh* (1965) and *The Squire of Val* (1967) – looked at the Norse saga which in the late 1940s and early 50s she suddenly realised had been played out on her doorstep. Taught English history by the PNEU, the fact that Kintyre had been a Norse territory by dint of Magnus Barefoot dragging a longboat across the isthmus some sixteen miles from her home had escaped her. Now she could describe a birlinn down to its last oar and argue over the finer points of its presentation for voyages of peace and war. Her research led her to examine minutely the sights, sounds, tastes and smells of an era, not simply their basic facts. Nor was she afraid to admit when she was wrong. As her knowledge increased she became aware of errors in the earlier volumes which she demanded should be changed in reprints.

She did nothing by halves. Her collaborators on the Badden Cist Slab, an article published in the *Proceedings of the Society of Antiquaries of Scotland* in 1961, were Stuart Piggott and JG Scott, two of the most respected men in the field of Scottish antiquaries at the time. By 1962, she had written *Mid-Argyll: a handbook of history*, and in the same year, the archaeological survey of Mid Argyll which she produced with Mary had also been published by the Society of Antiquaries and was even then accepted as the starting point for the survey by the 'professionals' which was eventually to be published in expensive official volumes decades later. She sent off articles to the *Scotsman* newspaper and stories to the BBC to ward off the wolf from the door.

Was she, as her cousin Helen Kenneth suggested, 'galvanised' for the life she found herself leading by the harsh realities of her early years? Had the lack of understanding of what she was going through as a child and teenager turned her into the sometimes driven woman she was to become? Marion was certainly aware that others neither approved of nor understood the choices she made. As early as 1949 she wrote a tongue-in-cheek poem addressed (but not delivered) to her friends and relatives in London.

Oh, I am the Clever Miss Somebody,
and praise has turned my head
I want you to meet Miss Somebody,
You'll think she's quite divine,
She's such an interesting girl to know,
(as well as a cousin of mine).
She comes from terribly far away,
(you remember that place where I went to stay?)
She farms all day, and writes all night,
And she's ever so gay when the lights are bright,
And her views are mine, so I know they're right,
Miss Somebody, how do you do?

The verses go on to say: 'Now tell me, you farm? How terribly fine! It's always been a secret wish of mine. . .' and 'Oh, writing for children! How clever that sounds!'. . . 'Now tell me my dear, whom I'm so glad to see, just how are things going , between you and me? Are you making much money or losing it all? How strange! You don't answer too easy and free. . . '

> How quickly she left us! Now what can it be?
> She lives all alone, dear – it's easy to see.
> Poor Someone! Extraordinary cousin to have –
> Well, I think poor Someone's terribly brave –
> Never a hint, though of course one could tell –
> And then there was talk of her not being well –
> Eccentric a little, that's all I could spot;
> And dowdy dear, too – that's with living a lot
> Alone in the country – a terrible fate!
> And chewing a straw and swinging a gate,
> And doing those things I should utterly hate
> To find myself having to do!
>
> I am Miss Somebody, I am alone,
> I am pleased as a b____ with a bone,
> When you've had your day, I can still have my think,
> (I am sorry you thought you perceived me to wink).
> I am the Clever Miss Somebody –
> Somebody,
> Somebody,
> Here we go round the Somebody

Marion knew what was said of her, knew what people believed she ought to do. This poem (there is much more of it) puts a brave face on it, but it still rankled in her old age when she wrote her letter to John, her heir, determined she would not impose her wishes on him as wishes had been imposed on her.

As her work was accepted, however, she began to believe more in her own capabilities and her own decisions. Free of her Durand grandmother (Lady Maude died in 1953) she consciously or otherwise became her father's daughter: a Campbell, a daughter of Argyll, a woman whose roots stretched back into the white mists of time. From this platform came her most popular book and her most controversial book: *Argyll: The Enduring Heartland;* and *The Dark Twin.*

In terms of the body of her work, these books are discussed later in this book. But in terms of the woman, the former can be easily reconciled within the framework of her passion and knowledge for this land which remains always a little apart from the rest of Scotland. While it speaks of the soul of Argyll, it reflects her on-going archaeological research which led in 1953 to her helping to found the Mid Argyll Antiquarian Society. She had been the first editor of its publication, *Kist,* which from very humble beginnings with many typing errors and Gstetnered pages, developed under her guidance into a respected journal containing papers of great value in the garnering of Argyll's history and pre history. When in 1977, *Enduring Heartland* was published, it was the distillation of that passion and knowledge – the record of a love affair with her homeland.

Dark Twin was something entirely different. This fiction was to alter her life as it was being written and would alter it again at the close of her life. The book took possession of her during its long period of gestation. She said it came to her in a series of waking dreams. She wrote down fragments on scraps of paper and eventually, laid them out on the floor and tried to make sense of them. She was never to deny an element of the fey – her friend Sir Ilay Campbell of Crarae recalled her climbing a hill behind his gardens and with a fellow antiquarian carrying out an apparently successful experiment to whistle up dark forces from the so-called 'witch's hill' on the far shore of Loch Fyne – and *Dark Twin* seemed to come to her from elsewhere.

It could, of course, merely have been the continued stress of selling off the Kilberry property which played tricks with her mind – in January 1956, the post office and croft in Kilberry, Ivy Cottage, a site for a garage and the Free Church Hall were sold for her by MacArthur Stuart and Orr to Messrs MacPhail Bros of Kilberry and the castle was once more proposed for sale. The Free Church manse was bought by Argyll County Council in 1956 for £750 and in February 1957, Keppoch Farm was sold. Marion recorded that a Mr Paul Hobhouse was interested in buying the 368-acre home farm and the castle but a Miss Hendry, who had bought Tiretigan Farm back in March, 1953, was interested in the farm only. She said: 'I would consider staying if Miss

Hendry bought the farm.' On April 10, 1957, Kilberry Home Farm and coach house were sold to Miss Hendry for £7,850 with houses, steadings and sheds. Keppoch Farm brought £7,000, but all of this merely paid off debts and did little to improve the quality of life for Marion, Mary and her mother.

Yes, she could stay on at the castle, but she could no doubt see the words of Colonel Henderson burning from the pages of a letter he had written in 1944 which said she would only get a 'thorough insight' into the whole position by taking on the management of the estate herself. Well, she'd had the insight and it had caused her nightmares. Some of them in the form of the waking dreams about inheritance, female heirs and lost love which were eventually to become *Dark Twin.*

The farms which were sold at this point were the last remnants of properties which had been in the family for centuries. They were long established within the Kilberry estate when the 1693 hearth tax was estimated. Parting with them weighed heavily on Marion's conscience even if their sale freed her still further to live her life as she pleased. She was to tell Nancy Nicholson in a BBC interview many years late that the *Dark Twin* came to her 'about the time I was giving up the farms'. She explained:

> I was working desperately hard trying to help employees find jobs and making the place look good. I was alone and no-one was in the house as a shock absorber. It was a book about the Iron Age, a tribal setting with two religions going on and a dual kingship. There was the reincarnation of a love affair and it all came out in snippets. Usually I have a plan. . . this thing – it just came and hit me.

She told Nancy she had 'the sight' and that her mother had 'had it strongly'. She also, she said, had 'the hearing' but that one should not seek it out. 'It comes to get you.'

Dark Twin is certainly strange enough to be seen as a book engendered by other forces. It is loved or hated, seen as a woman's book; as the book which is a blot on the landscape of Marion's more serious oeuvres. It could also, however, be read very simply as an autobiographical extract: the power in the kingdom in the east comes through the female line and is given to the youngest sister. If anything troubled Marion subconsciously more than the loss of the estate it must surely have been the breaking of the male entail and the fact that she was the third child of her parents and the only one to survive. Her mother had evoked the presence of Isabel and Ian often enough. Her lack of entitlement to the estate had been emphasised throughout her childhood and teens. Now she was throwing the whole thing up anyway, letting Daddie down, Mummie down, and leaving Archie and his heirs with nothing to inherit. *Dark Twin*, troubled in its inception, troubled in its presentation, is a book about inheritance, the defining factor in the young Marion's life.

Although it was to be written – or at least committed to paper – in the ember days of her farming exploits, *Dark Twin* would not be published until 1977, by which time her children's historical books and her historical and archaeological work had defined a neat category by which professionals and the public could label her. Marion was not a woman who liked to be pigeonholed, however, and while the academic world would come to spurn her because her embrace of the world was too all encompassing, this was the very quality which appealed to her friends, her growing coterie of young male admirers, and the wider reading public.

She described herself as a professional writer and amateur archaeologist but qualified that by saying: 'Technically I'm an antiquarian', and as one of twenty four honorary antiquarians in Scotland she gave a metaphorical and very ladylike two fingered salute to the 'scholars' she believed to be her detractors every time she reminded the world of this fact – and pointed out that she shared the honour with the Duke of Rothesay and the King of Norway.

She earned her stripes. She and Mary Sandeman visited around a thousand sites over a period of seven years and presented a paper in precise scientific terms. She played to the gallery every time she recounted those expeditions. 'Two wummen in their spare time wi' a tape measure,' she would say in a robust Scottish accent far removed from her own. 'We used Mary's hanky and a dressmaker's tape until we bought ourselves a proper tape.' This self denigration was always accompanied by a more serious reminder that they were 'women, amateur and unlettered – and I've had books turned down because I'm unlettered', was her stock dig at the detractors.

A thousand sites visited, digs undertaken, her craft marketing agency running on and on over two decades, her lectures, her politics and then: Auchindrain. This was perhaps Marion's most ambitious project and while she needed a lot of help from her friends to see it through, without her enthusiasm and drive, it would never have taken off in the first place. The seed of the Auchindrain project was perhaps sown when she did her first exhibition in the castle. That was followed by a travelling exhibition she devised with the local council which travelled first around local schools and then much further afield. Her 'tiddly' grey Vauxhall with its red leather seats became well known on the islands as well as mainland Argyll as she drove off to talk in draughty halls and school classrooms. As always, her research for these exhibitions was meticulous and if she needed a model of a medieval church, house or boat to illustrate a point about the Viking occupation of Mid Argyll she went to the top, demanding, for instance, assistance of the Norwegian consul in Edinburgh. Story boards and models were her stock in trade long before such display techniques became commonplace. She knew how to make these exhibitions appealing visually and through the written word. When she lectured, she used humour, analogy and a beautifully modulated voice to get her point over. Jargon was not her style: the language of the people was.

When her schools exhibitions proved popular, she suggested – as she had to the Ministry for Ancient Monuments when she wanted shelter for the Kilberry stones – a small museum. She was turned down on grounds of cost but the idea of creating a place where the heritage of Argyll could be brought to life was growing. With Sandy Fenton and Eric Cregeen, two men with a similar vision of presenting a vibrant testimony to the past, she originated the Auchindrain museum on the A83 between Furnace and Inveraray. This cluster of stone cottages was one of the last working farming townships in the area. It stands at the bottom of the former road from Loch Awe to Loch Fyne – never a very satisfactory highway and dangerous for carriages but used by drovers and armies alike down the centuries. It was on that road that the last woman to be killed by a wolf was found lying in the snow clutching the spindle with which she had dispatched her hungry killer as he took her life. Where better to bring the past to life in what Marion hoped would become 'the best folk museum in the world'?

Some serious negotiations with the Duke of Argyll's estates office were needed to come by the property. A trust was set up and Sir William Lithgow, son of Gwen Lithgow who had been so supportive of Marion and her mother during the war, was one of those who helped not only to get it off the ground but achieve its initial goals. As with any such project, there would always be an on-going need to raise funds, but Marion told the trustees:

> No other folk museum known to me has so many original buildings *in situ*. . . We have the opportunity to provide a new dimension in the study of history by preserving and restoring a complete 'piece of the past'. Nothing must be allowed to destroy the essence of the site but the essence must be brought out by good presentation and by making the place attractive to the hitherto uninterested visitor.

Marion's constant aim was for authenticity. In her books, in her research and now in her plans for Auchindrain, she was determined to present a true picture of Argyll. It was not enough to show the old run rig farming methods – the strip fields were still visible when the trust took over the township – or to present the black houses as they would have been when they were occupied by the close knit communities of the past. She wanted the old crops grown there – bere and flax – and the hay to be cut by scythe. But above all, she wanted Gaelic to be the language of Auchindrain.

She always claimed to be bilingual as a toddler, learning kitchen Gaelic from the servants. Her nanny Rena disagreed with this: the child would not have been allowed to learn any more than that pompous speech they had taught her by rote to deliver to the shinty prize winners from a table top in Kilberry. But as an adult, she was serious about learning the ethnic language of Argyll, wrote verse in it, and told the Auchindrain trustees: 'As long as we discuss and describe Auchindrain in English, we isolate ourselves from part of its essence.' She advocated Gaelic leaflets, signposts and 'at least some spoken

Gaelic among the guides' to achieve the atmosphere she wanted for the place.

The dream began in 1958 when Marion and Mary were working with the Antiquities inspectors. One of them saw just how much of the old techniques had survived at Auchindrain and there were at least eight complete buildings on the site. The local Antiquarian Society was inspired to conserve the place and Marion had taken the deputy head of the National Museum of Scotland to see it. Both saw its possibilities as a Scottish version of the great Scandinavian folk museums which Marion had visited before the war and they hoped to fit the museum around daily farming routine of the last Auchindrain tenant, Eddie McCallum.

When Mr McCallum retired in 1963, the Duke was all for bulldozing the place in the interests of modern farming. He told Marion and the Antiquarians that while he liked dreams he 'couldn't leave a bunch of derelict buildings rotting away alongside a main road'. By this time, Marion had fired not only the deputy head of the National Museum but Edinburgh and Glasgow Universities and local people of vision. Money from sources like the Carnegie Trust, which donated £5,000, was raised, artefacts were gifted to furnish the houses – but what moved Marion most about the development of the project from threatened township to active folk museum was Eddie McCallum's touching gesture of placing an item in each of the houses, including his grandmother's bride kist in which she had brought her blankets and clothes to Auchindrain as a bride in 1829, and a chair made in a neighbouring settlement.

The *Argyllshire Advertiser* reported in March 1967 that the museum had opened and Marion told the paper as chairman of the managing committee that while some people felt money was wasted on such a 'backward looking' project, others took the view that 'countries like individuals need to know their past in order to plan their future'. She saw Auchindrain as a microcosm of Scottish community life and was dedicated enough to spend a period of intense activity there, driving the eighty five mile round trip from Kilberry to oversee the transformation. Eventually, ill health – she had had another kidney stone operation in the early 1960s – meant she couldn't continue such input, but having been in at the birth of it all, she never lost interest in its progress. Eventually Argyll and Bute Council took over the museum: for Marion it would always be part of the enduring heartland of Argyll, from the 5,000 year old burial cairn on the skyline, along the track that follows a rock ridge crossing a glacial valley down to the arable land first cultivated 2,000 years ago, operated by a dozen families in Eddie McCallum's grandfather's day and compared by Queen Victoria to the farming systems operated in India.

In 1970, Marion wrote to the Duke of Argyll saying: 'My dear Ian, I am distressed to feel that you may think that the Auchindrain trustees have been planning to inveigle you into giving us still more territory.' As if! She assured him that funding of some £60-£80,000 was being sought from the Highlands and Islands Development Board. But her main point in writing was to dissuade the Duke from planting fir trees on strip-fields which were historically irreplaceable. Land elsewhere wasn't the point. She was passionate about preserving this last vestige of the farming heritage of Argyll as all around afforestation was swallowing up evidence of townships and farming methods. Her ability to write a 'My dear Ian' letter and to throw in some ancient Campbell history to satisfy the Duke's quest for clan background is today called 'networking'. To Marion it was part of being involved in something much older and more basic. For her, being Miss Campbell of Kilberry was never about having a title but about four centuries of blood ties.

CHAPTER TEN

The influential years

Cash flow would always be a problem, but Miss Campbell of Kilberry's status looked up enormously as the second half of the twentieth century progressed. Auchindrain was just one of the many pies into which she plunged not just a polite finger but an enthusiastic fist. The SNP's Eilean Mor project, the Columba Cave dig, the Ormsary archaeological finds and her own quest for acceptance as a historian through her biography of King Alexander III of Scotland were the major oeuvres. Nor was she ever without minor ploys, whether she was concerning herself with the state of public transport in Mid Argyll, editing *Kist,* or – in the very long term, advising others about displaying Argyll's historical and archaeological wares from the vantage point of the Auchindrain experience. When Neil and Ileene Duncan opened their heritage centre in Tarbert and David and Rachel Clough planned the Kilmartin House museum, they turned to Marion Campbell as as expert.

That she was so regarded must have pleased and occasionally puzzled her. Michael Davis was not the only one to divine the insecurity bred by her lack of letters, and the rebuffs which she would repeatedly experience at the hands of academia could only have reinforced it. Yet the people who cared about Argyll, about history and prehistory beat a path to the castle door and saw her as an expert in these fields. In 1954 she had been made Historical Adviser to the County Council following her *Treasures of Mid Argyll* exhibition which had been sponsored by the County Youth Council. From that had evolved a 7,000 year historical sketch, followed by *Mid Argyll : a handbook of history* published in 1962.

Often, of course, her enthusiasm for the past was fired by her needs of the present. In one of her many castle clear outs, she came across a coin – identified as Athenian tetradrachm and dated 460 BC – which had been found in the garden of a villa in Tarbert in 1885 according to her grandfather's papers. After much correspondence she sold it to the Hunterian Museum in Glasgow at its market value of £10. They displayed it and she got a pictorial record and a cast for local exhibitions. She told the Hunterian:

> I only wish I could make a gift of it to the Museum but I'm afraid in my circumstances I ought not to, if it is worth your while to offer for it. . . I hate to trade in antiques but there it is – if the coin helps to melt my entrance fee into the Society of Antiquaries it will let me off some of the hard work of writing and bring me nearer a little time off to get back to my Bronze Age dig.

This was a dig in which she had become involved at Ardrishaig and her name had been attached to many exciting finds sent off to Glasgow and Edinburgh throughout the 1950s.

In March 1959, she received a letter from the Royal Commission for Ancient and Historical Monuments about the inspectors who were coming to examine sites she had identified in Argyll which said: 'I am anxious that you should receive more recognition than a mere acknowledgement in the inventory for all your discoveries in mid-Argyll.' The suggestion was that she should prepare a detailed catalogue of her own to submit for publication in the Society of Antiquities' Proceedings under her own name and without illustration. When the London Society approved her work by admitting her to its hallowed membership (and demanded the six guinea fee for the privilege) her friend and fellow antiquarian Severene MacKenna, who lived in Tarbert and over the coming decades contributed extensively to *Kist*, told her: 'It is a nice little distinction to possess, rather like a small mattress between the hard ground and oneself.' But from Marion's stance, to be surrounded by young professionals working on projects such as a chambered cairn at Port Sonachan on Loch Awe in 1955 or the excavation in 1957 of a newly discovered burial cairn at Upper Largie near Kilmartin was an even more comfortable mattress between herself and the hard reality of a lack of a university degree.

There was scarcely an archaeological site in Argyll with which she did not have some valuable input praised by Scotland's universities and archaeological societies. Her labours brought an invitation to stand for election to the council of the Society of Antiquaries of Scotland in 1956. Her work on a cist on the island of Lunga was given official approval by Stewart Cruden at the Ministry of Works, and she was invited to talk to archaeological grants people who had already heard of her 'good work in Mid Argyll'. By 1958 she was driving a 12 horse power Hillman Husky and getting 7d a mile from Glasgow University for her field trips. All this while making sure the Kilberry fruit was picked and marketed.

Then she became involved in the Columba Cave dig. She had been alerted to the cave by a letter from Mr J.W. Stevenson writing from the Church of Scotland publication *Life and Work* on September 15, 1955. Mr Stevenson was investigating ancient Celtic sites in Argyll and had been told by Duncan Rogers, the owner of the Ellary Estate on Loch Caolisport, that Marion had a 'special knowledge' of such places. Mr Stevenson wanted to find evidence of a settlement of St Columba at Cove, near Ellary. Columba is credited with bringing Christianity to Scotland in the sixth century, with having anointed the first Christian king at Dunadd Fort in mid Argyll, and was reputed to have lived at a number of mainland Argyll locations before settling on the island of Iona and founding his monastery there. Had Cove been one of those places? Marion did not hesitate to try to find out.

She later listed those who joined her in the exploratory dig which led to a first report in 1959. Mary Sandeman was, of course, part of the dig, along with Miss E. Boyle, Miss E.C. Nisbet, Miss Kathleen Russell, Mary and Elspeth Campbell, R.G. Livens, Alan Gailey from Glasgow University Geography Department, D.R.D.L. MacNab, J.R. Hume and Ian Russell. When this enthusiastic crew turned up at the site, they found a ruined thirteenth century chapel and two caves. In the larger cave there were crosses cut in the rock face and other evidence that it had been used as a chapel. As Marion pointed out, these features had all been visible for many years and had been recorded in the Second Statistical Account of Argyll in 1846 and again by Captain T. H. White in 1868 when he stayed at Kilberry and visited various monuments in the area for his 1872 book of archaeological sketches. In the 1860s, Captain White found the cave used as a store by fishermen and Marion believed this had led to an unfortunate 'clean up' of a desecrated Christian site by well meaning late Victorians. Mr Rogers wanted the site tidied up for potential tourists which meant Marion's band of helpers had to get a move on. She said: 'All stratification had of course been lost by the nineteenth century operations. Tragic as this loss of stratification is, it did allow us to work fast.' Mr Rogers intended to display any finds inside the cave, a plan which worried Marion as she felt there should be protection for such valuable archaeological material. Bones were all to be re-interred inside the cave. She said:

> It is impossible not to feel regret that the cave could not be adequately examined before being filled up, and that the tip [of material dumped outside during the nineteenth century clean up] has not been completely searched... Mr Rogers wants it restored before next tourist season.

A Viking balance was discovered during the dig, identified by her friend Robert B.K. Stevenson of the National Museum of Scotland. It was a major find – one of just three found on the mainland and western islands – and perhaps what pushed Mr Rogers into allowing an ongoing dig over a period of more than a decade. At first he wanted the site cleaned up and shrubs planted in front of the cave. By this time, however, Marion had enlisted some of the major figures in the field to fight her corner. The Mr Livens mentioned on her list of helpers was a member of the Hunterian Museum hierarchy. John M. Coles, an archaeological expert from Edinburgh University, visited the site and made a trial trench at the back of the cave. She involved Professor Stuart Piggot of Edinburgh University's Department of Prehistoric Archaeology. At this stage, Mr Rogers had started to become impatient, but at the end of 1959, Mr J.B. Sidebotham CMG, 'a gentleman of considerable archaeological experience' according to Marion, visited the site and found a bone needle. Marion and Mary went straight to the site when Mr Sidebotham brought his find to them and they, too, found some bone fragments. Mr Rogers then agreed to hold off his prettification of the site and for seventeen days Marion pushed her helpers to sieve nearly all the material which had been replaced in the cave and half the tip outside.

The work progressed sporadically after that while Marion took her Viking exhibition on the road and lectured to the Antiquarians at Glasgow University ('a great personal triumph for you, as well as being a very valuable contribution to Scottish archaeology', was the verdict of Anne S. Robertson of the Hunterian Museum) but in 1962, she was told by the Society of Antiquarians of Scotland that she could apply for a grant of £50 to help with the excavation. She wasn't always entirely honest with Mr Rogers, telling him that they were merely riddling the tip rather than searching for skeletal remains, and he allowed further work to continue for the next three years.

Marion was not personally involved throughout the exploration. She had to withdraw in 1963 because of other commitments and illness and little more was done until 1972. Marion had become convinced that the cave was a fourth Obanian site, along with MacArthur's cave, Risga and Oronsay, which suggested prehistoric seasonal settlements of large communities. No longer was this about St Columba but about much more ancient inhabitants. Along the way she enlisted the voluntary help of Christopher Young, a young archaeologist from the Department of the Environment and his archaeologist wife Judy, and many others who were eminent in their field at the time or were to become so. The young professionals responded to her enthusiasm and provided some of the expertise she needed to progress her dig. In 1975, some coarse pottery was found on the site and Marion and Mary conserved fragments and all the other treasures in any container they could find.

Despite the grant, Marion never got round to formally writing up the Columba Cave findings and decades later a less indulgent Council of the Antiquarians asked her to provide a paper. By then, much else was exercising her energies and it was agreed that Professor Chris Tolan Smith of Newcastle University, an expert in Argyll caves, would take Marion's findings on board and write the paper.

After correspondence during the 1980s, he went to visit Marion and Mary in the 1990s and found them in continued straitened circumstances at Kilberry. Tracking down the castle had been an adventure in itself. The echoing hall where Marion's father had once sat reading in front of a blazing fire was by now damp and the Durand trophy skins from the Indian glory days were moth eaten where they hung spread-eagled on the staircase walls. The once grand drawing room echoed to his footsteps as he made his way towards a screened off area in the corner of the room, behind which he found two elderly ladies huddled over an electric fire.

The Raeburn oil painting of a former Campbell of Kilberry had disappeared in her father's day. The silver, which had started to be sold off in the 1920s, was now still more depleted. But Miss Campbell of Kilberry had been responsible for finding treasures which she now valued far more than family heirlooms: flints and bones which she had handed on to Graham Ritchie at the Royal Commission and which Tolan Smith found in the assortment of shoe boxes, cigar tins, chocolate boxes, a Yardley's soap box, Elastoplast cases, a whisky presentation case, a shortbread tin and Lady Hague Remembrance Day poppy boxes in which she and Mary had stored them decades earlier. Professional plans and day records were not her strong point, according to Tolan Smith – although there is plenty of evidence in her correspondence that she recorded the cave activities in a detailed way – and he said that she gave an equivalence to every item she found. The professor admitted, however, that Marion had the potential to hold her own among the less scientific professional archaeologists of her day, the kind of faint praise which would not have surprised her.

Meanwhile, back in the 1960s, across the loch from Ellary Sir William Lithgow's tractor man had turned up yet another find and despite the professed ill health she had pleaded as a reason for not continuing the messy dig at Columba's Cave, Marion was only too pleased to head to Ormsary to take a look. This was a very exciting find and was to become her next major project. In October 1962, Sir William wrote from his Kingston shipyard in Port Glasgow offering her help to excavate the site on his estate. 'By all means investigate... we have a Post Hole Digging Machine which is ideal for testing ground in search of 'cists' of this kind'.

Tolan Smith sees this flitting from site to site as filling a vacuum because there was no county archaeologist and the Commission, constrained by its budget, swept through Argyll without stopping to investigate new archaeological finds in any depth. Marion, of course, had no budget other than pathetically small grants which she picked up here and there – but now a site had been found on land owned by a man of substance willing to provide help. Marion and Mary wasted no time. She immediately involved Jack Scott to identify pottery and when it was clear that the pieces were from the Bronze Age, Sir William wrote to Kelvingrove Museum where Jack was curator of the archaeology department and asked if Glasgow Corporation would be prepared to lend technical assistance on the site at Clachbreac farm.

Marion was not slow to bring in other contacts – the men from the Inspectorate of Ancient Monuments were next on her list – but Sir William was keen that the work be kept in the hands of West of Scotland archaeologists and received a response from Dr Stuart Henderson, the director at Kelvingrove Museum, commending the 'excellent work being done by Miss Marion Campbell'. Future archaeologists like Chris Tolan Smith may have thought Marion to be a Miss Marples of the archaeological world, but the scholars of the 1950s, 60s and 70s admired her work and were pleased to have her head up projects they simply had no funds to initiate, let alone carry through.

Cists, skeletons, and a food vessel were found in good condition and Sir William sent a chauffeur with the food vessel in a plastic bucket to Glasgow for Jack to examine. He also set up an on-site caravan as a work place for Marion and her variable team, bought a Polaroid camera (then a very new piece of technology) to take photos at every stage of operations and considered carbon dating – another new technique. He was wary of publicity but got Marion to prepare a piece which appeared in the *Oban Times* of December 15, 1962 – an exhilarating pre-birthday present for Marion. It read:

> One of the most important Bronze Age finds ever to be discovered in the Knapdale district of Argyll has just come to light on the Ormsary Estate of Sir William Lithgow, Bt. During the past few days 11 graves situated close together

> have been uncovered in a field which was recently cleared of potatoes.
>
> It is the largest group of cists known to exist in the district and gives indication of what must have been at one time a large settlement.
>
> Miss Marion Campbell in charge of the digging believes that traces of an even larger settlement may yet be discovered.

The site was reckoned to date to between 1500 and 2000 BC and three complete decorated pottery bowls and the remains of a fourth were found along with burned and unburned human remains. Marion wrote to inform Stewart Cruden at the Ministry of Works what was going on at the site, telling him:

> 'Aunted, that's what I am, 'aunted! What a time of year to be landed with a major Dig.

This jokey horror at the situation could not conceal her glee that 'Bill' was laying on metallurgical analysis to test for a bronze-working site, a plastic-sheeted shelter for the site and her caravan. '. . . he is dead keen and very anxious to do the thing properly', she told Cruden. As the work progressed it became clear that this was a site of some importance and despite 'expert' opinion that flint did not occur in Mid Argyll, there was flint galore in the shape of axe heads and tools. Marion's theory was that there was a source upstream – or as she suggested, 'up-glacier', of the potato field.

Christmas intervened with the baking of mince pies and wrapping of parcels, but Marion's enthusiasm matched Sir William Lithgow's. In January 1963 when she wrote to Stuart Cruden, he responded that his whole office was delighted to have archaeological information without being 'urged to do something about it'. By March, Cruden was learning that the latest work at Clachbreac was 'really something' and that help WAS in fact needed, perhaps by way of a senior student to help Jack Scott who was in the background as technical adviser. Marion was planning to get back to business by mid-March after the worst of the winter weather and Sir William was offering to pay for carbon dating. There were ten cists and copper slag – or at least, she hoped it was copper slag, which would offer proof of Bronze Age workings.

In the middle of all this came the letter proposing her as a Fellow of the Antiquarian Society. She was asked for a relevant curriculum vitae and said: 'I feel it's very odd to put in two children's books among my 'work' but they do contain a good deal of hard research and they are poor things but mine own.' She added is a more serious vein: 'This is something I have always regarded as 'quite above my touch', and I feel there is very little I can put forward in my own support.'

Despite her lack of letters (and from this comment, self confidence), that CV was already impressive: she listed herself as one of the founders and first president of the Natural History & Antiquarian Society of Mid Argyll, the only honorary member of the Kintyre Antiquarian Society, a lecturer on local antiquities with the Glasgow University extra Mural Scheme, the planner and executer of two travelling exhibitions funded by Mid-Argyll Community Council, and she included the St Columba's Cave (despite never completing the paper) and Clachbreac excavations. Her publications then already included a small and already out-of-print popular guide to St Columba's Cave written in 1959, the Mid Argyll Handbook of History, written for the local society in 1962, and with Mary Sandeman, the authorship of a paper on Badden cist, a Field Survey of Historic and Prehistoric Sites in Mid Argyll, the first report on nine years of field work carried out by the two women which catalogued 724 sites of all periods, 232 of which had already been published as a paper for the Antiquarian Society. Marion and Mary had discovered 243 new sites, the subject of the paper she had read to the Society of Antiquaries Scotland in 1960 to such acclaim. She also included *The Wide Blue Road*, published by Dent in 1957 and *Lances and Longships*, out that year, and was able to say that *The Squire of Val* would be published in 1964.

In the nineteen years since she had left the WRNS, one broken reed coming home to look after another, Marion Campbell of Kilberry had become an author of children's books, a local historian of note, a respected authority on matters archaeological (whatever the academics of the future would say of her amateur status) and was now to become a Fellow of the Society to which she aspired but had thought herself too lacking in letters. She appeared to take it all in her stride, writing Clachbreac measurements on the back of a Players Medium Navy Cut fag packet with the old sailor logo and sending off iron ore to Dr William Macfarlane, the metallurgist at the Fairfield shipbuilding works at Govan in Glasgow for carbon dating. She and Mary, both heavy smokers, were often to be seen flicking ash around the site of a dig: they may have lacked precision but they oozed panache.

By 1964, it was clear that there was neither enough iron ore nor sufficient bone fragments for the technology of the day to be able to come to any conclusions, but Marion had answers of her own. She decided that rather than this being a prehistoric site of bronze manufacture or even a medieval one, that by chance an eighteenth century bloomery (many such sites were found along the coast where the first stages of ore extraction was carried out using charcoal kilns) had been set up near to the original prehistoric site. This flies in the face of those critics who claim she was too keen to romanticise her finds, but certainly endorses Ian Hamilton's view that a more formal education in history would have narrowed her vision and concentrated her interest on one short period in time. Marion was more keen to prove that huts and a stockade had surrounded the graves found at Clachbreac, which would have had major implications for Scottish prehistory – and what's more, people in high places were listening to her theories.

CHAPTER ELEVEN

Politics and people

Marion Campbell's archaeological and historical work was usually unpaid – except for the miniscule fees and paltry mileage payments she received for her lectures and exhibition tours. Her books, firing a new generation's imagination about the rich history of Argyll, brought her self satisfaction but no fat fees. And so her dealings with the powers that be in the world of antiquities were often double edged. She continued to part with Kilberry treasures – from flints to the National Museum of Scotland to exquisite linen to Kelvingrove Art Gallery. This oiled the machinery and brought valuable contacts on board – people like Stewart Cruden, the Inspector of Ancient Monuments with whom she had first corresponded over the shelter for the Kilberry stones.

Then there were the experts at the National Archives of Scotland to whom she offered Kilberry deeds from the sixteenth century to modern times, rent rolls and farm accounts from the late eighteenth century and unsorted nineteenth century family correspondence. And she was on first name terms with specialists at the Hunterian Museum, Glasgow Art Galleries and Museums, the National Museum of Scotland and the Scottish universities. Having offered exhibits she was in a good bargaining position to pick top class brains and beg sight of primary sources of information. These contacts were for her initially the professors she had never had because of that failed entrance exam – and she devoured the information she gleaned from them. By the mid 1960s, however, it was she to whom many of the professionals went first as a primary source of all things Argyll. In time, she would gift family papers to the National Register of Archives (Scotland) and

Edinburgh and Glasgow University libraries but in the early years she was always hoping they would send her a cheque by return post. Often, a certificate confirming her donation was all that arrived.

In 1964, she was at last elected a Fellow of the Society of Antiquaries at a meeting in London. She was congratulated by fellow Scots not only for strengthening the Scottish representation within the national Society but because 'no-one has deserved the honour more than yourself'. She had, of course, to pay a membership fee for this honour of being elected, which stretched her budget somewhat for many years. That same year, she decided not to seek re-election to the District Community Council. The District Clerk, Henry Robertson, recorded thanks not just for her presence on the council but her work with the travelling exhibitions and help with other projects.

While some lairds see it as their place to be figureheads in local politics and within the social structure of their stamping ground, Marion Campbell was always a doer. For her, being a district councillor meant putting her area on the map, and she did it herself with her balsa wood story boards. Being president of the local antiquarian association was about stout shoes and a trowel, not genteel meetings over a glass of sherry. Being a member of the Scottish National Party involved everything from keeping the voters' roll up to date for efficient canvassing (weekly trawls of the county's local papers to see who had married, who had died, who had moved into and out of the area) through fly posting to a commitment to the party's Eilean Mor project which led to a long association with William – Billy – Wolfe, a father of the modern party. Her commitment to the Scottish National Party was idealistic and perhaps stemmed, according to the one of the party's most senior figures, Professor Sir Neil MacCormick, from feelings rooted in the tradition of responsible lairdship.

Sir Neil met her in February 1974, that troubled political year which saw two general elections and was a triumph for the nationalists across Scotland. Marion was chairing a meeting for his brother Iain, the SNP candidate who won the Argyll seat, in the village hall at Ardfern. Sir Neil said: 'She was very vigorous and very welcoming. There were big turnouts for the political meetings then and again in the next general election that autumn. Marion was a forceful speaker as a chairman.' The two didn't meet again until 1980 when the Eilean Mor project was inaugurated. Marion wrote the publicity booklet for the project and gave what Sir Neil called 'a very instructive talk about the chapel and the archaeological significance of the monastic cell on the island.' Professor McCormick, a historian rooted in academia, said:

> If there was anything surprising about Marion it was one of the lairds taking our side politically. She was not in any way grand in her ways though she was a person of whom you would take note. As a university person I was perhaps surprised at how learned she was. She was an amateur but a gifted and well read one. A degree would have given her a formal passport and would have given her a more structured but not necessarily a more interesting approach to the sources. In a curious way she belongs both to academic history and to folk history. It is a shame if she did feel put down for not being a scholar.

The professor felt that Marion was a fundamentalist in her political outlook. She was for independence but quite pragmatic about the process. He shared what he called her 'eccentricity' of perceiving Scotland from its Gaelic, Dalriadic taproot but she was never distressed by any modernising of the party as it progressed towards the 1999 renewal of the Scottish Parliament. She was the honorary president of the Argyll and Bute party for several decades. In the spring of 1997, Sir Neil, who became a member of the European Parliament, found her frail but still keen to help win back the Argyll seat. She and Neil MacLachlan, a long-term Kilberry friend and neighbour, carried out poster warfare in Mid Argyll, with Marion fly posting over Neil's Labour posters. Sir Neil said: 'As a highly respectable lady in middle life, shinning up and down ladders putting posters up was part of the camaraderie of the election campaigns and the SNP invented that and for many years outstripped the other parties in its enthusiasm. Marion was a real activist.' In a letter to Lorna MacEachern at Drumlanrig Castle in Dumfriesshire in June 1974, Marion excused her lack of correspondence about the history of the Duke of Monmouth saying:

> I have got myself into a chaos of arrears because of a tiresome book I have been writing, over the last two years,

> about Argyll; I have now sent the typescript off to the publishers and can only hope that this is the final form. Apart from three weeks in February spent helping with the SNP victory in Argyll, I have had no spare time at all this year to keep abreast of all the other jobs, and now am toiling to overtake all my sins of omission – a vain hope as people won't stop writing to me!

Sir Neil sees the Second World War as a very formative period for so many women of Marion's generation – women without an academic qualification but having learned how to make things work. He believes Marion was one of the pillars of the party in Argyll and part of the great victory of 1974, when that victory mattered. It was one of the first seven, followed by a further four, seats gained by the SNP which gave the Labour government of Harold Wilson such a fright. Sir Neil said:

> That pushed the boulder over the top of the hill. It took longer to build the house than we thought but it was then inevitable that the Labour government would make commitments to Scotland which later John Smith and then Donald Dewar – both Mid Argyll men – took up. She was not the least among those who made that long-term victory and she will be remembered as a tradition-bearer who captured in her historical writing that Dalriadic conception of Scotland.
>
> It would also be right to see Marion Campbell as part of a particular set of people who as the small lairds of Argyll sustained the community. She belonged to the cadet chieftans of the House of Argyll, many of whom played an honourable part in sustaining Gaeldom. She and her like played a part with honour and dignity.
>
> By signing up for the SNP it was interesting and helpful in the transition from the old deference to the new egalitarianism. There was a sense that she could give a lead, that these were decent folk and we could vote for them. I am very proud to have known her.

By comparison with those heady, powerful campaigning days, the Eilean Mor project was a very gentle affair, but nonetheless important in the annals of the SNP. William Wolfe came from industrial Lanarkshire, but had a somewhat elite Tory background. He was a chartered account, was Scout Commissioner, a poet and a 'romantic' nationalist in the sense that, like Marion, he was not unaware of the economics of nationalism but perhaps did not concern himself with them.

In 1978, Walter Paterson Neill, a bachelor and lifelong nationalist from the Tayvallich peninsula died at the age of 62 and left instructions to sell his possessions and use the proceeds to set up a trust for the benefit of the cause of independence of Scotland, with trustees appointed by the SNP. The funds were used to buy Eilean Mor mhic ui Charmaig, a 44 acre island at the mouth of Loch Sween in the Sound of Jura, which became 'the SNP island'. At the time, Billy Wolfe was the SNP national president and he was appointed one of the trustees of the project. He sought the help of the Argyll SNP president, Miss Campbell of Kilberry, who very usefully was also a writer, local archaeologist and historian. Who better to tell the world about the island and to advise on sensitively maintaining its ethos while developing it as a cultural centre for the party?

A visitors' day to the island saw Marion and Grace Logan spreading the flag of the red rampant lion on its field of gold on the site of the altar in the chapel which had been renovated by John, Lord of the Isles in 1380. Mary Sandeman guided the visitors to the hermit's cave, which had been inhabited as early as the seventh century AD. Rev. David Montgomery, the then parish minister of Tayvallich, led the worship but it was Marion who was the catalyst that day, presenting the visitors with history tailored to inspire nationalism.

She continued to advise Billy Wolfe on Eilean Mor matters for the next twenty years and the pair developed a friendship. He visited Kilberry and frequently wrote to Marion – adding to her growing circle of influential correspondents. In September 1979, she suggested an excavation of the island sites and literary research as part of the SNP's cultural plans for the island.

In December of that year, Marion reached 60 – the state retirement age. About the only thing she retired from was her crafts marketing agency, which she had found increasingly burdensome over the years. Now she wanted still more free time to pursue exciting political, literary, historical and archaeological pursuits. As well as involving herself in the Eilean Mor project, her adult novel *Dark Twin* had appeared in 1974, *Argyll: the Enduring Heartland* had come out in 1977 and she was involved in writing a history of Kilberry Church and its history. She told Billy Wolfe on December 18, 1979, two days after that 60th milestone, that she was expecting three or four 'boys' from the Royal Commission on Ancient and Historic Monuments to be staying in the top flat of the castle in the coming months as their field work on Argyll had started. This seemed to be a matter of following up the 1954-63 exploratory work which Marion and Mary had done and which as a paper in PSAS XCV (Scottish Antiquaries' Proceedings) had become the 'bible' for the men from the ministry. She told Billy Wolfe that as these 'boys' from the ministry were going to be around, it would be a good idea to pick their brains about the finer points of Eilean Mor's archaeological history and even to commission them for further work to clarify any points left to be investigated.

What a long way she had come from those first letters to the Ministry thirty years previously in which she expressed surprise at the wealth of archaeological treasure on her doorstep and tentatively suggested that she might have a look at some of them. Now she was not only the source of information for the Ministry but its landlady as well.

Billy, perhaps more than any of the coterie of admiring males in her circle of correspondents, became a friend in a practical sense. It was he who offered Marion and Mary electric blankets in the wake of an January gale in 1980. He was the one who brought his electric saw and his useful son to help cut logs from blown down timber (Marion and Mary had, of course, tackled the trees with an axe themselves but Marion admitted they were 'twa auld weemen peckin' awa like hens' at this mammoth task). It was in him that she confided that the castle was to be one of a number of large Argyll properties to undergo a rates review and the one she told when the valuation was reduced by a third, confessing that it 'meant a lot' and that she could 'start breathing again'.

She was the voice of reason in regard to Eilean Mor. She cautioned against a Communion service in the island chapel in case it caused Catholics and Episcopalians problems. She warned that a particular environmental specialist might hinder rather than help the project because while his professional skills were not in question, his public relations skills were. She advised diffusing Tory jibes that 'poor Walter Neill' would be 'turning in his grave at the way the SNP treated his legacy'. A mythical property developer had crept into the Eilean Mor equation – an irony as the battle Marion was currently fighting was against the development of holiday chalets at Keills – and launched what she called a pre-emptive strike which put it about that by buying the island, the SNP had in fact saved it from such a fate.

There were open days for several years after that first gloriously *Braveheart* inauguration, but eventually, Marion's failing health prevented her from making the somewhat precarious boat trip to Eilean Mor. It grieved her to realise that she was not as mobile as once she had been – this was not a question of flitting from one interest to another, a trait of which she might possibly have been guilty in earlier decades when new projects temptingly tumbled into her life with dizzying regularity. In 1986, she confessed that she could no long travel independently and that many things, including the completion of the Columba's Cave paper, were becoming just too much for her.

This was not, of course, to say that she was retreating from work. She was simply prioritising. For decades she had been determined to write a biography of Alexander III, the man she saw as one of Scotland's most important monarchs. Her passion for him had begun when she was writing her children's books, and by the time *The Squire of Val* was published in 1967, she had researched a wealth of information which was far too complex to be fed into another children's novel. She decided to research still more and to produce a scholarly book – whatever the academics might think of her. She had become passionate about handing on Scotland's history – but not just for history's sake. She was asked to talk at a Girl Guide residential training weekend at Oban in 1982 on the theme 'To find our own identity so we have something to offer the world' and she told delegates:

> I was taught virtually no Scottish history in school once we got past tales of Bruce and Wallace. If only we can get the past across to the children as something real, something that actually happened, the way people lived, what an

> anchor that gives them for their future. Newer nations would give their all for a fraction of such a rich heritage as we have in Argyll and it is ours to explore and build on.

There was therefore no let up in the research that she did to produce what she saw as her major *oeuvre*. She tracked down experts in stained glass, pottery and architecture of the thirteenth century. She struck up correspondence with people who could help her fit together the complex jigsaw of Alexander's ancestry, political and social status and marital condition. She turned to her historian and criminologist friend Joanna Gordon, daughter of a Skipness family and niece of Angus Graham. Angus was for many years Secretary of the Society of Antiquarians of Scotland and of the Royal Commission on Archaeological and Historical Monuments of Scotland and had corresponded much with Marion about the Argyll Inventories for which the Campbell-Sandeman paper had become such a valuable source. Joanna first knew her at the time of of Angus Graham's interment in the family mausoleum at Skipness in 1980, when Marion rather put Joanna in her place because she had begun the proceedings on time – a very un-Argyll thing to do. Angus had been a Greek and Latin scholar and Marion had picked his brains to ensure, among other matters, the correct translations of documents. Her own Latin was up to making sense of the thirteenth century Tarbert castle building accounts but Angus Graham had a much firmer grasp on the classics. Not everyone was so kind, and Joanna, who became close to Marion as she struggled to place *Alexander III* with a publisher, said: 'She suffered lifelong misery because of her treatment by the academic world. . . She knew she wasn't recognised and it wrankled terribly all her life. The great moment was when she was made an FSA (Fellow of the Society of Antiquaries) – none of your FSA Scotland!'

Joanna said she developed an immediate affection for Marion (despite the rebuke about her un-Argyll promptness) because of her attractive and welcoming personality. In getting to know her better, Joanna became aware that Marion had 'reinvented' herself several times over to suit her circumstances and needs. She said: 'Autodidact applies to her very well.' She also described Marion as 'an excessivist' whose every project had to be 'tremendously validated by her great pushful personality'.

The two women became very aware during the struggle for publication of *Alexander* that *Dark Twin* was a blot on Marion's curriculum vitae in the eyes of academic publishers. This book, which had come to her in waking dreams and had been pieced together from the scraps of paper on which she had scribbled down the strange names and events of an early Scotland, was seen, according to Joanna, as having too fanciful an approach. Certainly, it is the one book which splits her followers into two distinct camps: *Twin* lovers and haters. But as far as academic publishers were concerned, even *Heartland* was too airy fairy to lend any substance to her reputation and perhaps its very popularity with the general reading public damned her as much as the book itself. *Heartland* is a very personal view of Argyll and includes folk history and myth, poetry and poetic description as well as factual accounts of the past. It is such an evocative book that other writers, including her journalist friend Jim Crumley, looked to it for inspiration. Jim sought permission to quote a lengthy passage: homage indeed.

This did not, however, impress the publishers to whom Marion submitted the idea of *Alexander*, let alone those to whom she sent the manuscript. This pigeonholing by the publishers of writers of different genres seemed seemed to penalise Marion particularly harshly. Joanna Gordon said:

> As a historian she was extremely diligent and she had a wide frame of reference. She was extremely neat and much more disciplined than the vast majority of historians. Sometimes she added two and two and made five but we all do it. She was a burrower and she laboured night and day on that book.

She wasn't, of course, even in her sixties and seventies, rationing herself to one project only. Her writing was frequently interrupted by genealogical research for the many correspondents around the world who wrote timidly, boldly and even rudely for information, photocopies of ancient documents, proof of relationship with the great and the good, the poor and the marginalised. So many people had left Argyll over the centuries: some to make their fortunes in places like

Jamaica, as Marion's own Campbell ancestors had done; some sailing steerage to a strange land having suffered the effects of a famine or a clearance of tenants by lairds 'improving' their lands. Those who wrote were not only Campbells but Macdonalds, MacTavishes, MacNeills and so many other families with roots on the mainland and in the islands. Unless they were excessively demanding, Marion answered their requests with a generosity that stretched her budget and curtailed her writing time. Joanna said she was a woman who didn't suffer fools gladly and that there were times when she acted the *grande dame.* But Alasdair Carmichael of Ford on Loch Awe, with whom she made the exciting 'Torran Bronze Hoard' find in the hills above the loch and collaborated on work for *Kist,* saw only wit, enthusiasm and 'an intricate personality'. Alasdair had said that the 'serene gentleness' of Mary Sandeman might 'sometimes prove a needed brake on the Campbell impulsiveness' of Marion. Now the impulsiveness was also curbed by increasing back pain which stemmed from the Blitz injury and a variety of smaller ailments which together compromised her mobility – but not her enthusiasm for a good cause.

She could, without compunction, wipe out a connection which she felt did not match up to her high standards. In the early 1970s, for example, she had become involved with Richard Demarco of Edinburgh Arts. Together, they cooked up a scheme which brought parties of people across to Argyll to look at various archaeological sites with Marion giving field lectures and guided tours. Marion lent him slides which led to healthy bookings for a four week course at Demarco's studio with a trip to Dunadd fort, clarsach music by Margaret Low from Oban and a meal at the then 'Melfort Motor Inn'.

After just six months of correspondence, she addressed him as 'Dear Ricky,' he wrote to her as 'Dear Marion'. Her notes for the students 'overwhelmed' him. He wanted to have the launch of *Dark Twin* at the Demarco gallery, she had offered to be a 'Native Guide' for his summer school. This was to be an entirely new concept of the summer school as an art experience and there were links with Edinburgh University. The first year worked – to a point. But it was to end in tears – or at least with Marion 'blazing angry' about the way she and Gunnie MacPhie, who had been hired to include a stone rubbing experience in the trip, had been treated.

Without her say-so, an assumption had been made that the students would start their trip at Kilberry – and stay in the castle. There had also been assumptions made about the size of Kilberry roads (not suitable for big buses and a hundred students, her physical ability to traipse across the machair, and a visit chez Gunnie at her farmhouse in Ellary. There was much, much more and the bad behaviour of students on the previous year's outing which, among others, upset worshippers at Kilmartin, was all dragged out for an airing. Marion's honeymoon with 'Ricky' was over. 'Gross discourtesy and lack of common consideration' was just one of the burning phrases which winged its way around the country. There was heavy sarcasm about the 'assumption that we will be delighted to be trampled over by anyone who condescends to be interested in country ways' and an accusation that 'if Ricky had the slightest genuine interest in the countryside he might take a little care not to treat it like this'. She wondered if she could be civil to him if she met him again. It was not a happy ending but she certainly knew when to call a halt if her beloved Argyll was being abused.

On the other hand, if there was a battle which could benefit Argyll, she wouldn't let go – and she would pull any strings she could. From the early 1970s she had lent her weight to the fight to save Tarbert castle not only from the aberrations of the planning department which seemed not to be averse to modern bungalows being erected under its shadow but also the apparent lassitude of the Ministry of Ancient Monuments which did little to preserve the building itself. On the eve of her birthday in 1972 she had swung into action by seeking the help of her many contacts in influential positions. She was able to persuade Professor D.M. Wilson, secretary of the Society for Medieval Archaeology, to write to Argyll planning department pointing out the castle's archaeological and historical importance. In September of the following year she enlisted the help of Stewart Cruden, Inspector of Ancient Monuments, Scotland, explaining that 'a wretched man' was trying to build a holiday bungalow alongside the walls of Tarbert castle. Plans showed that the site of the ancient burgh of Tarbert, erected by Bruce around 1328, would be infringed. This was the oldest royal castle in Scotland for which building accounts still existed (and of course, Marion had translated them from the Latin), dating from the last years of Robert Bruce. It was one of around five burgh sites not built over by later buildings and here was an 'incomer' wanting to change all that with his bungalow. In fairness, the Council had turned the man down but he was appealing against the decision and Marion wanted as many big guns lined up against him as possible. She also demanded of the County Clerk that an emergency excavation be carried out should this gentleman win his appeal. As always, she used every weapon in her armoury, closing her letter to the County Clerk:

> I write as a Fellow of the Societies of Antiquaries of London and of Scotland, and a Member of the Society for Medieval Archaeology.

She of course signed it Miss Campbell of Kilberry – as powerful a pebble in her sling as the rest.

Tarbert castle was not to go away for a very long time. A Trust was set up and in 1978 she tried to get the Department of the Environment to take it over to conserve the site and improve public access. The 1970s had not been a good decade financially for Britain and there was no more spare cash for such projects than there had been in the immediate post war years. In 1979, she confirmed to Argyll and Bute District Council that she was still against the plans for the holiday bungalow as the case came up for appeal. In 1982, the appeal was reactivated again and again she objected, telling the Council: 'It would be a monstrous act of vandalism to allow any development on the site.'

In 1988, a year short of her seventieth birthday, she was a powerful force behind a steering group formed at an angry public meeting that followed a decision reported in the *Argyllshire Advertiser* as one which would allow the castle to die. In 1989, a report was made about the feasibility of an archaeological investigation and Marion remained active as the situation rumbled on.

CHAPTER TWELVE
The irony and the ecstasy

Joanna Gordon believed that Marion Campbell 'would have made a wonderful ambassador's wife somewhere in the world'. The place Marion would have liked to have been was at the side of Walter John Campbell, the man she said was the love of her life. She had loved him enough to leave the castle to him in a Will made in 1951, for which he thanked her in a letter from the Cavendish Hotel in London on September 3. Yet this handsome Naval captain with his lean and chiselled looks, immensely handsome in uniform, had drifted out of her life in the mid-1950s – his nephew Jonathan Howard claiming that despite her great charm and intellect she was not glamorous enough for Walter and Marion insisting it was a parting for the best because of the madness in Walter's family. He sent her that 'useful' naval brooch without so much as a message. No correspondence is evident until the 1970s, when Walter – now styling himself John – wrote a number of apologetic letters. He had read *Enduring Heartland*, liked it and told her so. He had turned down a desk job at the Admiralty and instead had run an establishment for delinquent youngsters in Bristol.

There is hint enough in his 1970s correspondence that the two decades in which they had lived out their separate lives had not been cloistered for him. He was no stranger to gin and tonics as the sun dipped below the yard arm and perhaps this as much as anything would have troubled Marion had they married. As it was, there was now conciliatory correspondence which ended with Walter's death at Meridian Hall, Bristol, on October 31, 1978. On December 11 of that year, Marion heard from the Trust Division of Lloyds Bank that Walter John had left her £100 in his Will, along with a silver salver given to him by the officers of HMS *Cochrane* and 'the little Three Thousand Years old Phoenician vase'. She may have felt this was as unsympathetic as his postal gift of a Naval brooch but despite all that, his was the photograph on her bedside table at the time of her own death.

As she approached what the French call the *troisiemme age*, she was still beset by financial problems. The books, the Fellowships, the digs and crusades may all have brought her respect and status but they didn't bring home the bacon. Mary Sandeman's income meant the two of them could survive, but there was no cushion when disaster struck, as it frequently did in an ancient pile like Kilberry Castle. In 1985, Marion paid out over £570 for roof repairs and the first stages of treatment for dry rot in the tower. The second stage of treatment had to be postponed until an electrician came to cut off the electricity in that part of the building. The scullery wing was on the brink of collapse and the former conservatory was now pouring with water and, were the castle not a listed building, would have been better demolished. Marion wrote to her bank saying she really didn't know how she was to carry on. The old, old story of selling up was being recited again:

> Heaven knows, I don't want to sell the house after all the struggles to keep it, but it is sometimes tempting to think how much the contents are worth, even if it might be nearly impossible to find a buyer for the building.

Despite an appeal against a rates valuation, the bill for rates had more than doubled and she was looking forward to a grim Christmas if she had to pay up. Not that Christmas had ever been a lavish affair in the post war era.

In 1988, she wrote that letter to her second cousin John, grandson of Uncle Archie and the young man she wanted to take on the castle – if he would have it. She and Mary had experienced the worst July gales for fifty years and there were trees down all around the castle. She had been involved in lengthy correspondence with her 'maddening' publisher, and the two women had decided to move 'in the next year or two' into the former laundry cottage down the drive from the castle. Mary had bought the place as a tactful answer to the growing financial problems at the castle. The sale of the cottage put money into the

Kilberry kitty and it was a good long term plan to make life more comfortable for them both. But as Mary and Neil MacLachlan remembered, the two women had been circling each other cautiously without directly broaching a time scale. Neil, the Labour Party poster warrior, had lived at Kilberry since June, 1945 when his father went to work on the estate. He had watched Marion being badly served by farming advisers and when he and Mary married in 1965, they became Marion's friends and helpers. Mary often looked after Mrs Sandeman when the two younger women went off on digs and other ploys. Now in the 1980s, Mary found Mary Sandeman confiding that she didn't know how to get Marion to agree to move into the cottage, while Marion was wondering how she could capitulate and give up the castle. Ill health and increasing discomfort in the damp, chilly castle must have made the decision for them. Marion clearly saw she had to gift the castle to John as soon as possible so that death taxes could be avoided. But as she told John, it had to be his decision – she would not burden him with this millstone if he did not want it.

She told him:

> Don't ever think you can't tell me what you want and intend; meantime I'll try to put down what I think about my own plans. We are definitely moving to Mary's house in the next year or two, always supposing I last that long and she gets the improvements done that she wants (I am getting her round to thinking and talking about what these are). The idea is to take her furniture that's here now plus whatever we need of mine. I shall probably try to get some of the Durand possessions back to my cousins, especially Grandfather D's pictures (most of his were lost in the Blitz, and some of his grandchildren haven't got any). . . Grandpa D gave my Mother a lot of 'small treasures' because he thought she was the only one of the family who would keep them and look after them. . . Her good Beckstein piano is probably worth £2,000, and I do feel I am obliged to do anything but sell that (it was a wedding present to her from her brothers and sisters).
> What concerns me most is what's to happen to this house.

She had lived a life in which she was never free from that concern.

Now she was not only anxious that she had to survive for seven years so that John would avoid inheritance tax, but that she would burden him with 'other people's bygone tastes', always 'the snag about an Old Family Home'. She told John that the last time she had put the house on the market was in 1956 when the Cistercian monks turned it down as being less than comfortable.

> I have spent my life struggling to make ends meet – every time I made a fair bit from a book, the house roof opened and gulped it all down – and frankly I'm tired of having to count the coppers while tripping over ornaments and swords and whatnot which have to be looked after because they are worth a lot.
>
> I never got the capital Ivy thought she was leaving me, as I think you know already (she left so many small legacies to friends that we never managed to pay more than 75 per cent of them, so 'there weren't no core' for me) – so it would be rather nice to be able to motor along comfortably for what time may be left.

Marion little knew when she wrote that letter to John on July 27, 1988, with her health failing and in the middle of fruitless negotiations to interest publishers in *Alexander III* that she would not just motor along comfortably for 'what time may be left' but that in her final years she would be cruising at exhilaratingly high altitudes. That after a lifetime of counting pennies she would at last be able to breathe comfortably when the bank statement came through the letter box at Druim A'Bhuinne, the laundry cottage of her grandfather's day, into which she and Mary Sandeman moved at last when John and his wife Charmian came to live in Kilberry Castle. Marion was able to tell her lawyers in November 1988 that the move to the cottage to the seaward of the castle, which for years had been used as a gardener's cottage, would give Mary relief from carrying coal and logs to keep the draughty castle warm because for some time Marion had been unable to help 'apart from the cooking'. As she wrote to Mr McNair at MacArthur Stewart in Oban: 'We are both getting old.'

She was pleased that John, eldest son of Uncle Archie's son Colin, was her heir. That his hobby was bee keeping fitted with the Kilberry ethos – those years when her mother had tried to keep the place afloat with bees and market gardening must have sprung to mind. Her regret was that he would not come to the well-kept Kilberry of her youth.

> I have managed to keep this building in reasonable repair. We can't possibly keep the grounds as they were when my parents employed three gardeners.

She insisted to Mr McNair that she didn't want to pressurise John, but she was weary. She said: 'I feel we must get our own move cut and dried shortly, if it is to be made at all.'

It was not, of course, as simple as Marion and Mary moving out and John and Charmian moving in. There was a bond dating back to the 1950s which had to be discharged before the young couple could get the castle. Then there was the work to be done on Druim A'Bhuinne. An architect was employed by Mary, who had paid £3,500 for the cottage and a handkerchief plot of estate land – but things were at a standstill because she felt it was all too expensive. Marion, ever more forceful than Mary, wrote: 'If it were my house, I'd have got things a bit further forward, I would hope, but I can hardly harry an architect employed by Miss Sandeman.'

She complicated matters by offering Durand heirlooms to her relations from her mother's side while foreseeing nothing but fur flying if they all actually managed to get together for the carve up. She had Afghan rugs valued and she gave huge amounts of family paperwork to Murdo MacDonald, the Argyll archivist. It was a great purge, a time of change, a time of wondering yet again if she was doing the right thing. She certainly had more confidence in her decision making than she had had in her younger days and she was confirmed in having chosen her heir well when her friend Sir Ilay Campbell of Crarae met John, Charmian and their children in April 1990 and wrote to say 'What a nice couple' they were.

By June that year, Marion was organised enough to begin to worry about that lifelong problem – 'of Kilberry'. Would she still be able to use this title when she was living in the cottage, she asked Sir Ilay. He delved into the Lord Lyon's rulings on the matter, questioned their validity and advised her:

> Nowadays I should say it was a matter of choice or mutual agreement! After all, except for Baronies, the whole system of territorial designations only arose from the convenience of knowing who was who – or what! If I were you I would remain firmly 'of Kilberry' as long as you are around – through courtesy, if for no other reason – one you have definitely earned! After that it would be correct for John to use the designation, not only as owner of the house but as heir of the family 'on the spot'.

It is difficult to imagine who would have omitted to call her Miss Campbell of Kilberry, yet it was a point of order she was keen to establish. They had laughed at her at school for using the title. She had lost the property which gave her the right to use it when the trustees of the estate sold it from under her feet and now she was giving that property to her heir.

In August 1990, the two women moved into the cottage, each having signed a codicil allowing the other to stay in the property in the event of death. The move was a bonanza not only for the Durand family and the Argyll archives but for an odd mix of organisations, including the regimental headquarters of the Argyll and Sutherland Highlanders at Stirling. The cottage was small and the heirlooms and family documents were many. Those which belonged to the castle remained there – the rest were pruned to within an inch of their existence. There was no drawing room here – just a cosy sitting room. There was a dining kitchen – but then, when had the two women last entertained in style in the elegant dining room in the castle with its family portraits (minus the famous Raeburn which had been sold off even before the Jock and Marion's church mice days and was last spotted by the family in a Munich gallery in 1987). The kitchen and bathroom upstairs had a view of the encroaching woodland and the flora and fauna visible from these windows were in themselves worthy of the upheaval. Marion's study immediately became organised chaos and the work on *Alexander III* resumed.

By now, Marion was suffering from intense back pain, had several bouts of gout in her hands which sometimes made it impossible to type. A major heart attack in 1991 took its toll. Joanna Gordon said that she continued to suffer from a lifetime's bad diet which in later years manifested itself in a surfeit of white bread rolls. Even so, the move from the castle gave her fresh impetus and she embarked on a new round of politicking and campaigning. Paying an instalment of the much hated poll tax in 1991 she took the opportunity to complain to Strathclyde Council's director of finance about the planned reorganisation of local government. 'I opposed the creation of large Regions in 1973, but I now feel Strathclyde is doing a great job in very difficult circumstances and it angers me to see all that in jeopardy.' She supported Neil and Ileene Duncan when they sought advice about opening a heritage centre at Tarbert, and kept a finger on the pulse of the Tarbert castle campaign.

Also on her list of things to do was the publication of diaries her grandfather ('Old Kilberry') had kept meticulously in the latter half of the nineteenth century, and an analysis of the Depredations of the Campbells. This was the document which listed the looting and worse carried out in Argyll in 1685 by king's troops – ostensibly a civil war tactic to quash rebellion but in reality a settling of local clan scores.

It would be a few years yet before she could tell Michael Davis the county librarian and historian that there was going to be money in the kitty to publish these projects. That money was to come her way because of the strange book which was currently in part to blame for her inability to get her historical biography published. *Dark Twin* had been in her life even longer than the peacemaker king of Scotland. It had begun to impinge on her consciousness in 1953 when she was all alone in the castle, struggling to juggle being farmer and writer. It was pieced together from those jotted down waking dreams after Mary's arrival at Kilberry in 1954 and first sent off to her agent of the day, Anthony Shiel Partners, in 1958. It had remained a problem child to her for many decades.

Giles Gordon, then a young man working for Anthony Shiel, tried hard to place *Dark Twin* in those early days but without success. Giles was – on and off and in varying degrees of cordiality – to remain her agent for the rest of her days. One publisher had told him that he could make neither head nor tail of *Dark Twin.* Some seventeen or eighteen others simply returned the manuscript with a rejection slip. Giles eventually returned it to Marion who put it in a drawer with other unpublished efforts. She had been content then to get on with her children's books and her archaeological work and the children's books had proved a success until 1968 when Dent told her that the market had changed and teenage sex in high rise flats was the order of the day rather than historical adventure. She persevered, however, with *Peregrine's Gold, The Boatman's Boy* and a third which was not in that same series which she called *The Memory Well.* Then in the early 1970s, Giles decided to ask for *Dark Twin* again because Alick Bartholomews of Turnstone Press was launching his own imprint. Alick also took *Argyll: the Enduring Heartland* on board but Marion's ideas for a biography of Alexander III got nowhere with him. It was 1973 before *Dark Twin* was first published and it came out in 1975 as a paperback which horrified her not only because of its lurid cover but because it contained a surfeit of typographical errors. It was a book which sold around the world, puzzling many, enslaving others.

The first bite at *Alexander* came in 1989 but the publisher died before anything could be settled and she was out in the cold again. She revised the biography, but when she again began sending this manuscript off, it met with the same negativity which had first greeted *Dark Twin* – but for reasons more damaging to Marion's self worth than the rejection of *Twin,* a book she agreed was 'either loved or loathed' and that sometimes she was among those who loathed. Her dreams may have been the substance of *Dark Twin* but her heart and soul had been invested in *Alexander III.* Mainstream publishers turning it down she could understand – it was a serious, well-researched history not some blockbuster of a historical romance – but she was deeply wounded when Edinburgh University Press wouldn't even look at it because she wasn't an academic and Stirling University liked it but wouldn't risk its fledging reputation by publishing work from someone who had 'no letters'.

One of her closer friends of these later years, the QC Ian Hamilton who as a student was one of those who liberated the Stone of Destiny, was an encouraging mentor in that Sysyphus-like struggle which so many times saw her pushing the boulder of her manuscript up to the top of the mountain only to have yet another ambivalent publisher flick it back down again. In 1991 she had sent the manuscript of *Alexander* to Ian, who as the author of *A Touch of Treason* knew the market for historical books. He also admired Marion's writing, but when he saw *Alexander*, he was distressed to see she had frequently abandoned her own compelling narrative style in an attempt to meet the criteria of those academics who were so callously turning her down. With great generosity of spirit, he went through the book line by line, sometimes being harshly critical, at others exclaiming joyously in the margin:

> Oh lovely lovely, My Dear Marion... This is sheer Marion Campbell magic – sentence slips into sentence and I can feel the wind in my face...

Apologising for his 'insolence' in suggesting that she rewrite some passages, Ian wrote to her in November 1991 '... my view is that it is a great, indeed a major book' and added: 'Between the bits of erudition this story sings.' He scolded her for not reminding readers of historical detail she took for granted as common knowledge and was the essence of tact in reminding her to give sources:

> Marion your scholarship makes me weep with joy. Where on earth did you come across this gem – this atom of delight. Your footnote does not say.

Her own footnote on *Alexander* was to say:

> I have been tinkering with this book for too long, and I have made conscientious efforts to exclude an over-subjective approach. Now, I am told, I have been too impartial, and have offered no general assessment of my subject's character and personality... I still feel I'd recognise him the moment he walked into the room.

After interviewing Marion about her research for this opus I wrote in *The Herald*:

> 'Marion Campbell has lived with Alexander III for more than four decades'. She chuckled at the impertinence. She knew more about this man than many women know about their husbands and she wasn't going to give up on him.

> But then, her research for every piece of work she did had always been meticulous. She made notes on the first edition of *Wide Blue Road* pointing out that the Viking boats of the thirteenth century had fixed figureheads rather than the removable ones prevalent in times of peace. For *The Squire of Val*, she used architectural drawings of the chapel where Richard spent the night on watch. When it came to *Alexander III*, no stone remained unturned in her search for accuracy and a letter to the National Museums of Scotland asking for help with the coins and seals of the reign was typical of her attention to the most minute detail. But above all, Marion was a great storyteller, and that was the quality Ian Hamilton believed she had put aside in trying to please the academic publishers.

Marion's income in the early 1990s was in its usual shaky state and it was a godsend when journalist and author Jim Crumley, her close friend and admirer, persuaded the photographer and publisher Colin Baxter to give *Argyll: the Enduring Heartland* another whirl. Re-reading the 1977 version she realised the archaeology was twenty years out of date and set about rewriting it. It was the version she preferred – 'except, and it's a big exception, for the several serious misprints', she told Michael Davis some years later.

She had reason to remember these mistakes painfully:

> I was in the middle of its proofs when I found my dear Mary dead in bed one morning.

Mary's death on April 10, 1995, was not simply devastating emotionally: Mary MacLachlan, the Kilberry neighbour whose friendship stretched back to the days of Mrs Sandeman's ill health, came over to the castle that sad morning and Marion told her she had no idea how she was going to cope. Cope she did, however, finding comfort in turning Mary's writings for *Kist* into a book. Mary had written some delightful pieces about her childhood on Jura. Ever modest, it took Marion's chivvying to have them appear in the Antiquarian Society magazine. Now Marion undertook to give them a wider audience with evocative illustrations by the wife of Mary's nephew Sim under the title *When the Years were Young*.

Work was her saviour in the post Mary months – even the disheartening struggle to get *Alexander* into print. Jim Crumley and Billy Wolfe each tried to put *Dark Twin*, a book which enthralled them both, back in the bookshops in 1995 and this intensity of goodwill from her friends must have kept her afloat in the dark days after Mary's death. The loss of her friend of 63 years made 1995 a hard year and even a letter from Colin Baxter with a cheque for £300 saying how delighted he was with her reworking of *Enduring Heartland* could not have brought the same satisfaction that it would have done just a few months earlier. Even so, by the end of the year she had received another cheque from Baxter for £642.26p for *Heartland* sales and she was feeling relatively well off, given that Mary had left her part of an annuity as well as enabling her to live on in the cottage.

And then in 1996, the tide of Marion Campbell's lifelong hardships, and stuggle as a writer for acceptance, seemed at last to turn. The cause of a ripple of excitement was the arrival that February of some Americans at Kilberry. An American woman named Charner Wallis was yet another of the army of *Dark Twin* fans and she had asked friends who were visiting Scotland to trace the book's author. An actress with producing aspirations, she wanted to turn the strange Celtic tale into a film.

Jim Crumley wrote to tease Marion about being on first name terms with Mel Gibson before long and confirmed that the famous wrestling bear Hercules was still alive and living in central Scotland. He also knew where wild boar were raised. These would be essential bit part players for a film of *Dark Twin*. Giles Gordon, with whom Marion had parted company over the non-publication of *Alexander*, had come back into her life to try to have *Dark Twin* republished, and the idea of a film of the book was exciting the imaginations of Marion and Jim Crumley alike. In truth, however, Marion was more excited by Ian Hamilton's suggestion for yet another publishing possibility for *Alexander* and by the prospect of Giles Gordon finding a new publisher for her now out-of-print children's books. It had been a tough winter and she'd welded herself to her dilapidated old typewriter with its jumping keys and flighty ribbon to try to shake off her sadness.

On February 20, Jim Crumley wrote to her:

> I'm delighted to hear you have worked your way out of your depression, and you're right, it is the only therapy worth a damn. I'm particularly pleased that *Alexander* is alive and well again.

By April, he was writing:

> So you're going to be something big in the movies, the sideboard groaning under the weight of serried Oscars and Baftas! Splendid news! I would cheerfully gatecrash the Kilberry Inn gathering at the drop of a hat. . . You would certainly want someone to talk telephone numbers with Hollywood. . . I hope fervently that the whole project bears fruit – it will be no more than you deserve.

This letter preceded a meeting with Charner Wallis and teased Marion about the prospect of high powered Hollywood wheeling and dealing. As it was, at the end of April, Giles was wondering 'whatever happened to that American film person?' because there had been no contact with the agency's film department. Jim Crumley wanted to know what was on the cards, too, having practised his drawl and 'John Wayne walk in front of the mirror'. Marion was less concerned whether a movie would result, and more with the Mary Sandeman book, with the SNP's policy of independence in Europe, with her gout and arthritis and with the fact that her Baxter edition of *Enduring Heartland* had yielded no more cash.

By September, the Mary Sandeman book was published, despite many difficulties – and the American connection had been rekindled. A flurry of letters from friends demanded of Marion who was Charner Wallis? What was she like? and were her intentions honourable? Marion wryly commented that it was 'a pity to be "discovered" late in life' and sent off *Alexander III* to John Tuckwell, an Edinburgh publisher, saying:

> I would like to make one last attempt to get it into print – but I balk at yet another full rewrite without hope of publication. Yes, I am indeed that despised animal the 'amateur historian', but I am also a professional writer and I can, and will, work to a publisher's advice as to length and presentation. I have no letters (having gone into the Forces

instead of University in 1939, and having had no chance to remedy the omission since then).

Alexander was Marion's obsession. Charner Wallis's obsession was *Dark Twin* and Marion's children's books. The American had devoured all of Marion's published work and came back to her in October hungry for more. She wrote from 122 North Orange Drive, Los Angeles, confirming terms and conditions in which Marion assigned the film rights for *Dark Twin* which, in obfuscating legal jargon, Charner 'intended but was not obliged to adapt into a motion screenplay'. Marion was to retain the book publishing rights. Charner would pay a deposit on November 15, 1996, and a large number of US dollars on the first day of pre-production of 'said motion picture or on 1st July 1997, whichever is earlier'. The contract was long and complex and Marion was annoyed that it referred to English law – she was governed by Scots law, she pointed out in the flurry of other amendments and corrections which went flying back and forth across the Atlantic between her agent and Charner's legal people.

Charner then set out her intentions for *Wide Blue Road, Young Hugh, Squire of Val* and *Lances and Longships.* She planned four motion pictures and Marion was to receive another deposit on November 15, more on March 30, 1997, and still more dollars on the first day of pre-production of each of the four screenplays or on 1st March 1998, whichever was earlier. This contract was signed by Marion and Charner on November 3, 1996.

A Durand cousin wrote about all this excitement but congratulated Marion on her scepticism: 'How wise of you to be cautious about buying your Rolls!' Marion's concerns were still the Sandeman book, a piece about her childhood for a Save the Children fund-raising book – and by far the most important issue in her eyes, John Tuckwell's interest in *Alexander.* At the close of 1996 Charner Wallis had paid cheques for the rights to Marion's four children's books and *Dark Twin.* Even allowing for the fee due to her agency, Curtis Brown, Marion was – possibly for the first time in her life – approaching a Christmas she could celebrate without penny pinching.

None of this Hollywood business could deflect her from the work she considered essential and indeed, she saw it as much a means to allow her to work on the *Depredations of the Campbells* as a precursor to actually seeing her written work on celluloid.

This freedom perhaps gave her the sense of wellbeing she needed to go in May 1997 to the opening of the Kilmartin House museum. She had spent several years advising Rachel Clough, one of the founders, and offering exhibits to the new project, recalling the lessons learned at Auchindrain. She was an honoured guest at the opening party and assured her friends that all was well on the film front. She had received enough warnings to be cautious. An exiled Scot, Judge Willie MacCrea from New York State, with whom she exchanged lengthy letters for many years about matters political and historical, told her: 'Southern California is not called "La La Land" for no reason at all. It is likened unto a bowl of granola: what isn't fruit and nuts are "flakes".' Armed with this plethora of advice she was well prepared in June 1997 for the invasion of film people and she had the pleasure of discussing the need to spread payments of tax out over three years because her income had jumped so impressively.

But in typical fashion, it was a campaign against quarrying near Kilmartin which threatened archaeological treasures that was uppermost on her agenda. She may have been approaching 78 but she intended to inspect the site when work there recommenced. She even offered some of her new found wealth to the archaeological team charged with ensuring that no finds were disturbed by quarry work and told them:

> I have long felt and preached that the upper terraces of the Glen should be given much more attention! I worked on the Brouch an Drummin site long ago. Now unfortunately I am far too decrepit to be any help on the site, but if I could help in another way I would be glad to do so.

Tarbert castle was also still an issue for Marion in September 1997, and she seemed to leave others to feel protective of the books scheduled for filming. Jim Crumley hoped that she was managing to keep 'a tight rein' on the 'excesses of the Hollywood clan' while keeper of the Clan Campbell records Diarmid Campbell, then working in

America, worried that accents and vocabulary might stray too far from west coast Scots.

In all this flurry of activity, there was just one shining beacon for Marion. The contracts for the proposed films may have been lucrative by comparison with her previous genteel poverty but in terms of self worth, the most significant contract which Marion had ever signed was the one with House of Lochar to publish *Alexander III*. She was being urged to complete the analysis of the *Depredations of Clan Campbell* and to get down to writing an autobiography, but from her perspective, these were peripheral projects. Her *magnum opus* was complete, accepted by a publisher (House of Lochar was also to republish *Dark Twin* and her children's books after a deal with Scottish Children's Press did not come to fruition) and with not a word about her lack of 'so much as a BA'.

Many letters were flying to and fro between Giles Gordon, Marion, Charner Wallis and her lawyer Abigail Payne and there was puzzlement about the lack of filming activity while more and more options on Marion's books were sought – even on those never published, like the *Red Fox Cub* – but Marion simply felt buoyed by the whole process of being back in the thick of publishing activity. She dashed off stiff letters of complaint about badly typed manuscripts, confided her impatience with the film people in letters to Giles and despite increasing immobility was delighted to have a book signing for *Dark Twin* at the Tarbert Heritage Centre. In the November of 1998, she wrote:

> On top of that two long out-of-print children's books are due out again early next year, so all this plus *Alexander III* is going to keep me spinning until the filming starts again in April. Not bad for my 80th year.

Not bad at all, and she was clearly able to hold her own in the face of high powered Hollywood bargaining. A letter to Giles Gordon on December 1, 1998, scribbled rather forcefully on his own typed letter to her, insisted that the *Red Fox Cub* was not filmable – 'and I have told CW so' – and of *Memory Well* she added that she had 'often told CW I want, and intend, to rewrite this book'. She was bandying film terms about 'outline treatments' and 'options' as if she had been in the movie business all her days and she was certainly not going to allow liberties to be taken with her work.

Although Charner Wallis had crossed the Atlantic in pursuit of *Dark Twin,* the book with which she had been so taken as a student in the 1970s, it was *Wide Blue Road* which seemed to be heading first for the cinema screen and the local and national papers in Scotland recorded the fact. Marion and Charner were the subject of many interviews during this new wave of Marion's celebrity but Marion was still more concerned to assist *Alexander III* through the process of publication than to see her books on screen. She had told everyone it was now completed after forty years of research, writing and rewriting, but she could not help continuing to tinker to make it perfect. In January 1999 she finally tracked down the music for the wedding song performed for Princess Margaret of Scotland and King Eric of Norway in 1281. Charts were still to be finished and not one distant relative of the Scottish king was to be omitted from numerous family trees.

Ill health continued to be her enemy, but as always, she put up a fight. She refused to allow the shingles she suffered in the early part of 1999 to prevent her opening the Birlinn Bar at the Loch Fyne Oyster Bar – a local co-operative venture which fitted completely with her ideas of equality, ecology and local economy. Nor did the illness stop her communicating with academics interested in the Auchindrain museum – and certainly it could not get in the way of celebrating the return of a parliament to Scotland after 300 years.

Eilean Mor, Columba's Cave, letters to the *Scotsman* about the furtherance of Scottish interests, the tying of loose *Alexander* ends – and still she could find time to write a lengthy letter to her old nanny Rena, in her nineties but still able to take an interest in the progress of her charge from so long ago. 'My dear Miss Marion,' she replied, 'What a nice picture in the *Herald.*' She asked if Mr Campbell at the castle was the great grandson 'of Mr Archie who was such a nice gentleman and was a judge in India for many years' and hoped she would enjoy the book launch of *Alexander III* at Kilmartin museum. 'I'm sure you will look very smart in your new suit,' she reassured her. Once a nanny, always a nanny, even if the charge is 79 and the nanny 93.

The nice mannered little girl with the waist length hair was now, however, a woman with an edge to her tongue and seven decades of sticking up for her rights behind her. And when Charner Wallis asked for a sequel to *Dark Twin*, wanted to 'leave out the gloomy bits' and work towards a happy ending, Miss Campbell of Kilberry had no need of anyone to fight her corner. The words 'no deal' appeared in emphatic capitals attached to the conditions she charged Giles Gordon with seeking in the continuing quest for acceptable contracts.

She pushed all thoughts of such annoyances aside, however, for the long awaited *Alexander III* book launch on Saturday, October 23, at Kilmartin House. It was a fitting scene for the occasion. The museum in this picturesque village five miles to the north of the Crinan Canal reflected Marion's archaeological work and her support for David and Rachel Clough, the founding trustees, as they had brought the place together. A room in Kilmartin House was dedicated as the Marion Campbell Museum and many of her books found a home there. Magnus Magnusson, the television personality and recorder of Norse history was her choice to launch the book. Donny Henderson Schedlers, an American story teller who had been working in Kilmartin Glen for some time, read the story of Margaret, Alexander's queen – and the history of the king whose reign began as a child when his father died in Argyll was at last in the public domain.

Marion Campbell of Kilberry was very excited that day. She had a crommach made as a gift for Magnus Magnusson and was determined it would be a secret. It was carried from the Kilmartin Hotel, where she was to stay overnight, with much mirth on her part as she realised a shepherd's crook was not something to be hidden easily. She fussed that everything should be perfect, because this was her night of nights. The woman who claimed to be of the line of Diarmid, whose family had occupied Kilberry Castle for four centuries, whose grandfather was convenor of the earliest County Council of Argyll and who herself had driven 100,000 miles around the county during her ten year archaeological survey and with Mary Sandeman tramped over 3,000 miles of bog and hill to reach its most remote treasures, was reaching the most important milestone of her life.

There are those who would argue that recording 640 archaeological sites, 200 of which had been discovered by herself and her companion Mary Sandeman, was Marion Campbell's greatest achievement. At that moment at least, she would have disagreed. She had failed her entrance exam to Oxford and told her mother she had let her down again. She had left the WRNS sick and dissatisfied. She had been forced to pare back a five-farm estate to 18 acres and then retrench further into a gardener's cottage. She had been told young people no longer wanted to read about adventure and she had no contact with the reality of their lives. She was dismissed by academics because there were no letters after her name.

Yet here she was with the most talked about historical biography of the year being launched in an award-winning museum with a library named for her. This was the book which gave her the status she had sought all her adult life.

But even then, though her heart was with *Alexander* in the thirteenth century, her mind was racing ahead to the twenty first. As Alasdair Carmichael had written in the *Scots Magazine* of February 1972:

> Her interests and concerns are much more bound up with the living than the dead; with the future of Scotland than with its past.

The struggle to have *Alexander* published had been a cruel one. Marion once said: 'Writers don't become – they just are,' but this book had been a difficult task and Sir James Fergusson, author of the only other scholarly work about Alexander, the 'zealot for peace', had urged her to tackle it. Her reasons for persevering were not all personal: she didn't only want to prove her own worth but Scotland's. Alexander was the king who developed Scotland into a coherent and independent Scottish nation. The nationalist Marion insisted we must learn from the past to grow in the future and the fates conspired that she should complete it when there had never been a better time to put a book about a peacemaking, nation-building king on the bookshelves of Scotland.

If Charner Wallis had a role to play in all of this, it was to be the catalyst whose presence caused Marion's name to be once more in the public domain. Her interest in the children's books and *Dark Twin* meant publishers were interested in republishing. Giles Gordon worked extremely hard to ensure this would happen, but there had been a decade when Marion decided to go it alone and try to get *Alexander III* published herself. Now, there had been a happy outcome and the reviews were favourable. Susie Strachan, a young friend from the island of Luing wrote to Marion:

> *Alexander III* is wonderful. I could hear your voice throughout, strong and clear, making immense scholarship accessible and enjoyable. It's a rare work of history which manages to make characters come alive as yours did.

Lady Mary Macgrigor, whose articles in *Kist*, encouraged by Marion and successive editors, led her to becoming a published historical writer, believed Marion's contribution to Argyll and to Scotland was her dedication to making history – and archaeology – accessible. Another friend wrote in November 1999: 'Rather a'lot of success for an unlettered lady!' and the good wishes for the new millennium poured in with congratulations and plaudits. *Alexander* crossed the Atlantic and similar praise came from there.

But as 2000 got underway, Marion's health deteriorated. Many of the letters she received, like the cards for her eightieth birthday on December 16, 1999, were left in their envelopes. One of those apparent telepathic links caused Daphne Tullis, a friend from St Margaret's School in Edinburgh in the 1930s, to write to Marion on March 22. 'We last met in 1942,' she reminded Marion. She was impressed that at 80, Marion was starting a new phase of her life, what with all the publishing and republishing and potential film making, and she told her: *Alexander III* aches with the longing the Gaelic souls have for the land.' She hoped 'lovely Kilberry' would 'wrap her round with love and make every day precious and wonderful'. It was a warm thought and one that Marion needed as her health failed. This was still no frail old lady, however. A stick, an eye damaged by shingles and the pain of arthritis were not enough to keep her away from her typewriter, and on March 26 she was giving – and asking for – information about ring netting from folk historian Angus Martin in Campbeltown.

The saga of the children's books went on. Children's Press seemed likely to founder and Giles Gordon didn't want the books to become pawns in a bankruptcy situation. 'Let us speak (as opposed to pray)' he wrote to her at the end of March. But in April she was in Ward B at Oban Hospital. In May, when she was convincing friends and family alike that all was well, she received a thank you letter from a fellow patient who had found Marion an inspiration during their stay together in the ward.

It had been intended that Marion would have a short convalescence with Jilly Mackie-Campbell, one of the 'Coats girls' who had become neighbours when their parents, owners of the Paisley thread company, took property in Mid Argyll. Now Jilly and her older sister Lady Fiona Byatt, although a generation younger as girls, had become dear and supportive friends. The convalescence did not take place.

The staff at the hospital told callers that Marion was 'picking up nicely' but was 'still uncomfortable'. The end came as a shock to friends convinced she was invincible. Two days before she died, the writer and historian Neal Ascherson who wrote in her obituary in *The Herald*, that he had been visiting the same ward in the Oban hospital where Marion appeared to be in a coma. In conversation with the patient he was visiting, he said that no-one knew when a standing stone at Ballymeanoch had fallen. 'Well I know,' said Marion, pulling off her oxygen mask. 'It was in 1943, when a Shetland pony was sheltering against it from the storm. The poor beast was nearly scared to death.' She reassured Neal, who had first known her as a 'straight-backed woman with level blue eyes which never left yours, high colour in her cheeks, light chestnut hair, quick laughter', that her situation that June day was 'not as bad' as it looked. Neal wrote in that obituary that, unhappily, it *was* as bad as it looked and that 'Argyll lost its bard and its champion'.

EPILOGUE

Marion Campbell's death on June 13, 2000, was a blow to Argyll. She had been its champion and who was to fill the gap? Marion had not only served her county as a councillor for the old Mid-Argyll District Council for twenty years and then as chairman for four years until the reorganisation of local government in 1975 – she had put it on the map. To chart its archaeological past may have provided her and Mary Sandeman with ten of the most glorious years of their lives, romping around the county with their measuring tapes and tapping fag ash into burial cairns as they went – but this was also a vital and invaluable undertaking. Her historical charting of Argyll, through the papers of her own family and other primary sources, and her ability to turn that history into something alive has enticed visitors back to a corner of Scotland which had become neglected in the second half of the twentieth century. The Crinan Canal and the age of steam brought hundreds of thousands of people to Argyll in the era of Marion's grandfather and parents. Queen Victoria and Albert had put it on the 'Royal Route'. But the thrill of steamboat travel was eclipsed by cheap travel to warmer destinations and Argyll needed something more than scenery to inveigle people to visit. The discovery and exposition of a rich heritage provided that enticement and Marion Campbell of Kilberry was in great part responsible.

Although Professor Christopher Tolan Smith saw Marion as an amateur, even he admitted that she was 'was very good on the local scene, a great galvaniser of activity and enthusiasm' and he gives her 'nine out of ten on the local scene'. He said:

> Given that she had no professional training in the field she tended to get a bit out of her depth but there were no other people around to do anything. What should be recorded is that her major contribution was the Argyll Survey which

> she did with Mary Sandeman. It was a trigger for people like me and a benchmark for the Royal Commission. It was the ideal thing that two ladies could go out and do. She had all the contacts; the family network. She was certainly of value. She was very ready to contact people. John Coles was a lecturer at Edinburgh then before he went to Oxford. He worked with her. I am quite an admirer of her and her encyclopaedic knowledge of later periods. She was the classic amateur. She was in the wrong century really but was quite willing to step aside when she got out of her depth.

Others are more generous. Anne Kahane met Marion Campbell through her father, a representative of Glasgow University who was involved in the setting up of Auchindrain folk museum. Her father was impressed by the way Marion galvanised local people of influence, including the Duke of Argyll, the universities, and government departments to set up Auchindrain. Her father had known Marion from the early 1960s and saw her as the catalyst who made Auchindrain possible – a project which in its earlier days was a vibrant 'living' museum where visitors ate pancakes hot off the griddle while learning about ancient farming methods and crafts. Anne had been involved in many digs in Italy where she was doing academic work with the British School in Rome. She became a member of the Antiquarian Society of Mid Argyll and recognised in Marion her suspicion of the academic. She said:

> There was an edge to her but we got on. She wrote beautifully but it was her drive in getting the whole Auchindrain thing going which was a major achievement. As a means of interpreting a way of life of an earlier period it was very successful. She was very receptive to new interpretations. She channelled her enthusiasms and her objective curiosity and just got on with it – tremendously supported by Mary Sandeman.

Marion's enthusiasms, of course, included Scottish nationalism and she joined the SNP in 1961, which as Neal Ascherson pointed out in his obituary was a 'fundamental commitment made long before the party emerged from the political margins'. She was not a woman who jumped on bandwagons but one who deliberated deeply then made public declaration of intent – as she showed very clearly when she left the Scottish Episcopal Church to join the Presbyterian Church because she was convinced by the latter's egalitarian nature of the sharing of the Communion, writing a reasoned letter to the then canon at Christchurch in Lochgilphead explaining her departure.

Her nationalism stemmed in part from that ancient belief in Gaeldom that the land does not belong to man but that man is its custodian. She had a sense of duty and history which informed her political stance.

Ian Hamilton, Queen's Council and author, may well have admired these qualities in Marion but it was her writing rather than her politics which brought them together. He first struck up a correspondence when he published his *A Touch of Treason* in 1990 and sent Marion a copy. 'I was terribly impressed by her writing, particularly *Enduring Heartland.* It's a charming book. It is such compelling reading.' He confessed that if he had known she was a Scottish Nationalist he might have fought shy of sending her his new book 'because I find nationalists terrible, terrible bores – but she was an exception. She was never boring.' A friendship grew from that first correspondence and just as Ian wanted her judgement of his book, so Marion wanted his opinion of *Alexander III.* He said:

> She had a chip on her shoulder that she had never been to university. She had always wanted to be a professional historian and felt that she was at a disadvantage not having a degree in history and I used to tell her that one of the great handicaps that historians suffered under was having a degree because the degree focused on one particular point. She had the immense value of being steeped in history over not just a whole period but the whole of known history and beyond – and knowing the myths which famed historians reject because they only believe something if it's written down. Her imaginative interpretation may not have been entirely accurate but it painted the picture that history was about real people and not just about figures and movements of populations.

Of *Alexander III* he said:

> In the first draft she threw away every advantage she had in an attempt to compete with the historians. It was terribly difficult to say 'Marion, this won't do'. She put a tight corset on her imagination in that first draft.

Over tea at the cottage or in the Kilberry Inn, they talked of everything and anything, two witty intellectuals with a passion for words. Given back her confidence in her own style by Ian Hamilton, she went on to produce the book which would impress critics and historians alike. Ian had worried that his constructive criticism might lose him that friendship but felt the subject was important enough to take the risk. That Marion was prepared to rethink the whole book in the 1990s says much of her courage and determination. Ian Hamilton said:

> This was the book that was going to establish her as a historian among historians. Her chip wasn't hidden. It was said and felt very deeply and was something she had to be dissuaded from.

That the film versions of her books never happened during her lifetime was no surprise to Ian Hamilton, a man whose own book about the Stone of Destiny was under option for over a decade. Charner Wallis insists that her intention is still to pursue filming. She believed that her interest in Marion's books was the catalyst for the flurry of republications in the late 1990s and that publishers were jumping on her bandwagon. Ian Hamilton, whose passion for the place led him to Marion, sees her in less egocentric terms:

> She maintained her identity to the end as an author and articulate Scotswoman and we don't have enough of them. She was a great lump of yeast in the community and her influence continues.

When Martin Murphy, a free spirited craftsman, was commissioned to provide the shelves, table and chairs in the Marion Campbell library at Kilmartin House, he created furniture of great beauty from a variety of woods, amber, jet, arrowheads, flint and cow hides. He described it as a 'multi layered reminder of the 'enduring heartland' outside the window, about which Miss Campbell wrote so poetically'. He carved birds, mammals and plants on the shelves and chairs and on the underside of the magnificent table he wrote:

> This table was made during a wonderful idyllic summer in the year 2000
> By a captive spirit longing to be free.
> Trapped within these boards
> Is an entire sunlit landscape
> Untrodden
> But constantly dreamed of.

In 1942, Marion Campbell was in a naval camp in England, exiled from that landscape she loved so much. She wrote then: 'Of course, the ideal thing would be to live at Kilberry, do a bit of farming and a bit of archaeology and write – but I can't see that happening.'

But it did, Miss Campbell of Kilberry. It did.

Marion Campbell – the work

by David Adams McGilp

INTRODUCTION

In a writing career spanning five decades Marion Campbell published more than eighty works, drafted as many again and by the time her life ended, not long after the publication of her last book, she was truly regarded as a *grande dame* of Scottish literature.

The intricacies of her life are sensitively examined in the previous section of this book: family fortune and tragedy, ancestral responsibility, connections to ancient places and lost times, and these were also the themes of her literary endeavours.

From early historical fiction for children, through psychedelic historical fiction for adults to respected and treasured contributions to archaeological, historical and cultural bodies of knowledge, Marion's work was consistently characterised by an odd mixture of imagination and meticulous research. In her fiction, this style occasioned some uniquely complex plots and characterisations and curiously dramatic dialogues; and imbued her later historical works with an essence of sage conjecture.

Even if time and space allowed, it would be arrogant and presumptuous to critically dissect Marion's work chapter-by-chapter. Readers should decide for themselves whether a book is great, good or awful, and judge according to the quality of the writing, rather than their preference of genre. In this context, Marion could never be considered simply as writer of children's fiction, or historical fiction, or fantasy, or any single genre. Even the majority of her most respectable pieces have traces of cynical humour, and recurring themes and narratives populate elements of her work across all disciplines.

In any case, it would be impertinent and uncharitable to deny others the fullest intensity of experiencing Marion's writing for the first time by revealing plots; and those who re-read her work do so because they enjoy it just the way it was written. They neither expect nor need critical assumptions or opinions to assist them.

Nevertheless, it is a curious legacy. Marion Campbell's is a catalogue worthy of some exploration into the emotional and environmental conditions which motivated her writing, and an attempt to navigate thematic routes which reach across decades, centuries and millennia, real and imagined.

Of her published works, not all were books. There were articles published in *Kist*, the magazine of the Natural History & Antiquarian Society of Mid Argyll, *Proceedings of the Society of Antiquaries of Scotland*, booklets, guides, contributions, collaborations and editorships. All four novels published between 1957 and 1967 were for children. Her only adult fiction, *The Dark Twin*, was first published in 1973; the paperback edition appeared two years later and a second edition was published in 1998. Three of the original four novels have long been out-of-print but *The Wide Blue Road*, Marion's first book, was re-issued in paperback in 1999 to coincide with the expected release of an eponymous feature film.

In 1977 *Argyll: The Enduring Heartland* was launched to considerable acclaim. The book was reissued in 1986, and revised editions appeared in 1995 and 2001. Marion's *Alexander III: King of Scots* was launched at a grand event in Kilmartin House Museum in October 1999, eight months before her death.

The published articles included *Mid Argyll: An Archaeological Survey*. Written with Mary Sandeman, her life-long companion and collaborator, the survey occupied 125 pages of the *Proceedings of the Society of Antiquaries of Scotland* (Volume 95) in 1962 and was adopted as the prototype for the Royal Commission on Ancient and Historical Monuments of Scotland's *Inventory* series. Her contributions to *Kist* covered local, community and natural history, folklore, archaeology and even astronomy in articles which appeared from issue number two in 1971 to issue number 56 in 1998.

Marion Campbell will, of course, be remembered for more than her published work. For much of her life farming and estate management were daily routines; her affinity with Kilberry and allegiance to clan Campbell defined her local character; her membership of the Scottish National Party added vigour to district politics, and her willingness to protect the interests of rural communities has been an inspiration to two generations of Argyll's sons and daughters, and to those who choose to settle here. But if an individual must be judged by the tangible results of creative energy, then Marion Campbell will be a name which resounds beyond living memory for a body of work which has included seminal, authoritative and imaginative influences. That is not to say that all Marion's work should be accepted as exemplary in terms of content, style or consistent quality. She told stories, and as an exponent of that ancient and noble tradition she had some success. Her admirers were not confined to the Scottish feudal establishment or the academic and literary elite: children and adults from ordinary families could enjoy the adventure, fantasy, historical and atmospheric detail of these works just the same. Such is the appeal of Marion Campbell. Such is the mark of a great writer.

David Adams McGilp
January 2007

The Old Lady and the Books

I first met Marion Campbell by chance in 1992, in an optician's waiting room in Lochgilphead. I wanted to take a photograph of the setting sun from the top of the standing stone at Kintraw, and I asked her if she thought either Historic Scotland or the farmer would object to me leaning a ladder against it for maybe half an hour. She candidly advised me to 'just go ahead and do it', without a fuss; and be sure to let her see the results. I was flattered – she made me feel as though the endeavour was worthwhile. I never got round to taking the picture, but that encounter with Marion Campbell inspired me to take a keener interest in my surroundings.

I became a frequent and irritating borrower of materials from the Local Collection in Lochgilphead Library. Carolyn Mitchell and Ruth Morrison always trusted me with rare and expensive books: the Royal Commission *Argyll* Inventories – beautiful, precious things – *Statistical Accounts*, parish records and, of course, *Argyll: The Enduring Heartland.*

In the evenings when I was not socialising I was reading and learning about the places of my childhood: Tayvallich, Carsaig, Barnashalg, Ardnackaig, Dounie, and beginning to understand the significance of Kilmartin, Dunadd, Achnabreck, Keills and Eilean Mor. At weekends I visited these places, sometimes with friends, sometimes alone; so that I could experience them all over again, but from a new perspective.

The next time I met Marion Campbell was at Kilmartin House Museum, on the day of the launch of *Alexander III*. I had helped with the arrangements for the event, and during a run-down of the programme I told her about the influence she had on me. She was characteristically modest, and mildly embarrassed by all the attention.

Days later I was surprised and thrilled to receive a signed copy of *Alexander III* as a gift. I read it and was struck by the awesome scale of its undertaking, and surprised that the history of the thirteenth century could be so compellingly told.

Weeks later I wrote to her and asked if she would ever consider letting anyone write her biography. In a handwritten letter Marion replied:

> Dear David
>
> Thank you for your letter – and, inevitably apologies for a delayed answer (reasonable excuse for once – I was landed with proofs for the children's book reprint!)
>
> It's very flattering and gratifying to have someone wanting to do my biography, and thank you for that; but I have in fact been 'approached' by a publisher a couple of years ago. Giles Gordon my agent snorted and said, 'We could do better than that, I hope!' (referring to the publisher), but it set me thinking and I did do a little drafting for an autobiography-of-sorts. The project is still there, in the offing, and I still hope to give it a push some day.
>
> In the immediate programme I've (1) a million unanswered letters and (1a) a desktop edition of letters home from Jamaica and elsewhere, eighteenth and nineteenth century, from Kilberry connections; Mike Davis at the Library HQ is tidying up points of detail and we hope that can be wound up soon, under the title Letters by the Packet; (2) the Christmas once-a-year letters; (3) a fresh start, I hope, on a new edition of an 1836 print from a 1686 manuscript entitled Depreadations on Clan Campbell and their Associates in the Year 1685 (that's the short form of the title).
>
> This has of course been known, and read, for ages but never analysed; before I had to set it aside (because of *Alexander III*) I had identified most of the people and all but two of the places named, and done some work on livestock lists and household goods plundered – so with luck it won't need a vast lot more done. I also want to rewrite an unpublished children's book (contracted with Scottish Children's Press but far down the queue) which the film people want to do fairly soon. If I don't get it into order I

> risk having to produce 'the book of the film' accommodating whatever idiocies they have inserted! And they may want me to help with the immediately-next film after the one they'll be shooting early next year. Obviously I couldn't even give you interviews for a biography, let alone write an autobiography, in the first half of 2000. . .
>
> Meantime I look back on the Kilmartin event with a great deal of pleasure – and from what I hear, so do a lot of other people. Several of them had an eye-opener of the museum, so I hope it will have considerable knock-on effects.
>
> I'll look forward to seeing you some day, perhaps when the days begin to lengthen and we all start to emerge from hibernation.
>
> Yours very sincerely, Marion Campbell

A few months later Marion died, and so hopes of biography, films and new projects were laid to rest with her. Then, again by chance, Marian Pallister made frequent visits to Kilmartin House Museum, to research material in the Campbell of Kilberry archive for another book. We got chatting, and agreed that Marion Campbell was an extraordinary person, whose life and work were eventful and influential enough to warrant an affectionate tribute.

Argyll has had its fair share of literary characters and associations: St Columba, Adomnàn, Norman MacLeod, Kenneth Grahame, Neil Munro, John MacDougall Hay and George Campbell Hay, Naomi Mitchison, George Orwell, Angus MacVicar, Lorn McIntyre, Angus Martin, Alan Warner – some famous names, some great work. But none captured the quintessential Argyll in quite the way Marion Campbell did. There was as much passion and craftsmanship in Marion's pieces for *Kist* as was evident in *Argyll* or *Alexander III*. Marion always knew what she wanted to say, and had the skill, style and nerve to say it memorably.

During many years of stretched finances, Marion did feel compelled to write as a source of income. There were times when she bashed away on her typewriter, furiously connecting plot to character, checking her facts, editing, re-checking. Then there was the tense cycle of the submission process: synopses, draft chapters, acceptance or rejection.

There was the occasional delight of acceptance, followed by a frenzy of activity while final texts, illustrations and cover designs were discussed, print-runs and percentages worked-out, contracts agreed and signed. There were harder, darker moments when the sound of the mail van splashing through puddles on the drive heralded rejection: a succession of predictable excuses: not a big enough market, esoteric subject matter, too weird, too old-fashioned, too Scottish – always the helpful suggestion of another publisher who might be interested.

For years, when it came to publishers Marion played by the rules. She would write in the first instance to gauge interest from one publisher at a time. If prompted she would forward a synopsis, maybe a couple of draft chapters, sometimes ideas for notes or illustrations. It was quite common for her to wait months for a response, and if it was unfavourable, she would have to start the whole tedious routine from scratch. It was demoralising but Marion never felt humiliated. She knew she had the talent, and the determination, to take the germ of an idea and turn it into something outstanding: if a publisher showed no interest then it was their loss. It took a long time, but in the end she was right.

These scenes of creative exuberance and fiscal pressure were played out in an ancient, cold and leaking castle, surrounded by woods, fourteen miles from the nearest town, and between other commitments, amateur and professional. Marion and Mary needed to eat and sleep the same as every one else, they would do their best to keep warm, they would be welcoming and gracious to visitors. They enjoyed gardening, and when they were not otherwise occupied they would strike out for the hills and glens and forests in their quest to record Mid Argyll's monumental assets.

Marion was chairman of the South Knapdale Community Council and, of the Argyll constituency branch of the Scottish National Party. She was secretary and sales organiser of a crafts association which she helped initiate, and as a consequence one room of Kilberry Castle was given over entirely to knitting. She had managed three farms on the estate from 1945 to 1957: a considerable physical effort for a woman who suffered a back injury during an air-raid in Glasgow (rescuing a baby from a bombed building, it turned out); which caused her pain and discomfort to the extent that she was forced to give up sailing and fishing as hobbies.

She was instrumental, with Eric Cregeen, in the establishment of the Natural History & Antiquarian Society of Mid Argyll, and became its president. She wrote a play *The Civil War*, which was performed by the local drama club in the early 1970s, in her own words 'without any great impact'. And she messed around with poetry, 'not in the way other people are poets; I don't chisel away at it and put it together again.' She also claimed to have a certain distaste for the modern era: 'I don't so much enjoy the present day. I don't feel I have much to give children in that regard – the past is more interesting when you can write about Norsemen for example.'

Marion was certainly colourful, a little eccentric even; but the majority of her work was written with such candour and intuition that idiosyncrasies are overlooked, irrelevant, forgotten. She never wasted anything, and was eminently capable of modifying and refining ideas, settings and characterisations; a kind of honest recycler of her own research and original material, depending on the project. The recurring themes of birds, animals, trees and landscapes, royalty, nobles and serfs, kinship and folklore were no lazy or easy transfers. They were what she knew and felt; what she understood and loved; what she was best at.

But what use is a vat of knowledge without the ability to communicate it? Marion Campbell's command of language was exemplary, if a little archaic at times. Technically she was something of a pioneer – *The Dark Twin* was certainly *avant-garde* for parochial Scotland, even in the 1970s. *Argyll: The Enduring Heartland* has it all: economy of statement, depth of soul, humour, pathos, poetry and passion, atmosphere. Moments of genius created on the approach to old age, having cleared most obstacles from her writing path.

Recognition and success did not happen overnight: if they had, the Marion Campbell story would have turned out rather differently. In 1957 she made the decision to pursue a career as a professional writer. The decision was in part precipitated by the declining fortunes of the estate and the disposal of the farms; and in part by the acceptance of *The Wide Blue Road* for publication by J M Dent of London. Until then, Marion had regarded writing as a leisure pursuit.

In his affectionate bibliography produced for Argyll & Bute Council's Library Service, her friend Michael Davis describes the practice as 'a therapeutic release; a means of disengaging from farming worries.' This 'urge' to write was expressed by Marion in a wealth of unpublished material from tables of family trees and lists of royal successions to Gaelic notations and everyday observations. Each is complete and authoritative, characterised by relentless revision and evidence of thorough research. References and cross-references, footnotes and explanations appear everywhere, in neat handwriting, sometimes in ink, sometimes in pencil.

Throughout this extraordinary volume of material certain patterns emerge and minor obsessions become apparent. In many drafts precision, continuity and historical accuracy appear to take precedence over content or style. The reality is that Marion Campbell could afford to be preoccupied with such detail because she was genuinely capable of effortlessly elegant prose. Service men and women were forbidden from keeping proper diaries because of the security risk, but Marion kept a notebook and wrote essays. This example, in pencil, appears in a notebook dated August 8, 1943. Notably she made a single correction (nowadays mistakes and changes of mind are erased forever by the click of a mouse), demonstrating pride in the concept and confidence in its delivery – characteristics of Marion Campbell's style ever since.

On Facets

If an apple a day keeps the doctor away, it seems that an essay a day may avail against mental inertia; and unlikely though it is that the effort be sustained, at least one can make the attempt. Nothing justifies neglect, and the fact that one is temporarily unable to use a facet of the mind should not excuse one from keeping it polished. I have been fortunate in having more facets than I have yet fully investigated, indeed I have been tempted to think that there are too many and that I ought to occlude some of them (to vary the metaphor slightly), but I do not think that any justification could be found for deliberately burying a talent, even an apparently useless one. From this comes my habit of dabbling in every form of interest I encounter, and I thank God that hardly anything bores me. I am occasionally depressed to think how many openings will be before me when Peace returns, and for how few I have the knowledge necessary to develop them. The happiest choice would be to be anchored at Kilberry, where I could justify excursions into art, archaeology, music and literature as essential 'relief'. Once the die is cast and I am in a mould, it will be hard indeed to keep all the interests alive.

There is therefore all the more reason to plant seedlings from them now, before the tendrils have to be cut back.

The piece is frank, confident, and unapologetic. Marion affirms her gift for written language and acknowledges her eclecticism. Her mild reservation about the appropriateness of such a vocation is tempered by her resolution to learn, explore, understand and communicate. Part resignation, part dream, it explains her incentives with considerable skill and style. At the time her choice of profession was a real concern. Despite being educated at Queen Margaret Parents National Educational Union in Edinburgh, wartime service had prevented her from attending university and preparation for a career.

On the same day, in the same journal, she wrote:

On Familiar Spirits

For as long as I can remember, I have been finding my greatest pleasures in my own mind. This should make me an introvert, which I have heard is a narrow-minded and

> selfish condition. However, I hope I am neither of these, and indeed I justify the withdrawal to myself by the conviction that it has polished a lot of facets which would otherwise have remained inert. It is not so much that I go into the house and bar the door, as that I go in and go out again under the arches of the courtyard. I have never attempted 'to grow out of' the childhood world of pretence; but I have chosen certain habits and customs from there and made them grow up with me. Whether I could have done so single-handed, I do not know. Mercifully I have not had to try. So now, when I retreat into my courtyard of arches, there are fifty or so natures for me to choose from, and choosing one (or several) I can go out again into whatever situation has arisen to require it. In loneliness, laughter or sympathy; in anger, distraction; in homesickness, a home (Druim, Wood Manor or the Garden House); and everywhere familiar faces – Jill, Benny (always from the inside now, too much part and parcel of me ever to be seen objectively), Anthony with a birdlike interest, Pip and Ralph the good soldiers – the list could go on for pages. But there they are, the good company. They have averted, time and again, tears and darkness. I am not going to cut myself off from them now, though they may desert me one day when the inspiration fails. Certainly I've had my doubts, especially in adolescence when, like John Brodie, I thought 'it could not be right, it must be wrong' to live other lives so vividly. Now I don't think so; if the life of the body is circumscribed, the life of the mind must expand. So God rest ye merry, Gentlemen – your hold is not disputed.

Thus the double helix of empiricism and imagination is formed. On one hand the essay constitutes an early self-justification, and on the other it demonstrates ambivalence to criticism for cutting a new path. It is curious then, that for the rest of her life Marion would periodically be compelled to describe the surreal influences on her work and explain the geneses of ideas; and to defend her lack of a university degree.

The Wide Blue Road

Her outstanding junior historical novel.

Scottish Field March 1963

When this book was published in 1957, its thirteenth century scenes must have seemed incongruous to children of the post-war *milieu* and the embryonic space age. Ostensibly a thrilling Scots-Norse adventure, involving children being drawn near to danger by the selfish or misguided actions of powerful adults, this volume represents the first in what could be described as a series. (More than forty years later, Marion was to refute this during spirited correspondence between herself, her agent and the legal representatives of an American negotiating to buy the rights to several works.)

The principal characters are Richard (despised and virtually abandoned by his own father, gallantly adopted by a Scottish nobleman), Rolf (a captive Norse boy, wrongly accused) and Aithne (Richard's new guardian's daughter, impetuous and something of a liability). The formula is robust enough to encourage young readers, and the narrative has enough quiet authority to engender respect for the author's treatment of historical fiction. Interestingly Aithne represents the debut of a Marion Campbell trademark – the character whose name is not just difficult to pronounce, but difficult to work out how it should be pronounced. Marion was an acknowledged Gaelic scholar, and was possibly motivated to include the native tongue in protest at its omission from most mainland Scottish school curricula of the period. The story happens to be set in the time of the reign of Alexander III, King of Scots: a figure who held a special fascination for Marion probably from childhood, and certainly from the 1950s, until the publication of his biography at the end of the twentieth century. Children's fiction it may have been, but a life-long commitment to scholarly research in pursuit of believable narrative was established during her preparation for this work – a characteristic which awed and inspired generations of admirers, from children through amateur historians and archaeologists to famous writers and influential academics.

Yet *The Wide Blue Road* provides tantalising glimpses into Marion's worlds. Sir Hugh, Richard's mentor, is an Argyll man. Laird of *Dubhsgeir* on the rugged coastline he is at once feudal superior, moral arbiter and respected warrior. Naturally the unhappier circumstances of Marion's childhood, and the intermittent iconic presence of her beloved soldier father have some parallels with this adventure. More significantly perhaps, is the emergence of Hugh as a real hero of this tale, and of others to follow.

In 1994 Susie McGuire, an actress, broadcaster and performer, wrote to Marion, expressing her interest in adapting the unpublished *The Memory Well* for television. She was, coincidentally, a fellow Campbell, and child of former tenants of one of the Kilberry farms, and had enjoyed reading 'the Young Hugh books' and *The Dark Twin.* In her reply, Marion wrote:

> . . . in a roundabout way I was asked to send copies of the four Young Hugh *books* (I'm so glad you call them that), plus *The Dark Twin,* to Canongate for possible paperback reprint. . .
>
> I have two unpublished books besides [*The Memory Well*]; the last Young Hugh, called *Peregrine's Gold,* and an unrelated one called *The Boatman's Boy.*

All four of the books did, in fact feature Hugh, but *The Squire of Val* story is *all* about Richard. *Peregrine's Gold* was to feature some of the characters from *The Wide Blue Road* and *Lances and Longships*; but not Hugh, nor Richard. Marion's delight at Miss McGuire's description – '*Young Hugh* books' – is an acknowledgement of a reader's recognition of the *themes* of the books, rather than serialised plots involving one principal character. Indeed Marion herself described them as 'inter-connected, but stand-alone'.

A second edition was, in fact, published by the Scottish Children's Press in 1998, with cover design and illustrations by Andrew Hillhouse (which Marion considered were not only accomplished but also historically accurate). Marion admits to her own inaccuracies in her foreword:

> This was my first published book, forty years ago; there had been other attempts but they sank without trace, and deservedly. I began planning it ten years earlier on a visit to Sweden, after seeing the Sea History Museum in Stockholm. . . of course I had no reference books there, and made a list of things I must check. One haunts me yet: 'wasn't there some kind of sea-fight on the Clyde. . . ?' That's how little history I knew.
> The ignorance shows all through the book. . . Some of my blunders are excusable. . . I could pick holes, but that would only underline my mistakes. When old charts are handed out for classroom use they are stamped NOT TO BE USED FOR NAVIGATION; perhaps this book should be labelled NOT TO BE USED FOR HISTORY – but some parts are all right. . .
>
> Sorry about the mistakes, but don't let them spoil the story – it's not all so very far wrong.

To date there are no published records of complaints by 9–14 year-olds.

Unlocking the Treasure-House

In 1961 an article was published in the *Proceedings of the Society of Antiquaries of Scotland, Volume 94* entitled 'The Badden Cist Slab'. The piece was written by Marion Campbell, Stuart Piggott and JG Scott, and runs to fifteen pages of the august annual. The three contributors recounted the discovery and excavation of the decorated side-slab of a prehistoric stone coffin near Lochgilphead. While this was an important discovery (the slab was removed to Glasgow Art Gallery & Museum) the published work was unremarkable, following established principles of post-excavation reports, and sticking to the facts as they presented themselves. Marion, however, had been conducting her own investigations, with her friend Mary Sandeman, into the prehistoric monuments of Mid Argyll since 1954. *Mid Argyll: A Handbook of History* was published in 1962 (and the revised edition in 1974) – the everyman version of *Mid Argyll: An Archaeological Survey* published in the *Proceedings of the Society of Antiquaries of Scotland, Volume 95* the same year.

The *Survey* is generally accepted as the most significant and influential amateur undertaking in Scottish archaeology. One cannot pick up a book on the subject and fail to be confronted by references to *Campbell & Sandeman*: volumes six and seven of the Royal Commission on Ancient & Historical Monuments of Scotland's *Argyll* Inventory carry gracious acknowledgements of their contribution, and citations number several hundred. The volume of information is staggering: 640 sites visited and their features recorded, grouped according to monument type and accompanied by location details and a list of published references. That the exercise was completed at all is an extraordinary achievement – that it was undertaken by two local ladies criss-crossing the hinterland in a succession of disposable automobiles, and in their spare time, seems quite miraculous.

Some indication of their logical, methodical approach is evident from these extracts from the *Introduction* to the paper. This is unsentimental, matter-of-fact Marion Campbell non-fiction – clear, bold and embellishment-free:

> This investigation began in 1954 with an attempt to compile a list of known sites in our home area for our own information and for the use of the then newly formed Natural History & Antiquarian Society of Mid Argyll. We have restricted our work to the Local Government District, which is bounded on the south by Kintyre (and excludes most of the village of Tarbert Lochfyne with its castle), and on the north by a line drawn from the seacoast south of Loch Melfort, along the watershed to the southern end of Loch Awe, and thence from Braevallich, Loch Awe, along watersheds round the heads of Glens Aray and Shira, and to the shore of Loch Fyne just west of Dunderave Castle.
>
> Our method has been to compile a catalogue from all available sources: the Ordnance Survey 6" map; the List of Scheduled and Guardianship Monuments; the List of Ancient Monuments compiled by local informants for Argyll County Council and printed by them in 1915; published accounts; placenames, air photographs and local information. For each recorded site we prepared a looseleaf sheet and index card, and visited the sites as other commitments allowed. There are still some sites to be visited, and some entries in the catalogue are still not as full as we should wish, due to visits having been made, of necessity, in unfavourable conditions.
>
> We have recorded the National Grid position of each site located, checked any published data, re-measuring where this seemed desirable, noting changes since the published record, and recording any relevant information available. All measurements were made with a 6ft steel tape and a 33-ft surveyor's tape, as it proved impossible for two operators to handle a longer tape on exposed sites in bad weather. A prismatic compass was used for bearings, which have not been corrected as no deviation card is available; it should be noted that appreciable local deviation may be encountered in this area. . .

> . . . The catalogue is arranged in accordance with dateable sites elsewhere, without excavation except where stated; we offer it merely as a field guide and not as a final classification.

On reading it, it is hard to imagine either Marion or Mary having had any real doubt that they would satisfactorily conclude the project. Yet here is an odd contradiction: there is a trace of apology for imagined misunderstandings on the part of the reader, but Marion would never have agreed to the survey's submission had she not been entirely sure of its accuracy. This may have been the embodiment of Marion's disquiet at the prospect of academic disapproval, or simply a subliminal disclaimer. In any case she need not have worried – the paper was universally acclaimed as a great work, and archaeological academe recognised the pair as credible archaeologists. They may have been amateurs, in the truest sense, but they had achieved respectability. Published by HMSO, the authoritative *Argyll* Volume 6 was published in 1984 and had a retail price of £57, and Volume 7 cost £120 when it came out in 1992. *That's* respectability.

Lances and Longships

> A slice of Scottish history is vividly brought to life.
>
> *Glasgow Evening News* March 21, 1963

Hardly flushed with success (there were no remunerative advantages to the publication of the Survey), but modestly content with the proceeds from *The Wide Blue Road*, Marion submitted her second story featuring Richard de Brun and Sir Hugh of Dubhsgeir, and Dent published *Lances and Longships* in 1963.

Against the political desolation of the Norwegian defeat at Largs, Angus of Islay aspires to seize control of the Argyll islands. Opposing chieftans support a Scottish assimilation, and so the scene is set for noble adventure and murky power-broking.

Richard and Rory (*The Wide Blue Road*) enlist the assistance of Hugh and his house to harbour fugitives from this aftermath, and so unravels a convoluted story bristling with struggles for power and territory, tests of loyalty, battle scenes and chases, trickery, sovereignty, treaty and romance. Several of the characters who first appeared in *The Wide Blue Road* are to be found here: they are all a year older, fuller, more sympathetic. The historical elements of the thirteenth century background are integrated better with narrative and dialogue than in *The Wide Blue Road* – a sign that Marion was becoming more adept at fusing the precision of a historian with the creativity of a novelist. With the exception of serious articles published by the Society of Antiquaries of Scotland and her considerable contribution to *The Encyclopaedia of Scotland* (1994 J & J Keay [Eds.] Glasgow, Harper Collins), a vivid blend of fact and fiction characterised all her work. Her children's books were historical fiction; the only adult fiction was historical fantasy; the majority of articles for *Kist* contained playful anecdotes, and there were occasional references to the supernatural. Of her greatest works, *Argyll: The Enduring Heartland* is at once history, reminiscence and a collection of fictionalised occurrences. *Alexander III – King of Scots* is a biography, but written with the novelist's flair for evocative, and illusory, contemplation.

Young Hugh

Real characters, in real conflict.
The author knows exactly how this ship sails.

Times Literary Supplement June 1965

Between the publication of *Lances and Longships* and *Young Hugh*, Marion produced an exhibition catalogue called *Treasures of Mid Argyll: An Introduction to 6,000 Years of Settlement.*

Dent published *Young Hugh: A Year with the Norsemen* in 1965. The hero of *Young Hugh* is, of course Sir Hugh of Dubhsgeir (*The Wide Blue Road* and *Lances and Longships*), but, as the title suggests the story is set before the time of *The Wide Blue Road.* Set in the period 1241-1243, Hugh is just 14 years old, and living with his parents at Dubhsgeir (a castle on the western shore of Argyll), having recently undertaken apprenticeship knighthood training.

An old Norse friend of Hugh's father's sails in with his son (about the same age as Hugh), and they embark on a seafaring adventure out into the Atlantic and down the African coast, back to Ireland, Argyll, Orkney, Iceland and eventually to Norway. In the far north Hugh is exposed to his shipmates' complex family arrangements, contraband, shipwreck, betrayal and injury; and faces his first test of leadership. This high adventure, with teenagers in the mould of saga heroes, defying, influencing their seniors and ultimately getting their own way, is, on one relatively formulaic – countless authors have had success with young characters triumphing over parents, teachers and other figures of authority. On the other hand, *Young Hugh* demonstrates a maturity of character beyond his teenage years; the reason of experience often attributed to children and young adults who have broken with tradition, taken chances, taken risks. Could this be the persona of Marion Campbell, half-orphan, half-ingénue, itinerant chronicler and sturdy pragmatist? All things to all men: compiler of facts, story-teller, laird, stockwoman, politician, historian, poet, friend, upholder of ancient tradition, embracer of change. Marion was a woman brimming with ideas and incandescent with the desire to share knowledge of a past so overlooked.

The thirteenth century, and the reigns of Alexander III in Scotland and Haakon IV in Norway fascinated Marion. When drafting *The Wide Blue Road* in 1947, she found it necessary to research the Battle of Largs: by her own admission in the Introduction to *Alexander III* she was so startled by her ignorance of the period that she resolved to redress the balance. That she did is a matter of record, but the effect this research had on her fiction of the 1950s and 1960s was remarkable.

Marion understood the significance of the period, as well as she understood the significance of the age of Dalriada. Indeed the parallels between these historic episodes were not lost upon her, and she may have sought to inform readers of the definitive role played by Alexander III in her nation's history. Despite the end of the Dalriada era coming 400 years before Alexander's began, the overriding themes are startlingly similar: the power of politics over bloodshed, international influences and the unification of a recognisable Scotland.

Villainy, of course, had a part to play in Marion's fiction, as it did in real life. Beyond the best tradition of swashbuckling, younger readers are thankfully spared graphic descriptions of physical violence in any of the stories, but a sub-text of dark deeds, motivated by jealousy, acquisitiveness and megalomania, permeates each and every one. The perpetrators are usually family-members, aggrieved by the success or popularity of a sibling, or confounded by their hereditary place. There is no shortage of role models from history: sometimes Marion's characters emulate the selfish actions of kings or king-makers, at other times they shine as beacons of righteousness in a fog of deceit. Nobody's perfect.

The Squire of Val

> More exciting than any historical novel I have read.
>
> Barry Metcalfe *New Zealand Listener*

Marion felt it necessary to write a preface for this, the last story to feature Richard de Brun of Val:

> Some people may like to know exactly when this story is supposed to have happened. Although you will not find it stated in the book, the year is 1265. In that year Alexander III was King of Scots, Henry III was King of England and Louis IX was King of France. King Louis's youngest brother, Charles of Anjou, had just been given the Kingdom of Sicily by the Pope, and when the story begins Charles has just set off to win his new kingdom.
>
> Most of the characters in the story are not in the history books, apart from the obvious ones, King Louis and his courtiers. Mont St Michel is of course a real place, and you can go there today and see the buildings Richard saw, surrounded by later additions. Dubhsgeir in Scotland is Castle Sween on the map, and is well worth a visit. The barony of Val-les-Fougères is not on the map, but it must lie somewhere south of Mortain, north of Vitré, and southeast of Mont St Michel; so perhaps one might find it hidden thereabouts.
>
> The people in the story would talk Norman French, and I have used some odd words for which there is no handy English equivalent; in case you find these muddling, I have made a list of them with explanations, but I expect you can work out their meanings as you meet them. Like the date and the history, they don't really matter, but perhaps they may make the book more interesting and help to give the feeling of what it was like to be alive in Normandy seven hundred ears ago.

Hugh of Dubhsgeir makes his final, perfunctory appearance in *The Squire of Val,* published by Dent in 1967. Richard, a year older than he was in *Lances and Longships,* and further versed in chivalry, is recalled to defend Val, his father's seat. Inevitable adventure ensues, loyalties and mettle are tested, but a life-long ambition is realised in extraordinary circumstances. The format is familiar, and so are the characterisations: bright young things wrestle with internal conflict before running rings round their elders, supported by a cast of faithful feudal inferiors and estranged family, and motivated by ardent moral sensibilities.

Marion realised that Richard was getting too old to be of continued interest to the readership, so embarked on *Peregrine's Gold*; re-introducing some of the characters from the first two books, and re-visiting the spirit of Norse adventure in a Scottish historical tradition.

Critics could argue that the 'series' demonstrated an economy of effort: the same people doing roughly the same sort of thing between the same familiar places. One might equally surmise that Marion was consumed by material so thoroughly researched that she did not want to waste it. Either way, she would not be the first writer to be either published or successful for producing works of similarity. In many ways she was ahead of her time – today there are several creators of imaginary worlds and character sets who sell millions of copies and have become celebrities.

The Dark Twin

> Universally spirited, disciplined, pioneering. Miss Campbell's learning is unobtrusive, her touch light as a harpist's.
>
> *The Times* March 8, 1973

The Dark Twin is the story of Drost, black-haired child of the Middle Priestess, and the epic cruelty of his apprenticeship to serve as co-ruler with Ailill, his blond and treacherous sibling king. Drost's power of second sight is as much a burden as an advantage – the spirit of Yssa, his destined love, is lost, and confounding all endeavours to be united with his own soul. It is rich fantasy; beyond historical fiction, and alive with intrigue, secret knowledge and oblique characters.

First published by Turnstone Press in 1973, Marion Campbell's only published work of adult fiction so defies convention it is best described by the author herself. And it is, in an author's note which appeared in all editions.

> This book evolved at a time of deep anxiety and physical exhaustion, out of a series of brief waking dreams. Usually, when I am writing children's adventure-stories, I surround myself with timetables and factual notes; with this one, I floundered through the debris of a cutting-room floor from which there coiled up fragments of scenes and unintelligible dialogue. I was forced to make notes in order to get rid of these bewildering odds and ends; only after I had gathered a pile of loose-leaf pages could I be sure that the episodes had any connection.
>
> At that stage the characters were still nameless. I found the process of note-taking so tiresome that I assigned names, at random as I thought, to the main actors –

gleaning from Pictish and Dalriadic king-lists suitable barbaric sounds. The name 'Yssa' came out of the blue; I began to wonder (correctly, as I found later) whether I was dealing with a primitive version of Tristan and Isolde.

For several years I added more scenes, and at last began to arrange them into a coherent whole (if 'coherent' is the appropriate word). I had completed the section in which a sick man is found in a ruined hut, when I received a jolt which almost made me abandon the whole project; I read, in some review of a work on medieval literature, that 'behind Sir Tristram there stands the shadowy figure of Drust ap Tallwch the Tall'. Of this detail I could recall no conscious knowledge whatever.

Now, nine years after the book's completion, I can try to assess the material setting of the story. Its date is perhaps around 500BC. Iron is in use, though bronze is still the prestige metal; the burial-rite is cremation; new tribes have recently introduced new customs. The social organisation of kings, totemic tribes and wealth in cattle, is Celtic, with a substratum of earlier groups enslaved or dispossessed. The 'savages' of the closing section, who seemed grossly anachronistic when I wrote of them, might perhaps be some displaced pre-Celtic group reverting to a debased form of an ancient Mesolithic hunting culture.

Two notions, central to the story and still alive in folk-tradition, need explanation. 'The Apple Orchard' is a translation of 'Emain' Abhlach, the Arthurian Avalon. It was a kind of pleasant limbo, where spirits awaited reincarnation; Tir nan Og, the 'Land of the Young', was the Celtic paradise from which there was no return.

The concept of geas is more difficult to explain briefly. Geis (plural geasa) is something tabu; a forbidden act is geas. (The word is linked, perhaps, to the Latin *nefas*, 'do not, lest, . . . ?). Not only is it tabu, it is doomed to happen. A geis may seem absurd, a thing one is never in the least likely to encounter, but inevitably some chance will bring about the fated deed or meeting.

This book is in no way an attempt to construct an archaeologically probable picture of prehistoric life; it is a romance, in every sense of the word. I have tried to exclude

> any comment from a modern standpoint and to adhere to the atmosphere of pre-Christian times; beyond that, I have told the story as it came to me. Like any Celtic tale, the story has as many layers of meaning as an onion has skins; I leave it to the reader to peel off the layers, or not, as he prefers. 'It went by me, and I caught it as it flew'.

The description gives nothing away. The reader is prepared for confrontations with odd premises and unfamiliar surroundings. Mysticism, symbolism, myth, legend, fantasy and drama: retrograde science fiction to rival Clarke and Bradbury.

Richard Demarco and Alick Bartholomew
request the pleasure of your company at a party to honour
Marion Campbell of Kilberry
upon publication by Turnstone Books of

THE DARK TWIN

Tuesday, February 27th 1973
The Richard Demarco Gallery
8 Melville Crescent Edinburgh

In the *Glasgow Herald*, on April 14, 1973, Naomi Mitchison wrote this review:

> You might suppose, starting this book, that it was just another piece of fantasy fiction, very popular just now when we are trying every way to escape from an increasingly terrifying, ugly and mad world which has come into being without our willing it.
>
> How wrong you would be! The deeper I got into it the more certain I became that this was something which one might call intuitive history, and with which I myself am not familiar. I began to suspect this because of what I happen to have picked up about pre-Celtic and early Celtic civilisations. It all rang true. You can take it, I believe, that

> *The Dark Twin* is likely to be a more accurate picture of our forefathers in Scotland than any which have been produced, so far, by the professional historians.
>
> Not that Marion Campbell is anything but a professional in the sense that she is an archaeologist whose serious work had been done in the West of Scotland, especially Argyll. This means that, given an artefact, she knows how it will fit into the hand and into the life.
>
> Yet that in itself is not enough for the far more interesting warp and weft of intuitive history. This has to be based on very widespread evidence, coming from things, from places, from words, probably from music, possibly from the occasional illuminating dream, none of which tell a complete story, but all of which, in the process of falling through a sensitised or poetic mind, come together into a recognisable shape.
>
> This shape may well be, as here, a story of love and war and hunting, of tests and sacrifices, of friendship and treachery, of honey wine and barley cakes, above all of the Mother Goddess who later metamorphosed into St Bride, since Columba in his turn knew better than to challenge her.
>
> Simply as a story this is a good one, closely knit, full of clues and tensions, holding the reader all the time. Beyond that, with any luck, this book will lead you back into yourself and beyond yourself, down to the very beginnings of Scotland.

The first edition sported a cover by the illustrator Roy Tunnicliffe. A melancholy couple overlook a twilit landscape, their tender embrace enveloped by swirling robes and capped by windswept hair. It is the landscape of dreams, and Marion liked it very much. A Scottish Book Club edition was published by Club Leabhar, also in 1973, and in 1975 Alick Bartholomew of Turnstone Press agreed to the release of a paperback edition by Panther Books, an imprint of Granada.

Marion hated it. In a letter to rare book dealer Donald MacCormick, she enquires about locating copies of her out-of-print books, but explicitly warns:

> I do NOT want the abominable paperback (Panther) *Dark Twin* which is a mass of typographical errors, as well as

> having a jacket of manic inappropriateness.

And to her agent, Giles Gordon, in 1997 she wrote of the first edition:

> It really was miraculously fault-free – the appalling paperback, Panther, which I never even saw until it was out, amply made up for the hardback perfection! (Did you ever see that horror? I practically use the tongs to handle it).

Her complaints were, in part, about copy-editing and printing blunders which made it to publication. The narrative was complicated enough, and Marion felt that readers could be confused or misled by some of the more serious mistakes which made it onto the pages. Mostly, though, she was offended by the jacket design. A mysterious female humanoid emerges from the darkness above a scene of recent combat. A man in armour covers his eyes, or an injury on his face. He lies on a shield and holds a sword-like weapon in his other hand. Above him kneels another, virtually naked. His helmet and gauntlets are streamlined space age versions of gladiatorial armour; the gold and turquoise colour scheme matching the shield. He raises his head to behold the vision, dropping his club. Peter Jones's quasi-erotic airbrush interpretation owed more to high-camp interstellar fantasy than the inner-worldliness of the story, and Marion regarded the entire production with extreme distaste for the rest of her life. The episode demonstrates beyond dispute that the book itself was open to diverse interpretation, a consequence of which Marion was well aware.

A second edition was published by House of Lochar in 1998. This time its release was planned to precede the release of the film versions of *The Wide Blue Road, Lances and Longships, Young Hugh* and *The Squire of Val.* Errors in the text were corrected, a new cover was designed by Sophie Moorish (a mixed media montage of dark sky, rock-carvings, runic scrawl, relic and a haunting double-exposure image of a body kneeling, or crouching). Naomi Mitchison wrote this foreword:

> All historical writing has to be based on guesswork and on the ability of the writer to see deep into the period about

which he or she is writing. Even when the people of the past have left plenty of evidence, written or built or painted, we are still unsure. Go back even beyond this kind of evidence and build on the necessities of climate and soil and the probabilities that these people, our ancestors, had certain kinds of hopes and fears and perhaps love and thinking parallel to our own. When this is mastered there comes, at least for some people, the necessity to dream and plan, to let the words come and write them down. If the dream goes right, you may have made a true contact with the past and this, I think, has happened here.

The evidence in whispers and traces of a very early culture in the Highlands is there, but so deeply lost that only the poetic imagination can reach it and make it come alive. In this book tiny shreds of evidence have come together into the flow of a story which, to my mind, presents not only a historical possibility, but a gripping story. Are we entitled to make this jump into the past and write as though we had experienced it? I read it a time when I was working for two Government bodies; both the chosen members of these bodies and the civil servants who were supplied to us were deeply anxious to do whatever we could for the people of the Highlands, perhaps undoing some wrongs which had been done to them in earlier times. I read this book on my way to a meeting in Inverness. For a moment I noticed Marion Campbell sitting beside me. I had only just finished the book and it had me strongly in its grip. I began to ask her about the end of the book – I would like to have seen a few more firm knots tied. Perhaps you may feel that too. But she was, in fact, not there. Yet that was the strength of the writing. I wonder if this kind of thing may happen to other people who go head and shoulders under into this book.

How close, then, has she taken us into the past? It is not always an easy road. We have to adapt ourselves to certain other beliefs and ideas which may be under our own skins, unnoticed until they are called up. But do not fight them. Let them come and you will have an experience of the past – more especially if you are a Scottish reader – which will give you an extra eye for many things you will see and hear. Go to it then.

Sincere praise from a senior lady of Scottish literature – previous editions of the book may well have enjoyed longer runs and shorter periods out-of-print, had this endorsement accompanied them. Would it have meant as much a quarter of a century earlier? Or was the book ever (or always) judged by its cover?

In 1977, Roger Dean, the famous illustrator responsible for *Yes* album covers and a catalogue of teenage bedroom posters, suggested an illustrated version of *The Dark Twin.* Bound in any case by contractual obligations to Turnstone, Marion was concerned that a fully-illustrated version would be impossibly large and costly. Roger Dean then suggested a collaboration on another story, to be treated from the beginning as an illustrated book. Marion offered a work-in-progress *As I Heard Tell* – a collection of legends and traditional family tales – but the correspondence seems to have ended there and the project was never started.

The fact that *The Dark Twin* was in demand enough to justify a second edition twenty-six years after its first incarnation speaks for itself. During its wilderness years Marion received letters from people in far flung places, congratulating her on such a work; drawing parallels with their own literary or scholarly endeavours; always eager for information on the background to the story, sometimes offering scientific explanations for particular astronomical, climatic or archaeological details which appear in the story. These people were not cranks, and Marion remained in correspondence with some of them for as long as she was able.

ARGYLL: THE ENDURING HEARTLAND

> A love-book written by someone who is a poet, a delicately observant country woman, deep in local history and archaeology, above all a romantic writer.
>
> Naomi Mitchison *Glasgow Herald* May 5, 1977

In nineteen seventy-seven Elvis Presley died, a great fuss was being made over Queen Elizabeth's silver jubilee and Marion's concise but erudite booklet *Kilberry Church and Parish* first appeared. Turnstone published *Argyll: The Enduring Heartland* – one of two works for which Marion Campbell rightly deserves her place among the icons of Scottish literature. The first edition carried a foreword by the Duke of Argyll, and line-and-wash illustrations by Frances Walker. A limited, numbered edition signed by the author and the Duke of Argyll was available in a presentation slip case, the proceeds of which were donated by the publishers to the Inveraray Castle Restoration Fund.

Characteristically *Argyll* was far from straightforward: no mere folksy fondness for her surroundings; no simple account of cultural impact, rather a unique blend of fact and fiction, folklore and apocrypha, Gaeldom and anecdote, wisdom and poetry. The connectedness between Marion Campbell and her homeland is at its most palpable, most touching, in and between the lines of this work.

Marion's own introduction begins:

> This is a book about my home-ground.
> I wanted to call it *My Argyll*, because that is what it is – one person's understanding of past and present, one idea for the future – but the title sounded too selfish for a book that sets out to share, welcome, explain, introduce a beloved landscape to new friends.

Indeed no aspect of this 'beloved landscape' was overlooked. *Argyll* is a companion: a gloriously subjective and evocative guide to what makes the region special, rather than a catalogue of places and features.

Imaginatively-titled chapters paint vivid scenes of prehistoric humanity, Celtic mythological adventure, the glory of Dunadd and the legacy of Dalriada. Geology, geography and ethnography are established and reviewed between past and present, against a backdrop of dramatic natural beauty. Livestock, wild animals, birds, fish, trees and flowers are afforded prominent influence from the earliest times, in folklore, and the modern era.

Gaelic expression is celebrated, its status lamented. No hand-wringing woeful dirge, but a constant reminder of its impact on local culture; an understanding of its minority appeal, and warning against its neglect. Spirituality is explored and its marks explained: the dim past and modern fakery of druidism, the vigour and monasticism of the Celtic and early Christian churches. Sometimes there remains in this rich landscape a sacred site or even a church; sometimes the only clue is a placename.

The themes of Norse inheritance, territorial expansionism, royal succession and the power of kinship explode from the pages in energetic and passionate renderings of skirmish and battle, bargain and betrayal, power, glory and loss. Campbell histories and apportionment of estates are rattled off; the appeal and contribution of the island communities acknowledged; the infinite seascape revered, ancient and modern navigation of its routes respected. The spread of the gospel through the modern church, the unions with England, the Glencoe massacre, Jacobitism, the fifteen and forty-five, Clearances, campaigns and adventure, bards and heroes, travelling folk and enduring clan spirit – all exposed, explored, explained: all connecting or connected with the soul of Argyll.

In addition to the extraordinary depth of knowledge expressed in *Argyll*, and its moments of poignant poetry (Marion's own, and work by others), there are moments of warm personal reflection. A time of genuine community endeavour and apparent rural tranquillity is recalled with affection. The anachronism of feudal servitude is neither mourned nor ridiculed, but understood and accepted as natural change. This was a moderate and liberal view from a woman who twice inherited her West Highland estate, and had fond memories of her privileged ancestry.

The truly startling feature of *Argyll* is Marion Campbell's contemplation on the future, based on experiences of the recent past. The 1960s witnessed a dramatic increase in the popularity of the automobile, and opened up Mid Argyll in particular to trippers not arriving or passing through by boat. This trend increased in the 1970s and 1980s, as dramatic improvements were made to principal access routes from Glasgow (A82 Dumbarton to Balloch, Arden to Tarbet; A83 Arrochar to Inveraray and Inveraray to Lochgilphead).

In addition to visiting population increases, settlement in Argyll generally rose as young professionals relocated from central Scotland and elsewhere, eschewing urban career progression in favour of self-employment in a flourishing rural economy. Many of these settlers first discovered Argyll as holidaymakers, and were motivated to move permanently into the area by lifestyle choice, in a practical demonstration of ultimate experience consumption. New wealth was created during this period by, and in response to, improvements to the hospitality and leisure industries, local government reform and aquaculture.

There was widespread refurbishment and extension of existing hotels and the construction of new ones; creation and expansion of static caravan sites, self-catering units and emerging marina facilities. Sub-regional government headquarters grew, and new-build housing increased to accommodate the influx of personnel. Salmon, trout, mussel and oyster farms on varying scales occupied most sea-lochs from around 1973-1990, intensively supported by subsidy in the early years from the Highlands & Islands Development Board.

Marion understood and tolerated these changes, but forecast, in 1977, a bleak demographic dominated by a settled majority, homogeneous, intent on imposing imported cultures and values on native populations. Rather than confront this fate with hostility, Marion sought at every turn to coach newcomers in the traditional Argyll ways. These are the legacies of *The Enduring Heartland* – shrine for the faithful; *vade mecum* for the soon-to-be converted.

After the book had been out-of-print for several years, and in response to growth in demand, Marion's friend Jim Crumley, journalist and author of *Gulfs of Blue Air: A Highland Journey* (Mainstream, 1997), persuaded Colin Baxter to publish the second edition of *Argyll* and the revised text appeared in print in 1995. The photograph of Kilchurn Castle on the original cover was replaced by one of Castle Stalker, and the foreword and illustrations were omitted altogether.

The third edition was published in 2001 jointly by House of Lochar and Kilmartin House Trust. Marion did not live to see the final impression, but had completed a full list of amendments to the text before taking ill early in 2000. Things which had bothered or embarrassed her: dates, references and translations, and passages which she felt needed updating were taken care of and the corrected text delivered to House of Lochar in the autumn of 1999.

Martin Gallagher designed a new cover, this time featuring a main photograph of Kilmarie Chapel at Craignish, other sites of scenic and historical importance, and a roughly contemporary shot of Marion herself. It was a picture she liked: taken by James C Williamson, she regarded it as a reasonable likeness and suggested its use on several publications and to illustrate certain articles.

This time the honour of writing a foreword went to Neal Ascherson, author, journalist and part-time local resident. The esteem in which Marion was held by eminent writers, and the timelessness of *Argyll* are succinctly summarised in his opening:

> There can be no replacing Marion Campbell of Kilberry, whose death in the year 2000 deprived Argyll of its leading bard and champion. But at least, in her honour and to our own comfort, we can bring back her best-known book.
>
> *Argyll: The Enduring Heartland* had a way of becoming unobtainable. In most countries, it is the mediocre writing which vanishes; in Scotland, for some reason, it is often the

> important books (like the novels of Lewis Grassic Gibbon, out-of-print for decades at a time) which turn into samizdat-like objects, passed from hand to hand in home-made polythene covers. First published in 1977, *The Enduring Heartland* sold out long before demand for it was satisfied; printed again in 1995 after years of clamour and entreaty, the fresh edition in turn was snatched up so rapidly that once more the book became something to be borrowed from a friend, or to be waited for in a long list of applicants to lending libraries. The lack of Marion can never be made good. But the lack of her book can be filled, and it is a privilege and delight to welcome it in its third appearance.

There should be a day, not too distant, when every secondary school pupil in Argyll should read the book. Its intuitiveness and eloquence have not faded in nearly thirty years. There is no reason to suppose that its spirit be any more dilute in the thirty to come.

Nineteen eighty-four saw the reissue of *Mid Argyll: An Archaeological Guide* and the 'Kilbride Kists' paper in the *Proceedings of the Society of Antiquaries of Scotland* (Volume 114). The latter was written with Graham Ritchie, one of Scotland's foremost archaeologists, respected lecturer and author. Between 1984 and 1993 Marion published eighteen articles in *Kist* magazine and others in the *Review of Scottish Culture* (Number 5), and *Journal of the Clan Campbell Society* (USA) (Volumes 17 and 20).

In 1989 Marion was commissioned to contribute to *Discover Scotland,* a collectible supplement to the Mirror Newspaper Group's Scottish *Sunday Mail.* Here she defines Knapdale: two parishes on the western edge of Mid Argyll:

> Few things annoy a Knapdale native more than to be told he lives in Kintyre (worse, 'in the Mull of Kintyre', a lumpy headland at the far end of a long peninsula – visible from Knapdale in most weathers, but so are Gigha, Islay, Jura, Mull and often Ireland too, for good measure). We are not particularly grateful to be swept in with Mid Argyll, either, for we have our own ideas.
>
> On a general map Knapdale consists of two spikey promontories and a bulge, all facing south-west into the sea between Loch Crinan and West Loch Tarbert. The Crinan Canal marks the northern boundary, and the main Tarbert-Campbeltown road the southern. Between the two long ridges lies Loch Sween and its secret inlets and sheltered corners, wooded to the waterline or opening sudden vistas; next comes Loch Caolisport, 'the harbour on the sound', though it offers only perilous anchorage; the swell of coastline that opens to southward is Caolislate, 'the side of the sound' (the Sound of Jura, which opens to the

Atlantic), until you come to the point of Ardpatrick at the mouth of West Loch Tarbert and look across to Kintyre. The east side of Knapdale lies along Loch Fyne and was almost uninhabited until the last two hundred years; it lacked any road until the 1790s, where now the main road runs. The old routes for men and cattle ran high through the central hills, curving westward around the shoulder of Sliabh Ghaoil 'the Forest of Love', once a royal hunting ground.

The whole area lies aslant from north-east to south-west, a jumble of lava flows and older rocks cooked and twisted by long-dead volcanoes, scarred and planed by glaciers. In places, especially in Caolislate, there is a terrace of good ground along the coast, now lying some 30 metres above the sea and edged by grassy cliffs. The good soil was left by melting ice, the terrace marks the slow rise of the earth as it was freed from the weight of ice, the cliffs were formed by the beating of the newly-deepened sea. Along the loch sides lie some of the largest detached rocks in Scotland, some with local tales about quarrelsome giants who threw them about – more evidence for the power of the glaciers which swept them along like pebbles in a stream and shed them hither and thither as the ice-carpet melted.

A landscape which has come through turmoil to calm is matched by a thinly-spread population which has survived its own turmoils – raids from the sea, armies marching to war, refugees, new would-be masters, incomers with new ways to be adopted or adapted or gently but firmly changed into the way Knapdale works. There are no long-established towns; Ardrishaig, which now straddles the eastern end of the Canal, grew from a small farming settlement on 'the thorny point' to a rendezvous for fishing boats and then, once it got its pier, to a port of call for the Clyde paddle-steamers that were the handiest form of transport we ever had. (Up to 1939 they were used like local buses, with people boarding them at Tarbert to talk business between there and Ardrishaig, or crossing to Rothesay for a bowls match.) Another village grew up at Crinan, at the western end of the Canal, but the only other settlement of any size is Tayvallich around its horseshoe bay; boats again, you see. It's amazing that we have not all grown webbed feet by this time.

Knapdale today lives by farming and forestry, fish-farming and tourism, though as you explore you will find some more unusual enterprises flourishing – a couple of boatyards, an artist's studio among the woods, a fish-farming research station which exports its skills worldwide. Most of us live in a thin scatter of houses along or above the single-track roads – houses positioned for shelter rather than outlook, few of them far above the sea. Many are on long-occupied sites though few are above a century old. The older buildings were low compact affairs with thatched roofs; as long as a fire burned on the hearth they were snug enough, but once the hearth was cold the thatch began to sag. Two hundred years ago, when the area held probably tenfold more people than it does today, there were plenty of hands to demolish a deserted house and build another from its stones and timbers. A hundred years ago, the great new idea was to replace thatch with nice bright red corrugated iron sheets – so cheerful, so labour-saving. The sheets came ashore, clanging, from the little coasters that brought coal and fertilisers to the open beaches. (These were the 'Puffers', Para Handy's craft, that replaced the sailing schooners and smacks.) Now we depend on deliveries by truck, along roads that were designed for horses and carts.

The district was probably over-populated for its resources in the eighteenth century, when there was a boom in cattle (largely due to heavy Government buying for the navy and army) and a rising survival-rate with the introduction of vaccination against smallpox. There were few, if any, enforced Clearances and none of the horrors experienced in other parts of the Highlands, but there was a steady drift overseas and to cities – a trend now reversing itself. Survival must always have been a matter of sheer hard work, although conditions were relatively benign along the coasts. The pattern of life changed slowly if at all from that of medieval times, a pattern set up by long-settled families who knew how to use every available resource, and altered gradually by 'incomers' of the distant past who brought new initiatives – frontiersmen, in a word.

To see how it happened, look at a map, or look out from a headland on a clear evening. This is not a barren outpost on the edge of nowhere, but part of the fringe around a fertile expanse of navigable water. To the south, beyond Gigha, lies a low line of blue hills – the north coast of Ireland, stretching from Kintyre to Islay. Back and forth over these waters have gone voyagers, from the earliest hunter-fishers to the men who brought lime and took seed potatoes home to Antrim in our grandfathers' days. Something not far from ten thousand years of influences, ideas, progress and produce has been carried to and fro as winds and currents served.

There are no spectacular prehistoric monuments here to rival those around Kilmartin, but enough to show that the countryside has long been settled. Standing stones and burial-cairns, hilltop or coastal forts, not to mention a rich tapestry of legend, witness to the age of human activity. New finds turn up all the time – potsherds in a drain, a flint arrowhead on the tyre of a forestry plough. There is no way to reckon how many boatloads have come and gone, each new arrival drawn into local arrangements with his ways adopted, or not, depending on how they fitted local needs. The old history books with their 'waves of conquest' are generally discredited today; distant rulers change, established communities adapt.

In historic times three episodes used to be presented as 'conquests', but a closer look shows they were no such thing. Around 500 AD an Irish prince established himself as Righ (King) of Dalriada with his centre (or one of them) at Dunadd in Mid Argyll. He took charge of the area mainly because it was already full of people linked with the older kingdom of the same name in Ireland, not because he could mount an invasion. He was quite exceptionally successful, for his descendents are the present Royal Family of Britain. The next wave, according to the old books, was 'the Vikings' or 'the Danes' (as those books called them). Certainly raiding fleets from Norway did scour the coasts, as they did in Ireland, England, France and down to the Mediterranean – but raiders do not leave placenames. Other Norsemen came to settle, to suffer from the raids and to stiffen resistance. 'Knapdale' itself is Norse, so are Danna and Ulva at the mouth of Loch Sween, so is Turbiskill near Tayvallich (which must mean 'Thorbiorn's Well' or the like).

The third episode is less well-known, though it left more lasting effects. Another Irish prince, a cadet of the northern O'Neill, established himself in Knapdale around 1100 AD and won the approval of the King of Scots, Malcolm II (grandfather of Duncan whom MacBeth killed). One son of that prince had his stronghold where Castle Sween now stands, and was ancestor of the MacSweens who spread to Mid Argyll and north Kintyre; others founded the families of Lamont, MacLachlan, MacEwan, and a branch of Macneill, among others. These families provided local leaders, but they did not and could not displace the people who worked the land or fished the sea.

By the fourteenth century the Lords of the Isles had overall control of the mainland coasts facing their heartland of Islay. They were good overlords who gave peace, prosperity and good laws. A green mound near Crinan – perhaps prehistoric – is called Dun Domhnuill, 'Donald's Mound', a law-mound where the Lord of the Isles himself heard appeals against his local underlings.

In 1492 James IV deprived the Lord of the Isles of his mainland possessions and ordered his Chancellor, the 2nd Earl of Argyll to install reliable tenants. Argyll put some of his kinsmen in place, but was killed at Flodden before he could complete his reorganisation; some of the older leaders held on for another century. The reorganisation used to be evident in South Knapdale, where the lands were divided into wedges of coast and hill like slices of a cake, its centre reserved as a royal hunting ground. The whole district was controlled from Tarbert castle, and was known briefly as 'Tarbertshire'. Today the fleece of trees obscures the old divisions.

Forestry is a major employer now, but there have been other industries. There were lead and copper mines, small shafts and adits worked by pick and shovel a century or two back, and possibly worked in much the same way as by prehistoric miners. Stoneworking was a local skill; there are beds of fine-grained blue-green schists which, as an old mason said to me, 'Carve like butter while the quarry-sap is in them'. There are several collections of fine medieval carved stones – two in re-roofed old churches, at Keills and

Kilmory Knap – but the finest of all is not in Knapdale. It is virtually certain that the two main slabs for St John's Cross in Iona came from the quarry at Doide near Castle Sween. When you consider that the cross was erected in the eighth century AD and that its stones must have measured, before carving, not less than 3.5 metres by half a metre for the shaft, and nearly 2.5 by 1.5 metres for the head – each block over half a metre thick – and that they had to be quarried undamaged and then shipped from Loch Sween to Iona by boat or towed raft, you begin to get some idea of the skills involved.

A local 'school' of carvers later worked in Knapdale, with their own style and designs, under the patronage of the Lords of the Isles. The sane patronage encouraged trade; one Kilmory Knap stone bears a portrait of a Lowland merchant, identifiable by his pleated tunic and round hat, and others show the broad shears that were used for trimming the nap of fine cloth. Beside him stand men in chainmail and longer quilted surcoats, with swords at their sides and ships at their feet – the men who kept the peace for traders; but at Keills across the loch, one of the MacNeills chose rather to be remembered by his harp.

Today there are no weavers at Kilmory Knap – the last of them died in my childhood – and there are more sheep than people in Knapdale, despite the loss of hill-pasture under trees. The main farming trade is still, as it has always been, in beef-cattle. Until 1939 the cattle were walked to market, along the public roads or by hill-tracks used for many centuries, travelling from halt to established halt some fifteen miles a day. In the hey-day of the cattle trade, the eighteenth century, droves from Kintyre came through Knapdale on a high trail that swung west around the shoulders of Sliabh Ghaoil, past places called 'the hillock of the tents' and suchlike. Islay and Jura cattle came in by sea to Keillmore, where there is still a massive stone pier, its surface of stones set on edge to give the beasts a grip as they landed. From thence a track led up the spine of the land past Tayvallich; in places the ground is still worn, and no wonder, for it was not a new road the drovers were using. At a couple of places it is marked by a tall stone – and at least one of them bears Bronze Age cup markings.

> From Tayvallich they went on to cross the Add at its mouth, where there was a boat to carry the drovers and where the cattle swam, wading into the river on broad paved fordways that are still visible. There was a great annual market at Kilmichael Glassary, beyond Dunadd, where the droves for Falkirk and for Carlisle were made up, and the experienced long-distance drovers picked the stock that would travel best. These were men of skill and substance, whose word was their bond, and who might be on the road until midwinter, selling and buying as they went and returning to account for every animal to its breeder. The droving trade lasted, in a limited way, into this century, though the coming of the railways and then of cattle-trucks on the road brought the end of it.
>
> A man I used to know – a practical, up-to-date man, not given to whimsy – was on the hill one fine afternoon when he spotted a stranger coming down a path to a ford. The stranger wore a round blue bonnet, and carried something – possibly a folded plaid – on his shoulder. There was something a little odd about him, and it was an odd place for a hill-walker to be, so my friend waited to speak to him and make sure he shut the gate. The walker came on, down to a fold of ground, but did not come out of it. It was all rather strange, for where could he have gone? My friend later asked if anyone else had seen the stranger, and was met by one of those silences. Eventually, to set his mind at rest, someone said, 'That would be the drover'. Nobody knows what happened to that drover, or why he walks down to the ford on a summer's day. Perhaps, like the rest of us, he is loath to leave the flowers and birds of Knapdale, even for Heaven itself.

Her contribution transcended definition. The qualities for which Marion Campbell's writing was respected manifest themselves in what is an intense, microcosmic version of *Argyll*. Knowledge, and the sharing of it; scholarship; fond memory of times and characters gone; a willingness to embrace the supernatural; the bonds of family, friendship and the land and the uncertainty of the future come together in the expression of a laudable, and heartfelt desire. Marion was anxious to educate younger generations and future custodians of this land in the everyday detail of its history, as much as to the enormity of its significance. Similar crusading tutelage permeates the Young Hugh stories: behind the high adventure was thirteenth century Scotland, and Marion made sure children would glean something of the period from the books.

The article managed to populate the landscape in the imagination. Marion resisted the temptation to write a guidebook entry; instead she focused on the folk element, characteristic agricultural practices and local customs. Nor did she produce an enthusiast's field book, but rather a work which could engender enthusiasm in general countryside visitors. While the physical nature of an area, its history and people all affect its appeal, Marion succeeded in capturing the spirit of the place. That is a rare talent.

In the winter of 1989 Marion agreed to comment on historical information compiled for inclusion in the (then) Nature Conservancy Council's prospectus for a proposed Marine Nature Reserve at Loch Sween. She was asked to check the content and accuracy of statements, and shed light on some particular aspects: Castle Sween, the community at Oib and the 'Spaniard's Cave'. She was also asked if she knew the origin, and correct spelling of the Faerie Isles. In the letter which accompanied her complete rewrite, Marion tells it like it is:

> . . . As to the Faerie Isles or whatever – it is a completely bogus name so spell it whatever way you like. The only named 'island' on the 6 inch map is is Eilean a'Brèine, where *brèine* is the genitive of *Bràin* = foetidness, stink (does it catch decaying seaweeds?) I fancy that Victorian picnickers re-named the place, after getting all those nasty dirty crofters moved out – so 'Fairy Isles' belongs with 'Temple Wood' and 'Prince of Wales Wood' as a monument best forgotten!
>
> If you can do anything to stop people calling 'the Ob', 'the Oybe', I shall be very grateful – I seem to have had some success, but it doesn't last. The place is 'the Ob' – pronounced 'Ope' as in 'open'; *Oib* is (again) the genitive form. It simply means an inlet, a muddy creek, and it may perhaps be another Norse name (Norse 'Hope' has much the same meaning – or 'Hope' may be a Norse borrowing from Gaelic; I don't know what the experts say about it). . .

> There was a large Mesolithic mound at Tayvallich, where the cists were found (at the top of the car park in the middle of the village) – but the excavator was not very interested. I think it must have been a campsite on the crest of a ridge, overlooking both Tayvallich bay and Carsaig – perhaps when the sea was higher. There is a very little of it left against a rock to south of the site – probably full of microliths, like the soil that had been spread over the cists. Pity it wasn't found when there was time to riddle the soil. . .

Marion clearly understood that there was a very real danger of imported ideology diluting, or over time supplanting those local traditions which she held so dear, and was rightly contemptuous of any repertoire which masqueraded as authentic.

The notes on pronunciation and spelling may seem pedantic, but her concern was real enough, and she felt it her duty to protect what she could from bastardisation. The memory of the prehistoric mound at Tayvallich was a gift of secret information: Marion had extraordinary powers of recall: facts, figures, dates, occurrences, people; and places. With Mary Sandeman, Marion visited and recorded hundreds of sites; some no more than a scatter of stones, a ridge maybe, or furrow, but each a feature of fascination and a tangible connection to our ancestors. *People* created these monuments and their descendents have a moral responsibility to preserve them.

The proposed Loch Sween Marine Nature Reserve never became a reality, and the prospectus has long been out of circulation. Here is Marion Campbell's contribution:

> All prehistory from the Mesolithic (8,000 years ago) is represented in Knapdale. Seaborne contacts with Ireland led by 500 AD to a colony from the Irish kingdom of Dalriada, which formed its centre at Dunadd on the Crinan Moss and achieved independence with the support of St Columba; thence it spread to rule Scotland through a dynasty ancestral to our present Royal Family.
>
> 'Knapdale', like Danna (Danes' Island), Ulva (Wolf's Island) and Scotnish (Scots' headland), is Norse, named by eighth to eleventh century Scandinavian settlers. An

> eleventh century Irish settlement led by an O'Neill prince brought MacMurchaidhs, MacNeills and MacSweens (whence Castle Sween). The MacDonald Lords of the Isles held Knapdale after 1315 to 1493 (when it was forfeited to the Crown); this was a prosperous time. A Gaelic verse counts 'three blessings of Knapdale – the cruives (fish-traps) of Crinan, the deer-traps of Cruach Lussa, the Black Mill (horizontal mill) of Coille-bharr'.
>
> Ravaged by seventeenth century wars, Knapdale recovered and flourished, but harsh economic conditions and the 1840s Potato Famine led to forced Clearances for sheepwalks – themselves now under afforestation. Much tradition was lost, but sea-based industry is reviving with the rise of fish-farming.

A very special skill is required to impart such a volume of information in fewer than 200 words. Eight thousand years of history, cultural and linguistic influences, the Celtic church and the birth of a nation, places, people, poetry, the cycle of change and the passing of eras are adroitly wrapped up and offered as a neat packet, which, when opened, explodes with the very essence of these wooded fjords. Knapdale in a box. So-called experts in heritage interpretation stretch their creativity and clients' budgets to the limits in vain pursuit of such eloquence. That's what makes Marion Campbell's non-fiction so remarkable: it is a whole, and enriching, experience.

Magnus the Orkney Cat

Marion had another dream, waking herself up by saying aloud 'the cat's name was Magnus because he came from Orkney.' Describing the occurrence to her friend, the painter Kathleen Russell, the pair decided to collaborate on a children's story.

Kathleen's father took the draft piece to Paul Harris, a publishing consultant, who arranged for Canongate Press to publish it in return for production costs. Had Jack Russell not contributed to the project, it is doubtful that *Magnus the Orkney Cat* would have been published in 1993, or at all. But it was, as a story for very young children: 172 words of text and 33 full-page watercolour illustrations. It is a book by Kathleen Russell ('Words by Marion Campbell') – a contractual oversight for which Kathleen and her father made repeated apology, but which didn't cause Marion offence. However her copyright was not protected in the deal, nor did she receive any royalties; and she made it clear that such vague arrangements would not apply to a sequel which was planned, but never completed.

When the Years Were Young

The Natural History & Antiquarian Society never persuaded Mary Sandeman to republish her articles for *Kist* in book form, but after she died her nephews gave permission, and Marion was given the job of editing *When the Years were Young*. She managed to include unpublished draft material as well as text which had been clumsily cut to fit the magazine, and the Society published the little book in 1995. Marion paid for the design and production of the cover, but was hurt and irritated by the omission of her Editor's Note, which was sent to the publishers but not printed.

> I thank Mary's Executors and the Editor of *Kist*, the magazine of the Mid Argyll Natural History & Antiquarian Society, for permission to republish, and the Ordnance Survey for permission to base sketchmaps on OS maps (mainly the 1906 revision). Especial thanks are due to the late Alan Campbell for all his work in planning and producing this edition, not least the maps, and to Mary's niece by marriage, Margaret Sandeman DA (Glasgow) for her excellent drawings – many based on family photographs.

Her desire to include this note characterises Marion Campbell's good manners and attention to the correct form; and her willingness to acknowledge the contributions of others.

The second edition of *Argyll* appeared on the shelves the same year. Marion's only wish was that Mary had lived to see the end product. Of course she had read the chapters as they came along, and there had been just time to add Mary's name to those of her parents in the dedication. *Gus an bris an là* – 'Until the day break', a quotation from the Song of Solomon, which continues 'and the shadows flee away' which is often used in obituary notices. Marion and Mary had been friends for sixty three years, sharing Kilberry Castle for thirty years and Druim a'Bhuinne for five. Their enduring friendship outlasted her combined relationships with her parents (Marion lost her father when she was eight years old, and she was 26 when her mother died); and it was hard for her to recover.

In 1996 Marion wrote an article for inclusion in Una Cochrane's *A Keen Eye: Fact and Folklore on Scottish Highland Cattle.* Her *Scottish Cattle in Prehistory* is an authoritative and appealing guide to bovine migration, husbandry, trade and breeding from around 8,000BC – 800AD. The piece has its speculative, even controversial elements, but was written with typical affection and affinity.

Those same years witnessed other dramatic changes. Between tracking down long out-of-print early works, drafting articles for newspapers and magazines, submitting synopses, gardening, housework and catching up with correspondence, exciting opportunities presented themselves.

The Orkney Press expressed interest in the re-issue of *The Dark Twin,* and in 1996 an American film producer called Charner Wallis tracked down Marion Campbell, having read and been profoundly affected by the book. She considered the story would make an excellent film, and so embarked on an energetic campaign to secure the rights. In the lengthy and lively course of contractual correspondence which followed, Ms Wallis's company, Fairbourne Films successfully obtained additional and subsidiary rights to motion picture versions of *The Wide Blue Road, Lances and Longships, Young Hugh* and *The Squire of Val,* and paid Marion significant amounts of money for the privilege. There was an initial *frisson* of excitement at the prospect of filming; there were pre-production meetings at Kilberry, production schedules drawn up, merchandising deals investigated and much attention by the press. But it never seemed clear where the bulk of production finance would come from, and those much-anticipated first days of principal photography came and went without action.

In the Spring of 1998 Fairbourne Films tried to acquire options on the unpublished *Peregrine's Gold, The Boatman's Boy* and *The Memory Well.* Marion wanted to wait at least until the first film was made before tying up any more books, and a moratorium was imposed on negotiations.

In the summer of 1997 Georgina Hobhouse of House of Lochar

wrote directly to Marion expressing familiarity with and admiration for her published works, and hoping to be allowed to publish a new edition of *The Dark Twin*. She also intimated a keen interest in Marion's biography of *Alexander III*. That same summer Marion signed a seven-book deal with the Scottish Cultural Press (Scottish Children's Press) for reprints of the *Young Hugh* books and three new titles – *Peregrine's Gold, The Memory Well and The Boatman's Boy*; and Mainstream approached her about the possibility of commissioning her autobiography. Things looked set to improve.

Alexander III: King of Scots

> The author's voice is a bardic companion.
> Susie McGuire *Scotland on Sunday* February 13, 2000

Marion Campbell started to pull information together for her *magnum opus* in the1950s, when she first began to write historical stories for children and wanted to research the Battle of Largs. This is a solid book in the grandest tradition; its bright yellow jacket somehow at odds with the gravity of the content, yet hinting at a fresh approach. It certainly commands attention.

In the middle of the thirteenth century Scotland was effectively annexed by England, but the Scots harboured ambitions of freedom and independence. On the death of Alexander II (in Argyll of all places) Alexander III was made king at the age of eight and betrothed to Margaret, Henry III of England's daughter, at ten.

It is common to find that people could not place the reign of Alexander III in history; if they recall anything it's that he was thrown from his horse and killed in Fife. Marion's knowledge was similarly limited when she first began to write *The Wide Blue Road,* but she was soon fascinated at the wealth of material available, and accumulated notes for nearly fifty years.

The main significance of the reign is its foundation for the Wars of Independence with England. The intervention of Edward I was precipitated by the death of Alexander's grand-daughter and heir, Margaret the 'Maid of Norway'. But Alexander managed to establish an era of prosperity which later generations remembered as 'The Time of Peace', in which the Isle of Man and the Western Isles became Scottish territories by treaty. Two major invasions were threatened by England but were never mounted: the only war in forty years was with Norway, which ended at Largs in 1263.

Marion evokes national events in church and state, buildings, foreign trade and social life, and provides valuable insights into Alexander's family connections, particularly with his father-in-law, Henry III of England. The text runs to 120,000 words: 24 chapters with notes, and appendices on the royal itinerary, Royal Burghs, monastic foundations, coinage, and the Treasures of Scotland reportedly removed from Edinburgh Castle in 1296. She provides genealogical tables to guide the reader through the intrigue of ancestry; maps to explain complex territorial arrangements and help pinpoint locations; and there are carefully chosen plates and illustrations. Marion explains the consuming affair in her introduction:

> In this age of specialisation it is a monstrous impertinence for an amateur to embark on historical biography. My excuse must be threefold, that there has been no recent study of King Alexander, that I have taken an interest in his life and times for forty and more years, and that I am writing, not for the professionals but for people like me who were taught little or nothing of their country's history in their schooldays.
>
> I grew up between two sorts of history. There was the schoolbook kind, lists of the kings and queens of England and events from Magna Carta to the Corn Laws, into which intruded such irrelevancies as the battle of Flodden, the execution of Mary Queen of Scots, and the doings of a romantic incompetent called Bonnie Prince Charlie. Against that there was kitchen-history, forever associated with the scent of baking, with Somerled landing his salmon before tackling the Norsemen, the Good Sir James Douglas, and the Prince (it was long before I connected him with the shortbread-tin 'Charlie'). From these ravelled materials I assembled an outline-notion of Scotland's past, always with the belief that before 'Bruce-and-Wallace' there was little besides Shakespeare's *Macbeth.*
>
> In 1947 I began drafting a first children's novel about castles and ships: the plot called for a sea-fight, and hadn't there been something at Largs? I was quickly horrified at my own ignorance that I got down to reading anything and everything about the thirteenth century; luckily that led me to Sir James Fergusson's *Alexander the Third,* a work of

> profound scholarship lightly handled.
>
> For years I followed the trail, visiting surviving buildings, assembling family-trees. I began to hope, as the children's books mounted up, that one day I might produce a fuller study. When the first volume of *Regesta Regum Scottorum* appeared in 1960 I told myself it would be madness to proceed without the volumes for Alexander II and his son; in 1991 it became clear that I would not be around to write at all if I delayed much longer, so here I am.

Characteristically conversational, stimulating and modest – her introduction gives no clue as to the insight and intuition demonstrated in the text of *Alexander*. His reign may have been peaceful, but Alexander's life was crowded with incident. Marion's infectious enthusiasm for a little-known king in a forgotten era is one of the book's greatest strengths. It is a biography which appeals to people who don't usually read biographies; a chronology for those who normally find history unrewarding. The book combines the wisdom of a fable (the cycle of destiny: responsibility and achievement, vulnerability and tragedy) with the immediate realism of a live news broadcast.

Alexander had a very long gestation, and the original manuscript underwent several revisions, rewrites and edits before its eventual publication. The book had something of a troubled career. Serious work on assembling the mass of notes into a biography started in the 1970s and Marion hoped that it would make it to print by 1986 (the 700th anniversary of Alexander's death). At the time she was represented by Giles Gordon at Anthony Shiel, but they parted company after the agency failed to arouse interest in the subject among London publishers. Canongate rejected the idea on the grounds that there would likely be an insufficient market for such a little-known subject. Stirling University Press and Edinburgh University Press refused to consider the text (on account of a lack of formal qualifications, Marion was convinced); Birlinn did not show any interest. Charles Skilton Ltd accepted the completed book and production was well advanced when Mr Skilton died. Marion accepted the camera-ready pages and page-proof index in lieu of settlement for breach of contract to publish.

The Orkney Press, already in the process of re-issuing the children's books and *The Dark Twin* all in paperback, took the material on, but progress was glacially slow and Marion asked for her manuscript to be returned in 1991. Marion's friend, Ian Hamilton QC, had read the manuscript and recommended it to his own publisher, The Lochar Press, who were tempted but turned it down as not economically viable. In 1996 Marion approached the Tuckwell Press, who accepted *Alexander III,* but the terms of contract could not be agreed and in the summer of 1997 there was still no publisher on the horizon.

Giles Gordon, reinstated as Marion's agent, but now working for Curtis Brown, negotiated with House of Lochar on the Isle of Colonsay, and the contract was signed in January 1998. Long-time friend, writer and broadcaster Magnus Magnusson made the introductory address at the launch of *Alexander III* at Kilmartin House in October 1999, and cited the work in his *Scotland: The Story of a Nation* which was published by HarperCollins the following year.

Marion Campbell died on June 9, 2000 leaving few ambitions unfulfilled. Her earliest curiosity about her immediate surroundings developed into a love of archaeology, and through her eagerness to share her knowledge, we have a better understanding of the wealth and diversity of ancient monuments in Argyll. Her specialist research into the thirteenth century produced lively and believable fiction which may yet make it to the big screen. Over time her obsessive fascination with period and detail enabled her to write authoritative and respectable articles, and culminated in the completion of her life's work; affording her a great deal of personal satisfaction and the rest of us an instant classic.

The themes she explored were revisited, sometimes after decades, but many of her questions remained unanswered. Philosophy is no stranger to ignorance. In many respects she was ahead of her time – the celebration of egalitarianism and denigration of intolerance and cruelty are as evident in her fiction of the 50s and 60s as in *Alexander III.*

She was capable of leading us to appreciate the connections between past and present, present and future; and her concerns for her own neck of the woods apply with equal emphasis to national and international affairs. Someday, somehow, she hoped, politicians, policymakers and the indigenous and settled residents might work together, sensibly and practically to create a sustainable future.

In a way she created sustainability for her books. The nineties were clearly her decade. Despite losing her dearest friend and leaving the castle for the last time, she was prolific. Amongst her unpublished material were a television drama *Roddy the Post,* several submissions to *Scottish Field* and the *Scots Magazine,* reworkings and expansions of *Kist* articles, a guest appearance on BBC Radio Scotland and the publication of the essay 'First Time on Any Stage' in *A Scottish Childhood.*

As if there wasn't enough to keep her occupied, Marion found time to meet other commitments: revisions to *The Memory Well, Peregrine's Gold* and *The Boatman's Boy,* a collection of emigrant correspondence from the eighteenth and nineteenth centuries (*Letters by the Packet*) and a gracious foreword to Rachel Butter's *Kilmartin*:

> Here are the keys of a treasure-house, layer upon layer. It is an honour to be asked to write this foreword, and also a chance to reflect on the changes I have seen.
>
> In the early 1950s I was farming and sharing my home with a life-long friend. Our parents had interested us in local history, and we kept meaning to visit the cairns and standing stones we passed on our way to market, if only to fill gaping holes in our knowledge. We made a list, and quickly realised there were far more places on maps than we had noticed, others suggested by placenames, others mentioned in books but unmapped. . .
>
> We began by knowing nothing, trying to educate ourselves; in the end the Society of Antiquaries of Scotland made me an Honorary Fellow. Those were good days, but we never imagined there would be a centre of excellence at Kilmartin as there is now (often as we wished for one), and a book such as this was not in our dreams.
>
> But you, you lucky people, you have it in your hands. May you have as much joy of it as we had in our wanderings!

The eventual publication of *Alexander III,* and the posthumous release of the third edition of *Argyll* confirmed Marion Campbell's literary immortality. With strong titles in print, and a catalogue of potential reissues it is hard to imagine her name disappearing from the shelves. It is ironic that recognition, success and a degree of financial security should come so close to the end of her life, after so many episodes of frustration, delay, desperation and long periods out-of-print.

Tidemarks

Marion Campbell made sporadic attempts to chronicle her own life, but was usually too busy with other writing commitments to contemplate it for long. In January 1979 she created an introductory chapter, and reproduced it in the autumn of 1995. She called it *Tidemarks*, the name she favoured for her autobiographical musings. It must remain forever unfinished, for this is as far as she got:

> The morning after a big tide the shore is clean. Far up, under the curling lips of the broken turf, lie the banks of kelp that hide plastic cups and the child's lost spade and the old shoe. From there to the edge of the whispering foam are only the miniature riverbeds where the sea has drained back, and the asterisk footprints of wagtails and ringed plover, and the fat triangular prints of ducks and gulls. All the rest is white sand, with here and there a little wreath of yellow seashells or a snow-white feather. Whatever was there yesterday has gone, under the seawrack where you may yet find it or out to sea whence it may return on another tide. It was here, and it is not. Yesterday there were barefoot prints and bootmarks, and a fishbox that somebody has carried home, and a bit of nylon net that was just the job for the garden; but to look at it now, this is as blank a beach as ever Robinson Crusoe saw.
>
> So I sit down on a gray whaleback of a rock and I try to fix those images in my memory, before the next big tide takes them all away and with them the remembering, dreaming mind. Perhaps some of them were never more than illusions, a gull's pacing that looked like a line of writing, a drowned body that turned out to be merely a lump of seaweed. While they were there they were worth a look, but they have gone and soon there will be new things to find, new stories to read, whether or not anyone comes to read them. The only certainty is that you never know what will turn up.

Acknowledgements

This book has been informed by numerous letters and documents and by many people. Our sincere thanks to everyone for their generosity with time, for allowing access to correspondence, notes, articles, manuscripts, synopses and reviews, which we can only interpret as their personal tribute to Marion Campbell of Kilberry. Sadly, Mrs Betty Durie died a few months after our conversation. People who offered their help include:

John and Charmian Campbell of Kilberry
Murdo MacDonald, Argyll archivist
Lady Fiona Byatt
Sir Ilay Campbell of Crarae
Sheena Carmichael
Michael Davis
Betty Durie née Learoyd
Margie Fletcher née Brown
Joanna Gordon
Ian Hamilton QC
Jonathan Howard
Helen Kenneth née Campbell
Anne Kahane
Sir William Lithgow,
Jilly Mackie-Campbell
Professor Sir Neil MacCormick
Lady Mary MacGrigor
Councillor Donnie MacMillan
Mary and Neil MacLachlan
Jane Nelson
Margaret Rickman née Lithgow
Charles Sandeman
Rena Sinclair née Mackay
Professor Chris Tolan Smith
Daphne Tullis
Charner Wallis.

Kilmartin House Museum and the Natural History & Antiquarian Society of Mid Argyll gave access to published works in the Marion Campbell Library.

Bibliography

1955 'Looking at the past around us'
[in *MacTalla,* Argyll teachers' magazine, Spring 1955]

1956 'The Natural History & Antiquarian Society of Mid Argyll'
[in *MacTalla,* Summer 1956]

1957 *The Wide Blue Road* Dent, London; Dutton, New York

1961 'The Badden cist slab' (with S Piggott and JG Scott)
[*Proceedings of the Society of Antiquaries of Scotland,* Vol. 94]

1962 *Mid Argyll: A Handbook of History*

1962 *Mid Argyll: An Archaeological Survey* (with M Sandeman)
[*Proceedings of the Society of Antiquaries of Scotland,* Vol. 95]

1963 *Lances and Longships* Dent, London; Dutton, New York

1964 *Treasures of Mid Argyll: An Introduction to 6,000 Years of Settlement*

1965 *Young Hugh* Dent, London; Dutton, New York

1967 *The Squire of Val* Dent, London; Dutton, New York

1971 'Tales from Auchindrain' [*Kist,* Vol. 2]

1972 'Magnus Barefoot & The Treaty of Tarbert' [*Kist,* Vol. 4]

1972 'Butterwort' [*Kist,* Vol. 4]

1972 'Harvest and Hallowe'en Customs' (with B Foreman and A Fraser) [*Kist,* Vol. 4]

1973 'St Columba's Cave' (with C J Young) [*Kist,* Vol. 6]

1973 *The Dark Twin* Turnstone Press, London; Club Leabhar, Inverness

1974 'The Battlefield of Carse' [*Kist,* Vol. 8]

1974 Mid Argyll: A Handbook of History (Revised)

1975 *The Dark Twin* Panther, St Albans; Dutton, New York

1975 'Kilberry Castle in 1857' [*Kist*, Vol. 9]

1976 'Note from Kilberry Rent Roll, 1750' [*Kist*, Vol. 11]

1976 'Rock Carvings at Dunadd' [*Kist*, Vol. 12]

1977 'Moth Note: Choerocampa Elpenor' [*Kist*, Vol. 13]

1977 *Argyll: The Enduring Heartland* Turnstone Press, London

1977 *Kilberry Church and Parish*

1978 'Meteors at Kilberry' [*Kist*, Vol. 15]

1978 'A Fresh Look at Auchindrain' [*Kist*, Vol. 18]

1980 'The Boar Hunt' [*Kist*, Vol. 19]

1980 'Early Crosses at Keills' [*Kist*, Vol. 20]

1980 'Cnochan Uamhach Megalithic Chambered Cairn' [*Kist*, Vol. 20]

1981 'A Professional Visit to Mid Argyll in 1773' [*Kist*, Vol. 21]

1981 'Another Kind of Cairn' [*Kist*, Vol. 21]

1981 'The Western Voyage of Alexander II' [*Kist*, Vol. 22]

1982 'Aspects of Industry in Mid Argyll' [*Kist*, Vol. 22]

1982 'Domestic Animals and the Law in Ancient Times' [*Kist*, Vol. 24]

1984 'Argyll's Contribution to Scots Law' [*Kist*, Vol. 27]

1984 *Mid Argyll: An Archaeological Guide*

1984 'Cists from Kilbride, Mid Argyll' (with J N G Ritchie) [*Proceedings of the Society of Antiquaries of Scotland*, Vol. 114]

1985 'Some 18th Century Dykers' [*Kist*, Vol. 29]

1985 'Eilean na Circe: First Impressions and Second Thoughts' [*Kist*, Vol. 30]

1985 'Psalms and Protests' [*Kist,* Vol. 30]

1986 'Kilmichael of Inverlussa : A Notable Discovery' [*Kist,* Vol. 31]

1986 'The Kilmahumaig Stone' [*Kist,* Vol. 32]

1986 *Argyll: The Enduring Heartland* (Paperback) Turnstone, London

1987 'Baravalla' [*The Highland Breeders Journal*]

1987 'Robert I and Tarbert Castle' [*Kist,* Vol. 34]

1988 'Argyll's Rising: 1685 and After' [*Kist,* Vol. 35]

1988 'Stray Items from Kilberry Castle Archives' [*Kist,* Vol. 35]

1989 'Haste Post Haste' [*Kist,* Vol. 38]

1989 'A Farm Manager's Cash Book' [*Review of Scottish Culture,* No. 5]

1990 'Campbell Settlement in Jamaica' [*Journal of the Clan Campbell Society* (USA), Vol.17]

1990 'Carnasserie Castle' [*Kist,* Vol. 39]

1990 'Idolatrous Images' [*Kist,* Vol. 39]

1990 'The Night the Sea Came In' [*Kist,* Vol. 40]

1991 'But Yesterday' [*Kist,* Vol. 41]

1991 'The House that Baxter Built' [*Kist,* Vol. 42]

1993 'Cup-and-Conundrum Marks' [*Kist,* Vol. 45]

1993 *Magnus the Orkney Cat* (with K Russell) Canongate /Paul Harris, Edinburgh

1993 'Letters from Canada 1834-1836' [*Journal of the Clan Campbell Society* (USA), Vol. 20]

1993 'The Faint Footprints' Part I [*Kist,* Vol. 46]

1994 'The Faint Footprints' Part II [*Kist,* Vol. 47]

1995 *Argyll: The Enduring Heartland* (Revised) Colin Baxter, Grantown-on Spey

1995 'When the Years Were Young' (Editor) Natural History & Antiquarian Society of Mid Argyll

1996 'Scottish Cattle in Prehistory' [U F Cochrane, *A Keen Eye: Fact and Folklore on Scottish Highland Cattle,* Busdubh Publishing] [*Kist,* Vol. 4]

1996 'The Rooky Wood' [*Kist,* Vol. 52]

1996 'Mistress Jean' [*Journal of the Clan Campbell Society* (USA), Vol. 23]

1997 'The Unseen Neighbours' [*Kist,* Vol. 53]

1998 'Local Defences' [*Kist,* Vol. 55]

1998 'Molly Molloy' [*Kist,* Vol. 56]

1998 'First Time on Any Stage' [*A Scottish Childhood,* Vol. 2, Save the Children/HarperCollins, Glasgow]]

1998 'The Old Woman and the Books' [*Journal of the Clan Campbell Society* (UK), November 25)

1998 *The Dark Twin* House of Lochar, Isle of Colonsay

1999 *The Wide Blue Road* Scottish Children's Press, Edinburgh

1999 *Alexander III: King of Scots* House of Lochar, Isle of Colonsay

2001 *Argyll: The Enduring Heartland* House of Lochar/Kilmartin House Trust

2004 *Letters by the Packet* Argyll & Bute Council Library Service, Dunoon

Index

A

Achaglachgach 49, 50, 52, 59, 68
Alexander III / *Alexander III: King of Scots* 18, 20, 23, 155, 171, 172, 180, 182, 184, 185, 186, 188, 191, 192, 193, 195, 199, 200, 206, 209, 210, 211, 224, 226, 227, 255, 256, 259, 260, 261
anxious mother 38, 53, 68, 89, 120
Arbuthnot, Ivy (father's cousin) 10, 12, 14, 46, 61, 62, 64, 74, 75, 77, 78, 79, 91, 92, 96, 97, 180
Ardrishaig 55, 69, 83, 118, 130, 156, 242
Argyll and Sutherland Highlanders 25, 182
Argyll County Council 37, 148, 221
Argyll: The Enduring Heartland 148, 170, 184, 186, 206, 209, 213, 224, 236, 239
arthritis 188, 195
As I Heard Tell 235
Ascherson, Neal (writer, historian) 196, 198
Auchindrain 17, 151, 152, 153, 154, 155, 190, 192, 198
Auxiliary Territorial Service (ATS) (Territorials) 13, 31, 80, 81, 82, 84, 91, 92, 93, 94, 95, 98

B

back pain 107, 174, 182
bad diet 183
Badden Cist Slab 146, 220
Bartholomew, Alick 184, 232
Baxter, Colin 186, 187, 239
Boatman's Boy, The 184, 218, 254, 255, 261
Bonham-Carter, Margaret 64
Byatt, Lady Fiona, née Coats (*see also* Coats, Fiona) 125, 131, 132, 196

C

Caledonian Ball 84, 90
Campbell, Archie (uncle) 36, 37, 42, 44, 47, 48, 49, 50, 51, 52, 55, 57, 59, 61, 62, 63, 65, 73, 74, 75, 79, 115, 134, 137, 145, 178, 180, 192
Campbell, Diarmid 190
Campbell, Sir Ilay 148, 181
Campbell, John (Jock) (*see also* father) 24, 25, 27, 31, 33, 40, 41, 43, 57, 59
Cambell John (heir) and Charmian 24, 131, 140, 180, 181, 182
Campbell, John Walter 15, 39, 117, 131, 138, 141, 177
Carmichael, Alasdair (writer) 174, 194
Castle Sween 227, 245, 246, 248, 250
childhood 43, 46, 61, 63, 86, 90, 134, 150, 189, 209, 216, 217, 218, 246
Clachbreac 161, 162, 163, 164
Clough, David and Rachel (Kilmartin House Museum founders) 155, 190, 193
Coats, Fiona (*see also* Byatt, Lady Fiona) 140
Coats family of Paisley 131, 196
Cochrane, Una 253
Columba Cave 155, 157, 159

Cove 157
Craighouse (Jura) 84, 90, 124, 125, 126
Cregeen, Eric 151, 213
Cruden, Stewart (inspector of ancient monuments) 157, 162, 165, 175
Crumley, Jim (writer) 173, 186, 187, 188, 190, 239

D
Danna 244, 249
Dark Twin, The 18, 140, 148, 149, 150, 170, 173, 174, 183, 184, 187, 189, 191, 192, 193, 195, 206, 213, 218, 229, 231, 232, 235, 254, 255, 259
Davis, Michael (librarian) 135, 145, 155, 183, 186, 214
Dean, Roger 235
Demarco, Richard (artist) 174
depression 90, 98, 110, 142, 188
Diarmid's Grave 52
Dunadd 157, 174, 209, 237, 244, 247, 249
Duncan, Neil and Ileene 155, 183
Durand, Marion, (*see also* mother) 24, 25, 26, 27, 28, 29
Durie, Betty née Learoyd 54, 69, 78

E
Eilean Mor 17, 19, 155, 166, 167, 168, 169, 170, 171, 192, 209
Ellary 157, 160, 175
Episcopal Church 59, 99, 170, 199
Eton 27

F
father 42, 43, 44, 45, 46, 49, 50, 51, 52, 53, 54, 57, 63, 66, 68, 69, 73, 81, 82, 83, 94, 99, 101, 103, 108, 125, 126, 130, 133, 140, 143, 147, 160
Fenton, Sandy 151
Fergusson, Sir James 194, 257
Finchairn 58
Ford Hotel 58, 59, 64

G
Glasgow Art Galleries and Museums 165
Gordon, Giles (literary agent) 183, 187, 191, 193, 195, 196, 210, 233, 258, 259
Gordon, Joanna (friend and historian) 135, 172, 173, 177, 182
gout 182, 188
Graham, Angus 172

H
Hamilton, Ian QC 103, 164, 184, 186, 187, 199, 200, 259
Harrow 27, 51, 52
Haviland, Beryl 59
health/ illness 39, 65, 68, 69, 79, 80, 89, 92, 93, 95, 97, 98, 111, 112, 113, 114, 120, 126, 133, 153, 159, 160, 171, 179, 180, 192, 195
heart attack 182
Henderson, Colonel (estate factor) 59, 62, 74, 75, 91, 92, 96, 99, 102, 108, 110, 114, 118, 121, 122, 123, 127, 128, 138, 149
Highland and Agricultural Society 28
Highland Cattle Society 28
history and prehistory 135, 155
Hobhouse, Georgina 254
Howard, Jonathan 139, 177
Hunterian Museum 156, 158, 159, 165

I
Iona 157, 246

K
Kahane, Anne (editor) 198
Kelvingrove Art Gallery & Museum 161, 165
Kenneth, Helen (cousin) 55, 73, 75, 78, 146
kidney stones 112, 120, 123, 130, 142, 153
Kilberry piping book 52
Kilberry stones 136, 137, 151, 165

Kilmartin House 155, 190, 193, 200, 206, 209, 211, 239, 259, 264
Kilmichael Glassary 247
Kintyre Antiquarian Society 136, 163
Knapdale 45, 91, 161, 241, 242, 243, 244, 245, 246, 247, 249, 250

L

Lances and Longships 145, 163, 189, 218, 223, 225, 228, 233, 254
Learoyd, Betty 82, 83, 84, 87, 93
left-handedness 53
Ling, Jeanne (ATS officer) 83, 84, 93
Lithgow, Lady 100, 117, 123, 133, 137
Lithgow, Sir William 152, 160, 161, 162
Lochgair 65, 66
Lunga 157

Mc / M

MacArthur's cave 159
McCall Smith, Dr Bryce (family doctor) 58, 63, 65, 123, 129
McCallum, Eddie (last Auchindrain resident) 153, 154
MacCormick, Sir Neil (historian and nationalist) 142, 166
MacCrea, Willie 190
MacDonald, Murdo (Argyll archivist) 24, 135, 181
Macgrigor, Lady Mary 195
McGuire, Susie 218, 256
MacKenna, Severene 156
Mackie-Campbell, Jilly 196
MacLachlan, Neil & Mary 167, 179, 186
MacPhie, Gunnie 174
Magnus the Orkney Cat 251
Magnusson, Magnus 193, 259
marriage, attitude to 130, 133, 144
Martin, Angus (local historian) 195
Memory Well, The 184, 218, 254, 255, 261
Mid-Argyll: a handbook of history 146
Mitchell, Carolyn 209
Mitchison, Naomi 211, 231, 233, 236
Morrison, Ruth 209
mother (*see also* Durand, Marion) 40, 42, 43, 46, 48, 49, 53, 54, 56, 61, 62, 63, 64, 65, 66, 68, 69, 72, 73, 74, 75, 78, 80, 81, 82, 83, 84, 85, 86, 89, 90, 91, 92, 93, 94, 95, 97, 98, 101, 102, 103, 107, 109, 117, 118, 119, 120, 121, 123, 124, 127, 130, 132, 135, 137, 141, 144, 149, 150, 181, 194
motherhood, attitude to 125
Murphy, Martin (artist) 200

N

National Museum of Antiquities 134, 142
National Museum of Scotland 153, 158, 165
National Register of Archives (Scotland) 165
natural history 73, 137, 206
Natural History & Antiquarian Society of Mid Argyll 163, 206, 213, 221, 252, 264

O

Oban cattle sales 37, 38, 125
Ormsary 73, 100, 117, 155, 160, 161
overweight 89

P

Parents' National Educational Union (PNEU) 11, 53, 67, 72, 78, 80, 145
Peregrine's Gold 184, 218, 228, 254, 255, 261
Piggot, Stuart 146, 158, 220
Port Sonachan 156
Proceedings of the Society of Antiquaries of Scotland 146, 206, 220, 241

R
rates (local authorty taxation) 10, 52, 66, 132, 134, 170, 178
religion 89
Risga 159
Ritchie, Graham 160, 241
Robertson, George (estate trustee) 62, 65, 72
Royal Commission for Ancient and Historical Monuments 136, 156
Russell, Kathleen (painter) 157, 251

S
Sandeman, Charles 122, 123, 125, 143
Sandeman, Mary 72, 79, 82, 86, 90, 93, 100, 104, 105, 106, 107, 110, 117, 118, 119, 122, 123, 124, 125, 132, 137, 138, 139, 141, 142, 144, 146, 149, 150, 153, 157, 158, 159, 160, 161, 163, 164, 169, 174, 178, 179, 180, 181, 183, 186, 187, 188, 193, 194, 197, 198
schooling 53, 64
Scotnish 249
Scott, Jack 161, 162
Scott, JG 146, 220
Scottish Cattle in Prehistory 253
Scottish National Party (SNP) 19, 20, 142, 143, 155, 166, 167, 168, 169, 171, 188, 198, 207, 212
servants 31, 38, 44, 45, 51, 52, 66, 96, 152
shingles 192, 195
Sinclair, Rena (nanny) 49, 52, 53, 54, 59, 61, 63, 64, 67, 68, 69, 90, 152, 192
sleeplessness 90
South Knapdale Community Council 212
Squire of Val , The 145, 163, 171, 186, 189, 218, 227, 228, 233, 254
St Margaret's School 11, 67, 71, 72, 73, 78, 118, 119, 135, 195
Strachan, Christian (headmistress) 71, 79
Strachan, Susie 195

T
Tayvallich 169, 209, 242, 244, 246, 247, 249
teenager 14, 25, 86, 89, 146, 150
Tolan Smith, Chris 159, 161
Tuckwell, John 188, 189
Tullis, Daphne (school friend) 72, 195

U
Ulva 244, 249
Upper Largie 156

V
Victorian values 30

W
Wallis, Charner 18, 187, 188, 189, 191, 192, 193, 194, 200, 254, 264
When the Years Were Young 186, 252
Wide Blue Road, The 135, 138, 145, 163, 186, 189, 192, 206, 214, 217, 218, 223, 225, 226, 233, 254, 256
Wolfe, William (Billy) (nationalist and friend) 19, 168, 169, 170, 187
WRNS 91, 93, 94, 95, 97, 98, 99, 100, 105, 109, 111, 112, 118, 121, 127, 129, 130, 131, 133, 143, 163, 194

Y
Young, Christopher 159
Young Hugh 145, 189, 218, 225, 233, 248, 254, 255